PCs
for Non-Nerds

GEEK

Keith Aleshire
Brad Koch

NRP
NEW RIDERS
PUBLISHING

New Riders Publishing, Carmel, Indiana

PCs for Non-Nerds

By Keith Aleshire and Brad Koch

Published by:
New Riders Publishing
11711 N. College Ave., Suite 140
Carmel, IN 46032 USA

Copyright © 1993 by New Riders Publishing

Printed in the United States of America   2 3 4 5 6 7 8 9 0

```
Aleshire, Keith, 1963-
   PCs for Non-Nerds / Keith Aleshire, Brad Koch
          p. cm.
   Includes index.
   ISBN: 1-56205-150-4 : $18.95
   1. Microcomputers. I. Koch, Brad. II. Title.
   QA76.5.A3685 1993
   004.165--dc20                                    93-16741
                                                        CIP
```

Publisher   *David P. Ewing*

Associate Publisher   *Tim Huddleston*

Acquisitions Editor   *John Pont*

Marketing Manager   *Brad Koch*

Product Director   *David P. Ewing*

Managing Editor   *Cheri Robinson*

Developmental Editor   *Peter Kuhns*

Editors   *Patrice Hartmann, Steve Weiss, Rob Lawson, Nancy Sixsmith*

Technical Editor   *Daniel Gray*

Book Design and Production   *Amy Peppler-Adams, Lisa Daugherty, Dennis Clay Hager, Roger Morgan, Juli Pavey, Angela M. Pozdol, Susan Shepard, Alyssa Yesh*

Proofreaders   *Terri Edwards, Howard Jones, John Kane, Sean Medlock, Angie Trzepacz, Suzanne Tully*

Indexed by   *Loren Malloy, John Sleeva, Suzanne Snyder*

About the Authors

Keith R. Aleshire is a Phi Beta Kappa graduate from the University of Minnesota School of Journalism. He has worked for various high-tech firms, including Minnesota state government's central computer center, Northgate Computers, Digi International, and LaserMaster Corp. He has been a senior producer and columnist for Prodigy Services Co. and writes for several computer and technology magazines. In 1992, the PRODIGY service's Computer Club he produced received the Computer Press Association's award for "Best On-line Computer Publication." He is president of Computer Consumer Services Inc., an Eden Prairie, Minn., consulting and documentation company.

Brad Koch is presently the Marketing Manager for New Riders Publishing (NRP), responsible for promoting and developing new sales channels for New Riders' critically acclaimed, expanded book line. Prior to becoming the Marketing Manager, Brad was NRP's Acquisitions Editor. In this position, Brad developed the concepts for many of NRP's best-sellers, including *Inside OS/2* and *Inside Novell NetWare*. Brad was instrumental in planning the highly successful Windows, CAD, and networking lines of books published by NRP in 1991 and 1992.

About the Artists

Talmage Burdine attended Herron School of Art in Indianapolis and has worked as a free-lance illustrator for many years. He lives in Indianapolis with his wife and child. He said to tell you he works cheap.

Chris Rozzi earned his BFA in Fine Arts at Wabash College and continued to study in illustration at the Herron School of Art. Currently, he is an associate exhibit artist with The Children's Museum of Indianapolis and a free-lance illustrator. Mr. Rozzi enjoys comic books, hiking, scuba diving, and spending time with his fiancée, Susan, and her cat, Lagniappe.

Acknowledgments

New Riders extends special thanks to:

Pauline Aleshire, for her support during a very stressful project.

Talmage Burdine, for creating imaginative cartoons under tight deadlines. "Hurry up and be funny!"

David Ewing, for giving Brad a chance to stay up nights and to sacrifice his weekends for something like this. Keith thanks Dave Ewing for selecting him for the project.

Dan Gray, the best technical editor east of the Delaware River.

The makers of MJB coffee, for our caffeine-induced writing sprees.

Bruce Hallberg, for his contribution of Chapter 7. When it comes to ghost writers, Bruce is one of the best!

Terry Hall, for his puzzles. Mr. Hall is the Vice President of Media Productions in Wheaton, IL, and has been a professional puzzle designer for several years. Mr. Hall uses computers in most of his design work, and has published several complete books of crossword puzzles, word searches, and other puzzles. His most recent puzzle books—*Tyndale Crossword Puzzles, Volumes I and II*—were published by Tyndale House Publishers, Inc.

Tim Huddleston, for helping with the cartoons, drawings, and all the other stuff in this book, and Rob Lawson, for being there in an emergency.

Brad Koch, for the thousands of meetings he had to endure to set the Non-Nerd series in stone. Keith would also like to thank Brad, his partner in crime.

Lisa Koch, for her patience and for breaking the TV before the project started.

Mother Nature, for making caffeine.

Amy Peppler-Adams, for her imagination and hard work putting this series together.

Don Petersen, and Fourway Computer Products, Inc., for getting Brad started in this whole business.

Trademark Acknowledgments

New Riders Publishing has made every attempt to supply trademark information about company names, products, and services mentioned in this book. Trademarks indicated below were derived from various sources. New Riders Publishing cannot attest to the accuracy of this information.

ACT! is a trademark of Contact Software International, Inc.

Ami Professional is a trademark of Samna Corporation, a wholly owned subsidiary of Lotus Development Corporation.

CorelDRAW! is a trademark of Corel Systems Corporation

Crosstalk is a registered trademark of Digital Communications Associations

Harvard Graphics is a registered trademark of Software Publishing Corporation

HyperACCESS/5 is a registered trademark of Hilgraeve

KnowledgeMan is a registered trademark of Micro Database Systems, Inc.

Warning and Disclaimer

Contents at a Glance

Contents

Introducing the Computer

D on't put this book down. This is the perfect book for first-time computer users, first-time purchasers, or normal people who think working with their computer is like tangling with the business end of a porcupine. Keep reading and find out:

- Is this book for me?
- What will I learn if I read this book?
- Do I have to read the whole book? (No.)
- So, what's in this book?

Is This Book for Me?

Get this book if you are planning to purchase your first computer, or if you are new to computers and need to use one at home or work. Don't get this book if you are already a computer guru, expert, or super-experienced computer user.

If you are buying your first computer, count on *PCs for Non-Nerds* to show you how to select the right computer for your needs and how to avoid getting ripped off when purchasing a system. We even help you decide where to buy a computer system!

If you are just beginning to use a computer, or have been confused by the manuals or other computer books, this book is the help you need. *PCs for Non-Nerds* will quickly demystify the computer, while giving you the answers you need to use your computer productively. We know you don't care to know every conceivable technical detail about computers—you have better things to do than read computer books!

What Will I Learn If I Read This Book?

The goal of this book is to prevent the computer from ruining your day (or even just a part of your day). We've done our best to include the information that most users need to solve common computer problems that every computer user encounters at least once. However, we have left out the billions of details that the vast majority of computer users don't want to know.

NERDY
DETAILS

We haven't left out all the technical information. If you want to learn a little more about why your PC works, instead of only how to fix it when it screws up, read these nerdy detail sections as they appear throughout the book. One caution: reading all of these nerdy details could start you on your way to becoming a true computer guru!

The authors know that you don't read computer books for fun or entertainment. People read computer books to get their jobs done faster and better. But you shouldn't have to to read through boring, mind-numbing text to find the answer you need. That is why the information in this book is presented in a friendly, conversational tone that never gets too serious. We'll leave the truly important topics like world peace or how the Cubs are doing to other books.

Do I Have To Read the Whole Book?

No. You don't have to read the whole book. Read just the parts that answer whatever question you have at the time, or the parts that tell you what to do when your computer starts trying your patience.

This book is a reference. When you have a question (or your computer has a problem), use the index or table of contents to look up the answer you need. Then turn to the pages listed, get your answer, fix your computer, and get back to what you were doing before your computer started testing your patience. Simple.

STOP!

Any time you see a Stop section like this one, be certain to read it carefully. These sections serve as warnings and provide important tips for keeping your computer from really ruining your day. They also tell you how to avoid making a bad situation worse.

Part One: Buying and Installing a Computer

The three chapters in this section cover computer fundamentals, how to choose and purchase a computer, and how to set up your computer once you have one. Specifically, you learn:

- That there are only three "computerese" terms to know, and three myths to forget, before you can start using your computer productively and make smart purchase decisions.

- How to decide which computer is best for you, and who has the best deal.

- How to unpack and set up your computer like a pro (even professionals never get it exactly right on the first try).

Maybe your computer is already set up. If it is, you are ready for Part Two!

Part Two: Blast Off!

There is only one chapter in this part—making it very easy to read. This part is all about turning your computer on and off. Here's what you'll learn:

- How to perform the "smoke test."

- What goes on when your PC boots.

- How to find out where you've been "booted" to.

How to turn off your PC without losing any data or polluting your hard drive, and how to fix it when you forget and pollute your hard drive anyway.

 What to do when things just don't seem right.

Now that your computer is running (hopefully), you need to know where you are and what software is on your computer. That's the next part covered in this book.

Part Three: Software—Getting Things Done

Your PC is useless without software—like a CD player with no music! This part tells you how to survive your first few encounters with your PC's software. These systems are covered:

 MS-DOS—you'll learn just enough DOS to get your work done, but not enough to do any damage.

 Windows—learn how to move around, start and stop programs, and how to keep from getting lost among all those windows.

 OS/2—again you'll see how to move around, find help, start and stop programs, and how to exit OS/2 gracefully.

We'll also tell you how to purchase and install new software—even if you haven't ever purchased software before.

Part Four: Things You Have To Deal With

This part teaches you all about the parts of the computer you have to contend with on a daily basis. This is where you'll find a bunch of helpful tips and tricks that can make working with your computer enjoyable:

 How the guts of your computer affect your everyday work, and what to do when things go wrong.

 What all the different types of monitors and video options mean, and how to take advantage of them.

- How to manage your keyboard, mouse, and other things you can't keep your hands off of.

- How to keep your disks and disk drives healthy, and how not to trash important information.

- What the heck ports are (they have nothing to do with boats), and how to connect things to them.

- How to keep from going insane while trying to get your printer to do what you want it to do.

SAVE THE DAY!

> Throughout the book, you'll see sections just like this one that contain hints and tips that can help you "save the day" when your computer threatens to ruin somebody's day. Who knows—maybe you'll save your boss's day and get a big raise!

With these chapters at your side, your computer doesn't stand a chance because you'll always come out the winner!

Part Five: Chapters That Didn't Fit Anywhere Else

Portable computers and networks are more popular than ever, and many people will end up working with one or the other. If you're scared or intimidated, this part will show you:

- Why laptop computers are so popular, and how best to use one (if you have to).

- How networks function, and how not to be intimidated by using one.

Who knows, you may be lucky and never have to read any of these chapters!

Part Six: Finding Help

Even technoids need help once in a while, and you will too. Computers don't listen to reason or threats, and sometimes they just get confused on their own. This part teaches you:

What to do when your computer's choking. This chapter teaches you how to give first aid to your computer.

Who ya gonna call? Who can help when your first-aid efforts don't work. (Don't dial 911!)

If whatever ails your computer is terminal, you may need the information in the next section.

Part Seven: Upgrading Your Computer

There are hundreds of cool gadgets you'll eventually want to add to your computer. Some make your computer easier to use, others make your computer work faster. The chapters in this part will show you:

Popular things that are easy to add to your computer.

Popular things that are not as easy to add to your computer.

How to upgrade your computer so that it performs like a new computer.

TRICKS

When you see this icon, you've found a trick to make using your computer easier and less frustrating. And you can do this magic without a magic wand!

Time To Get Started!

Because you aren't going to read this whole book, take a look at the table of contents, or road map, on the inside front cover. Both the map and the table of contents help you find where to look when you have a question. Now, go ahead and put the book down—until you need it.

PART 1

Buying and Installing a Computer

GEEK

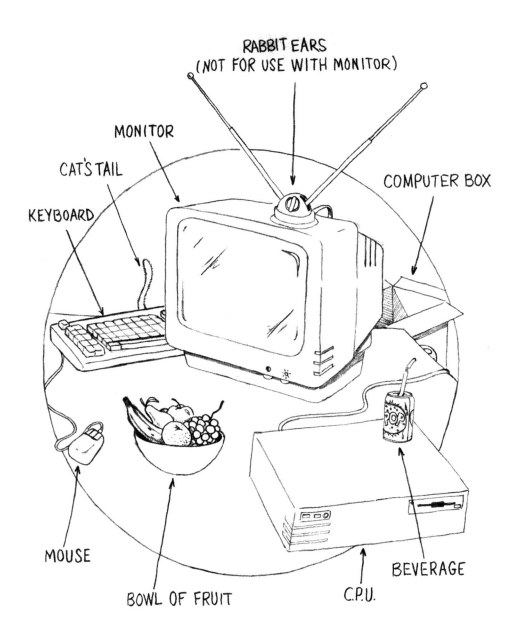

RABBIT EARS
(NOT FOR USE WITH MONITOR)

MONITOR

CAT'S TAIL

KEYBOARD

COMPUTER BOX

MOUSE

BOWL OF FRUIT

C.P.U.

BEVERAGE

CHAPTER 1

Can You Repeat That—Slower and in English?

$\mathcal{S}$o, you're preparing to use your first personal computer and you're a little nervous about making a disastrous mistake, or pressing the wrong button at precisely the wrong time. If you haven't made it that far, you've probably just been blitzkrieged with a non-stop, 1000-buzzwords-per-minute sales pitch from some department-store computer salesperson who looks too young to drive, let alone help you spend a couple thousand dollars on a computer system.

Wish you had some help cutting through the hype and fog? Relax, you're not alone. Last year over 10 million people purchased new PCs. These people all managed to survive, and now are more or less in control of their computer.

This chapter helps you become a veteran computer user. Think of this chapter as the computer equivalent of baseball's spring training. It's not very long and not very hard, but it will help you master the fundamentals that are crucial to success. This chapter helps you determine:

 Just what is a PC?

 The very few really useful PC-related words

The different types of PCs

 Two-door, four-door, and hatchbacks—PCs come in a lot of different body styles

 Computer anatomy—just the outside parts

 Operating systems species (including extinct ones)

 What PCs can do

 What PCs cannot do

If you already know this material, feel free to skip it. Unlike baseball's spring training, this chapter isn't mandatory and it doesn't require any windsprints or push-ups. Unfortunately, you also won't get in shape or get a tan by reading.

Huh? Terms You Need To Know and Myths You Can Ignore

New computer users face two challenges. The first is to become familiar with important computer terms; the second is to overcome nervousness about making mistakes.

The bad news about computer terms is about 100,000 of them already exist, and computer geeks are inventing more terms every day. Fortunately, you'll only need to learn a few of these terms to become an effective personal computer user. These terms are just like the terms and buzzwords you learned when compact discs (CDs) replaced LPs (long-playing albums), and when VCRs were first introduced. PC terms aren't any more difficult than these common terms; they're just newer.

Read through the following definitions. There aren't very many, and they are short. Once you have the hang of these terms, the rest of this chapter will be a breeze.

 Hardware. Hardware refers to the mechanical and electrical parts that make up a computer system. Computers, printers, keyboards, modems, monitors, mice, even powcr cords are all considered hardware. If it uses electricity or moves, it's hardware.

Software. Software is just a very, very long set of instructions, stored in the computer, that controls the hardware in a computer system. Hardware is useless without some kind of software to tell it what to do next. WordPerfect, MS-DOS, Windows, Lotus 1-2-3—these programs are popular software packages that you may recognize.

NERDY
DETAILS

You see the interaction between hardware and software every time you go to a grocery store with the laser-scanning checkout devices. The scanner, keyboard, and screen that displays your totals are hardware. Software controls these hardware devices. The software controls the scanner that scans the packages and looks up their prices and item descriptions. The software also controls the keyboard that the clerk uses to fix mistakes made by the scanner, and software tells the display screen what numbers to display.

 Data. Data is information created with a computer. Letters, budgets, charts, inventory lists—all these are data. Data may be manually typed (when you type letters and spreadsheets, for example), or data already in your computer may be updated or changed by software programs. Data is the stuff you don't want to lose.

That's it for definitions. Hardware, software, and data are the three terms you need to begin to understand PCs. Each of the terms in the rest of this book will relate to either hardware, software, or data.

PC Horror Stories That Aren't True (Honest!)

You need to dispel some common myths that tend to make people nervous about using a PC. Once these myths are off your back, you can relax and begin to enjoy learning about your PC.

Myth #1: If I press the wrong key or type the wrong command, I may physically hurt the PC.

Wrong. The only way you can hurt your PC physically is by tossing it on the floor or hitting it with something big and heavy—a baseball bat for instance. Other than a direct, physical attack, you can't hurt your PC just by using it.

Myth #2: If I press the wrong key or type the wrong command, I may accidentally lose or damage some important data.

This is possible, but not likely. The only way you can damage data is to ruin it deliberately. Big mistakes require you to know enough about the computer commands that you can actually delete data. By the time you've figured out how to hurt something, you'll know enough not to do it.

With current software, even the biggest mistakes can be fixed and usually cause nothing but inconvenience. In addition, most programs stop you and ask, "Do you really want to do this?" before something major happens, such as deleting an entire letter or using the same name for a file. If you aren't sure you want to make the change, say no. Check out Chapter 5 for a list of commands you should avoid.

Myth #3: Small children naturally learn about PCs more quickly than adults.

This is a popular TV myth that just isn't true. What is true is many children have had more time using computers, especially in school, than have most adults. Children also are not neurotic enough to worry about hurting the computer—the money for the computer didn't come out of their allowance!

Many kids learned how to use a computer by banging away on the directional keys and pounding on the space bar in the middle of some computer game. Don't feel like you need to be a kid to understand computers; you just need to quit worrying and start experimenting.

PCs Look Alike and Other Similarities

All personal computers (PCs) have three things in common:

1. PCs are hardware. You can use PCs to accomplish a number of tasks. Like cameras, microwaves, and stereos, PCs are another type of electronic device. Unlike TVs, telephones, and video games, which are made to perform only one function (displaying TV, communicating with another person, playing games), PCs serve a number of purposes.

2. Computers are considered "personal" if individuals can afford to purchase them, or if businesses can afford to provide them to individual employees.

3.   A computer is considered a "PC" if it is an IBM or IBM-compatible computer. Other kinds of affordable computers are available, but they are not referred to as "PCs." For the rest of this book, when you see the words "PC" or "computer," these words refer to IBM and IBM-compatible PCs.

PCs are more powerful and less expensive than ever. Businesses now consider PCs as productivity tools similar to photocopiers, fax machines, and other modern office equipment. Today, many consumers view PCs as just another appliance, the same way they think of VCRs and microwave ovens. These individuals use their PCs at work and at home for work and entertainment.

Three major types of computers are available:

- IBM PC and IBM PC compatible computers—PCs

- Apple Macintosh computers—Macs

- Non-IBM compatible and non-Macintosh computers

IBM and IBM-Compatible Personal Computers— What Does It Mean To Be "IBM-Compatible"?

A computer is "IBM-compatible" if it can use the same hardware and software as a personal computer actually manufactured by IBM. The IBM PC is considered an "industry standard" computer. Industry standard means that everybody knows how IBM built their PC and can now legally design and manufacture computer systems that are capable of using the same software and hardware as IBM's PC.

GEEK

NERDY
DETAILS

When IBM built their first PC, they used parts obtained from a variety of sources, and thus were not able to protect their design from being legally duplicated by other computer companies. Apple, on the other hand, designed and built their Macintosh so that they could prevent others from legally building Macintosh-compatible computers. (That is why Macintoshes generally cost more than PCs.)

Is There a Difference between "Compatibles" and "Clones"?

If you've started looking for, or using, a PC, you may have heard the terms "PC-compatibles" and "clones" and wondered what they were. Companies that build "IBM-compatibles" design and build their own PCs from scratch. Companies that produce compatible PCs usually are larger than, older than, and irritated (scared?) by companies that produce clones.

PC clone companies assemble their PCs from hardware manufactured by other companies. Clone companies typically are smaller and more capable of implementing and taking advantage of rapid improvements in technology. Clone companies do not have costs associated with inventing new products, enabling them to sell their computers for less. Clones assembled by reputable companies represent a great value and have achieved excellent quality levels equivalent to compatible PCs.

Why Aren't Apple Macintoshes Called "PCs"?

Apple Macintosh computers are not called "PCs" because they are not IBM-compatible. Macintoshes may look like PCs, but they can't use the same software or hardware as PCs. That's not all bad. Apple Macintosh computers are known for their ease of use and graphics capabilities.

Even Macintosh users don't refer to their computers as "PCs"; most Macintosh users call their computers "Macs." Maybe this is because Mac users spend a lot of time trying to be different and tend to be a little artsy. Many Macs are used by advertising agencies, musicians, desktop publishers, and others whose work is more creative.

SAVE
THE DAY!

Software companies have started making their software available for PCs and Macintoshes. This software usually works identically on either computer and gives Mac and PC users the ability to exchange data and to work with each other's programs. If you need to work with people who use Macs, check out software that works well on both types of computers.

Non-IBM Compatible and Non-Mac Computers

Atari and Commodore also produce affordable computers, but these products have not been widely accepted in business. These computers instead have found their niche as entertainment machines in special applications.

Other machines in this group include computers called "workstations." *Workstations* are high-performance PCs specially designed for scientific and engineering use.

Crash Course in PC Anatomy— Just the Outside Parts

With computers, as with humans, it is good to know which parts are which before you begin touching them. Before you do anything with a PC, you need to know what the basic parts do and what they look like. The following list defines the various parts of a computer system.

 Case. Computers cases come in several different sizes and shapes. Like car manufacturers, PC companies can alter a PC's design to meet different needs. When customers demanded more room for their families and luggage, car manufacturers responded by designing station wagons (and even gave some of them those really cool wood side panels). The station wagon is similar to other cars—it has an engine, four wheels, and brakes—but it also carries more of your belongings (or those of your friends when they ask you to help them move).

Computer manufacturers have met the demands of computer users by designing different cases (similar to car bodies) for their PCs. The most popular designs serve different purposes:

 Desktop. This is the most common type of PC. A PC is called a "desktop PC" if it is small enough to fit on the top of a desk and most of the controls can be reached while sitting in front of the machine.

NERDY
DETAILS

Many computer manufacturers still do not quite understand what makes a PC a desktop computer. Companies still put buttons and switches on the back of the computer where you can't reach them unless you wedge your head between the wall and your monitor.

 Tower. Tower PCs are the largest type of PC and stand on the floor. Tower computers are designed to be upgraded easily and have a lot of room to add things. Towers are most often used by businesses as part of a larger system, although they look cool standing next to your desk and are a convenient place to set things.

 Laptop. Laptops are portable computers small enough to be carried, but too big to fit in a briefcase. This type of PC is called a "laptop" if it is small enough to be placed on your lap and light enough that blood still flows through to your feet. Using one on your lap, however, is never very easy and is highly overrated.

 Notebook. Notebook computers are smaller versions of laptops. Notebooks fit in a briefcase and are easier to travel with than most laptops. Notebooks also weigh less than laptops—most weigh less than six pounds. Notebook computers are great for travel, but their smaller keyboards and screens are hard to use for extended periods.

 Subnotebook. Subnotebooks are even smaller than notebooks! Most of them look like severely overgrown calculators. These PCs are typically used for a specific purpose such as running a single application program.

See Chapter 9 for more information on what's inside a computer case. Most computers have these components:

 The Monitor. The computer monitor looks like a TV without antennae or tuning knobs. The monitor shows you what your PC is currently doing and gives you visual feedback. Chapter 10 has more information on monitors.

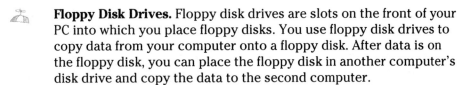 **Floppy Disk Drives.** Floppy disk drives are slots on the front of your PC into which you place floppy disks. You use floppy disk drives to copy data from your computer onto a floppy disk. After data is on the floppy disk, you can place the floppy disk in another computer's disk drive and copy the data to the second computer.

Keyboard. Everyone should know what a keyboard is. In case you forgot, a keyboard is the long flat thing with the alphabet and numbers printed on it that looks like a typewriter. See Chapter 11 for more information on keyboards.

Lock. Almost every new PC comes with a lock. When you lock the system, it turns off the keyboard and in some PCs prevents you from taking the cover off the machine.

SAVE
THE DAY!

The best thing to do with a key lock is to leave it open and hide the keys—you may want to tape them to the back of the computer. If you need to lock your system, leave one of the keys where you will not lose it.

Most locks (or keys) have a number on them that tells locksmiths (and burglars) which key fits the lock. Write this number down on the sheet provided in Chapter 5. If you ever lose both keys, you may be able to get a replacement from the computer manufacturer.

 Reset Button. When you press the reset button, the computer is quickly turned off and then on again. In addition, any data you have not saved is lost.

SAVE
THE DAY!

Occasionally computers become confused, suffer a type of brain spasm, and suddenly stop working. If your computer is running and your data is on-screen, but nothing works, your computer is "locked up."

To fix this problem, first thank your computer for turning any data you were working with into toast, then press the reset button. The reset button is a great feature because it wins every "dispute" with the computer.

Turbo Button & Light. Many computers can run at two speeds: normal and slower than normal. The turbo button enables you to switch between normal and slow speeds. (Don't worry if nothing seems to happen when you push the button. Some PCs only run at normal speeds and include the light just for kicks.) If the turbo light is on, your PC is running at normal speed.

NERDY
DETAILS

The only time you would want to run at the slower speed is if your program is easier to use at a slower pace. For example, you may want to slow your system down when you are playing computer games. That way the bombs drop on you a little slower and give you more time to get out of the way.

 Hard Drive Light. This light indicates that the computer is using the hard drive. This light is included to reassure people that the hard drive is actually working and to serve as a "wait-a-minute, I'm processing" signal. Hard drives are covered in Chapter 12.

 Mouse. A mouse is a device you roll around on your desk. As you move the mouse, it moves a little pointer around on-screen. After you get used to the mouse, it makes your computer easier to use by enabling you to choose options and move data around the screen just by pointing to what you want to do and clicking the mouse buttons. By using a mouse, you can quickly move to any part of the screen. Mice and other rodents are covered in Chapter 11.

 Power Switch. The power switch usually is near the PCs power cord. This switch turns on and off your computer. In case you wondered, "0" means off and "|" means on.

NERDY
DETAILS

The "0" symbol indicates an open electrical connection, one through which current cannot pass—"0" means off. The "|" symbol indicates a closed electrical connection that electricity can pass through—"|" means on.

 Ports. Ports arc the place where you connect things to your computer. Your monitor plugs into a port and your keyboard plugs into a port. Ports can be male or female, depending on whether they have pins or holes. Your PC probably has one or all of the following ports—serial, parallel, keyboard, mouse, and game ports.

Expansion Slots. Expansion slots provide you with room to add extra devices to your PC. Sound boards and internal modems are popular upgrades that use expansion slots.

The Fan. The fan in the back of your PC prevents your PC from overheating. The fan is part of your PC's power supply. The power supply adapts normal household current for use in your PC.

Operating Systems— Different Brains for Different Species

An *operating system* is software that controls your PC's hardware and enables your PC to work with other software programs. Operating systems are the brains of your PC; the hardware is just the body. The operating system controls the basic activities of PC hardware, much like your brain controls your breathing and heartbeat.

Operating systems also mimic your brain in that they enable the PC to communicate with other software programs. Operating systems do this by breaking down the complex instructions from other software programs into tiny chunks that hardware can understand. Operating systems you should know about include the following (included are their unofficial scientific names):

DOS (Userus Confuserus)

DOS is the most popular operating system for IBM-compatible computers. DOS comes in two identical flavors, MS-DOS and PC-DOS. MS-DOS is from a company called Microsoft (that more or less invented it) and works on all IBM-compatible computers. PC-DOS is IBM's version of MS-DOS.

Windows (DOS Graphicus)

Windows is a program that makes DOS easier to use by providing you with a friendly, graphical interface (what you see on-screen). Windows is more than just a pretty face, however; it also enables you to run more than one program at a time, and makes it much easier to share information among applications. Most new PCs (except those from IBM) come with Windows pre-installed so that you do not have to install it yourself.

OS/2 (IBM Graphicus)

OS/2 version 2.1 is IBM's answer to the Windows/DOS-based PC. OS/2 is more powerful than Windows, and does almost everything Windows does (it does some things better). OS/2 even runs Windows programs! OS/2, however, takes up more room on your computer's hard disk drive, and requires a faster PC to perform the same as a Windows-based PC.

UNIX (Nerdus Exclusivus) Yuck!

UNIX is the oldest of the PC operating systems, and still the most powerful—kind of like a modern-day dinosaur. UNIX originated on mainframe computers and was translated (called "porting" by programmers) for use on PCs. Like a dinosaur, UNIX is big, powerful, and a little difficult to order around. UNIX is used mostly by scientists and engineers who need its communication and processing power and do not mind cleaning up after a dinosaur once in a while.

NERDY
DETAILS

UNIX does have some friendlier versions. Like DOS, which combines with Windows to create an easy to use operating system, UNIX can combine with several programs. These programs are called interfaces and include OpenLook, Motif, and X-Windows. Even with these programs, UNIX is still more complicated than DOS, Windows, or OS/2.

Macintosh (Graphicus Nonserius)

The Macintosh operating system is easy, elegant, and consistent—it is what Windows and OS/2 hope to become. The problem with the Macintosh operating system is you can only use it on an Apple computer, and Apple computers aren't IBM-compatible PCs.

Extinct Species—Don't Buy These

When someone's computer becomes old, almost useless, or obsolete, what does he or she do? The owner sells it! The owner usually sells it to someone who is unaware the computer is old and useless. Machines that use the following operating systems are old and obsolete:

- 🔧 **CPM.** CPM was created by Digital Research. If you are looking for a used computer, and the add says it is a CPM machine, skip it and look for another computer.

- 🔧 **Strange DOS Operating Systems.** Right after IBM shipped PC-DOS (a renamed version of MS-DOS), there were a bunch of companies who tried to establish a "DOS" version of their own. These versions of DOS were similar to, but not exactly like, PC-DOS and MS-DOS. These companies failed completely. Unfortunately, some of their machines are still out there. If the computer does not run PC-DOS or MS-DOS, don't buy it.

What Personal Computers Can Do

Personal computers are simply tools designed to help people organize information and accomplish a wide variety of tasks. PCs are more sophisticated than circular saws, calculators, or typewriters, but PCs resemble common machines in that they are used by humans to build things, analyze numbers, and create documents.

PCs are used for a wide variety of tasks. At first, software for PCs was mainly business-related and was used for writing letters, storing and retrieving information, sorting lists, creating graphics, and analyzing financial numbers. As PCs became more powerful, they began to be used for more sophisticated applications—teaching pilots to fly complex military fighter aircraft, or predicting weather patterns, for example.

PCs are also a great form of entertainment—one look at a software store's shelves proves that games are big business on PCs. PC games such as SimCity by Maxis, Inc., can mimic the way cities grow (and decay), while others can lead you through intricate adventures. In the world of PC games, there is no limit to what you can do with your PC.

What Personal Computers Cannot Do

What's the main thing personal computers cannot do? PCs cannot think for themselves—they are not capable of independent action. PCs perform only the actions that you or the software tells them to do.

Contrary to decades of Hollywood images, computers cannot:

- Come to life after being hit by lightning and take over your body.

- Be used by teenagers to break into the USA's missile defense systems and start World War III.

- Figure the next winning POWERBALL number—although a lot of people are working on this one!

- Hurt you. A PC is similar to a rock; it hurts only if it falls on you or you fall on it.

"WELL, IF YOU DON'T LIKE THIS ONE...
I GOT A '89 YUGO OUT BACK THAT I CAN SELL YOU...
FOR THE SAME PRICE."

CHAPTER 2

Choosing and Purchasing a Computer

Do you have some money burning a hole in your pocket? Are you wondering what to do with that giant tax refund (if you're lucky enough to get one)? Maybe you're thinking about buying a personal computer for your home or small business? If you are, this chapter has some good news and some bad news.

The good news is PCs are less expensive and more powerful than ever before; it really is a great time to buy a PC. PC prices are dropping rapidly because of a cut-throat price war that forces PC manufacturers to drop their prices in an attempt to get (or keep) your business.

The bad news is that purchasing a PC is far more confusing than ever before. With everyone and their cousin selling PCs, it's hard to know who to believe. Many people now compare buying a new PC to buying a used car—let the buyer beware!

NERDY
DETAILS

"What's the difference between computer salespeople and used car salespeople? Used car salespeople know when they're lying!

Things really aren't that bad, but as a first-time PC buyer, you do have quite a bit to overcome. First, you must decide what you want to do with your PC. Second, you must learn and understand a ton of new terms and buzzwords. After all this, you must shop around as much as possible to be certain you find the PC that meets your needs and to avoid being ripped off.

This chapter first helps you decide what you want to do with your PC. It then demystifies the terms and buzzwords that computer salespeople use to confuse non-nerds like yourself. Finally, this chapter shows you how to select a computer that best fits your needs and even provides tips on where to purchase your PC. Specifically, this chapter shows you how to

 Evaluate your needs accurately

 Choose software that does what you want it to do

 Define your software's requirements

 Find hardware that best runs your software

 Decide where to buy your PC

 Determine if your PC purchase is tax-deductible

If you have already purchased a PC (or "liberated" one from your office) and know everything you want to know about PCs and purchasing PCs, feel free to skip this chapter.

Four Steps to PC Perfection

Purchasing a PC can be just as confusing as purchasing a car. Like cars, PCs come in many different styles and from many different vendors. Some PCs offer more power than others, some may promise superior expansion capabilities, while still others are like Yugos—spewing oily smoke and moving more slowly than anything else available. The options and possibilities can seem endless, which is why many new PC buyers feel overwhelmed when deciding which type of PC is best for them.

Fortunately, you can follow four steps that help you select the right PC at the right price from the right vendor, without relying on a 19-year-old salesperson, or spending weeks trying to memorize every possible PC option (you've got better things to do, right?). The four steps are pretty logical:

1. Decide what you want to do with the computer

2. Find the software that best does what you want

3. Figure out the software's general requirements

4. Buy a computer that best runs the software you've chosen

How Can I Pick Out a Computer When I Don't Know Much About Them?

The following sections help you complete these four steps. Each section gives you the knowledge and information you need to make the best PC purchase decision. These steps make choosing a PC that matches your needs as easy as possible. By the time you finish, you'll even have a "PC checklist" that you can use when shopping for your PC.

SAVE
THE DAY!

Be prepared to list the software you need. A PC without software is just an expensive doorstop. That is why you should begin your search for a PC by defining what software will do the things you want. Purchasing a PC without first deciding on what software you need is a great way to waste money. Unless you have a couple thousand dollars to waste, choose your software first.

First Step— What Do You Want To Do?

Before you get to the really fun part of buying a PC, you must decide what you want to do with a computer. The best way to do this is to make a list of the things you want to do with your PC. You don't need to write out every single thing you can ever imagine (or could imagine Madonna) doing with a PC. Instead, just list on paper your immediate, major needs (you might want to update this list later).

If you already know what you want to do with your PC, you can skip to the next section. If not, or if you're curious about what other people do with their PCs, check out the following list. It shows you the most popular things you can do with a PC and the type of software necessary to do those things. Get a pen and make a big check mark next to anything you think you'll need (unless you're reading this in the bookstore or you've borrowed it from a friend or your local library).

 If you need to create letters, form letters, reports, memos, or simple newsletters you need *word processing software*. A word processor is the computerized version of a sophisticated typewriter. Modern word processing software packages have built-in spell checkers, grammar checkers, and thesauruses. Many word processors can create documents with multiple columns and graphics images. Almost every computer user has some kind of word processor.

 The addition and subtraction of money, the use of rows and columns of numbers, and the sorting of information are all done with *spreadsheet software*. Spreadsheets look like big pieces of computerized graph paper. Each square can contain numbers, text, or formulas. Spreadsheets are much better than paper ledgers or chalkboards because they automatically recalculate totals and percentages whenever a number is changed.

 If you need to store, sort, update, and retrieve large amounts of information, you need *database software*. Database software can store simple recipe files or complex inventory and accounting records of a large company. If you need to maintain a large mailing list or inventory a bunch of equipment, you need a database.

 Pie charts, graphs, and presentations are all things done with *graphics software*. Graphics programs create everything from simple business graphics and organizational charts to artistic and dazzling photorealistic images. If you need to draw or chart things, you'll need graphics software.

Need to send a file across the country pronto? Do you need the latest greatest financial news? Or maybe you just want to play checkers with your buddy across town. To do these things you'll need *communications software*. Communications programs work with a modem, which lets you communicate with other PCs (or friends with a PC and a modem). You can also use these packages to connect to popular information services such as Prodigy, CompuServe, and America On-Line.

NERDY DETAILS

If you're interested in obtaining information on Prodigy, CompuServe, and America On-Line, you can reach them at the following phone numbers:

CompuServe	(800) 848-8199
America On-Line	(800) 827-6364
Prodigy	(800) 776-3449

Make sure you read all the microscopic fine print on the contracts with these services. It's easy to forget how much time you've spent connected to these services—possibly resulting in a phone or credit card bill that could put a dent even in Ross Perot's wallet.

 If you want to create sophisticated documents such as brochures, color advertisements, or wedding invitations, you need *desktop publishing software*. A desktop publishing program called PageMaker was used to create this book—cool, huh?

 Sales reps, managers, and receptionists need to track appointments and schedules. If you need help with these kinds of tasks, you can benefit from *scheduling/client management software*. This kind of software can help you stay organized and prevent you from missing important meetings.

 If you manage large projects that involve a lot of people and dozens of individual deadlines, you'll love *project management software*. Project Management programs are designed for you to manage large, multiperson, multistep projects effectively.

This is not a complete list of all the cool stuff you can do with a PC. Instead, just the most common, popular uses for PCs and their corresponding software categories are listed. Don't worry if you didn't see a description that meets your needs; many other software categories exist. These other categories include accounting/inventory management, computer-aided design (CAD), programming languages, multimedia, system utilities, and more.

Second Step—What Software Best Fills Your Needs?

After you've decided the general types of software you need, you can look for the specific software packages that best meet your requirements.

Typically, two or three software packages dominate each category. These dominant software packages offer a couple of advantages. First, by sticking with the major software packages, you can more easily take advantage of software training offered by local community colleges or computer training centers. Second, the dominant software packages give you the most flexibility when it comes to sharing information with friends or coworkers.

A sampling of the most popular packages for each category are listed in the following table.

Table 2.1
Popular Software Packages
for DOS, Windows, and OS/2

Application	Best DOS Choices	Best Windows Choices	Best OS/2 Choices
Word Processing	WordPerfect	Microsoft Word for Windows	DeScribe Word Processor
	Microsoft Word	Ami Professional	Microsoft Word for OS/2
	Q&A	WordPerfect for Windows	
Spreadsheets	Lotus 1-2-3	Microsoft Excel	Informix Wingz for OS/2

Application	Best DOS Choices	Best Windows Choices	Best OS/2 Choices
Spreadsheets (cont'd)	Quattro Pro	Lotus 1-2-3 for Windows	Lotus 1-2-3 for OS/2
		Quattro Pro for Windows	Microsoft Excel for OS/2
Database	Q&A	Microsoft Access	KnowledgeMan
	FoxPro for DOS	Paradox for Windows	R:Base for OS/2
	Paradox	Microsoft Foxpro	Sybase
Graphics	Harvard Graphics	CorelDRAW!	CorelDRAW! for OS/2
	Freelance Graphics	Microsoft PowerPoint	Freelance Graphics for OS/2
	Tempra Pro	Harvard Graphics for Windows	
Communications	ProComm Plus	ProComm Plus for Windows	HyperACCESS/5
	CrossTalk	CrossTalk for Windows	
Desktop Publishing	*Not worth the bother*	PageMaker for Windows	PageMaker for OS/2
		Microsoft Publisher	Ventura Publisher for OS/2
		QuarkXPress for Windows	
Project Management	Timeline	Microsoft Project	Microsoft Project
Sales/Client Mgmt	ACT!	ACT! for Windows	ACT! for Windows

NERDY
DETAILS

Thousands of different software packages are available—even programs for bird-watching! If you don't see something you need in the preceding list, it's because this book doesn't have enough pages to list all the different software packages currently available.

Most of these major software packages are available at software stores, mass market stores, computer dealers, and mail-order firms. See Chapter 8 for details on how to find and purchase software.

DOS, Windows, or OS/2—
Eenie, Meenie, Minie, Moe

Which operating environment to choose? Simple. Pick the one that best runs the software you've picked out. If the software you want is available for more than one operating system, you'll need to evaluate your budget and future needs to make a good decision.

Currently, most users and businesses are investing in Windows and Windows-based software. Windows' popularity has skyrocketed and most major DOS software packages have been rewritten to take advantage of Windows. By choosing Windows you also are choosing DOS because Windows runs in conjunction with DOS. The Windows/DOS combination gives you the most flexibility and access to the most software. For more information on operating systems, see Chapter 1.

OS/2 has only a fraction as many users as does Windows, but OS/2's popularity is growing quickly. OS/2 offers powerful 32-bit processing and other advanced features that Windows lacks. These features, combined with the capability to use Windows, DOS, and OS/2 at the same time, have convinced many people to switch to OS/2. If you are interested in OS/2, ask for a demonstration of both Windows and OS/2, then pick your favorite.

NERDY
DETAILS

PC operating systems have not kept up with advances in PC hardware. DOS and Windows both communicate with PC hardware in 16-bit chunks—they are 16-bit software packages. Most new personal computers, however, are capable of communicating in larger 32-bit chunks.

Communicating in larger chunks allows an operating system to do more work, and to do it faster than computers communicating in smaller chunks. OS/2 is the first user-friendly, widely available operating system for PCs that communicates in 32-bit chunks (in other words, it's a 32-bit operating system). Windows will soon offer a new version, called Windows NT, that offers 32-bit processing.

In either case, both Windows and OS/2 overcome the weaknesses of DOS (we won't bore you with a list, but believe us, DOS has plenty of weaknesses) and gives you much greater flexibility in what you can do with your computer. Don't forget, though, that Windows works best with software written specifically for Windows and OS/2 works best with software written specifically for OS/2.

Check Out the Features on That Software!

Before you settle on a particular software package, try to get someone to demonstrate it for you. Perhaps a coworker or friend has the software, or maybe one of the local computer vendors has the software on display. A demonstration gives you a chance to see how the software works and may help you decide which features are truly important.

If you can't find anyone to demonstrate the package you are interested in, call the software manufacturer. The software manufacturers will send you information on their products and might even tell you where you can buy their products. They may even send you a demonstration disk so that you can test drive a program before you buy it!

SAVE
THE DAY!

The way a company treats you when you want to buy something is at least as good, and probably better than, the way they will treat you when you need help. If the company is too busy to help you buy their software, you can bet they will be way too busy to answer any questions you may have later.

Third Step—What Hardware Does Your Software Need?

After all that soul searching about how you're going to use the PC, it's finally time to shop for your PC (unless this chapter convinced you that a big screen TV with a "computerized" remote control would be a better investment).

Still with us? Now that you know which software package(s) you want, all that is left is to find a PC that runs the software you've chosen. To do this, you need to review the hardware requirements of the software package.

The requirements of a particular software package are usually printed in very small letters on the outside of the software box. These requirements specify the necessary operating system, RAM, disk space, video options, and if the software requires any additional hardware such as a mouse or joystick.

Don't think you're going to remember all the fine print on the software box? This book can help. Flip to the back of the book. A tear-out card titled "Configuration Cheat Sheet" can be found there. This card serves as a checklist you can use to write down the requirements of the software packages you've chosen. Later sections in this chapter give you hints on how to understand all the stuff you've written and how to sift through the half-truths and hype. Just this once, try to read all the hints, because not all the answers are obvious.

Rip It Out and Write It Down

The card you just ripped out of the back of the book has room for you to write down all your software's specific requirements. When you fill in this card, it will be a big help when you are shopping for a PC. The following hints apply to each question on the form. These mini-explanations help you fill in the blanks and may make you feel a little more confident about your purchase decision:

Operating System Questions: This one is easy—just write down which operating system your software requires—Windows, OS/2, or DOS. Remember that Windows requires DOS to run.

RAM Questions: This one isn't so easy. If you are planning to use Windows or OS/2-based software, your PC can never have too much memory. To estimate how much memory you should have, take the largest amount of RAM required by any of the software packages you have chosen and add 2M to that number. If you are going to use only DOS software, a system with 1M of RAM is fine for most applications. Some sophisticated DOS software (computer-aided design, number crunching), however, may require more memory. If you are interested in learning more about RAM, see Chapter 9.

NERDY
DETAILS

Does the software package say, "Minimum Memory Required:"? Minimum memory requirements refer to the absolute lowest possible amount of memory the software requires to work. For Windows and OS/2 software, this minimum amount of memory is usually just enough for your software to crawl along at an infuriatingly slow pace.

Hard Drive Questions: The hard disk permanently (or until it decides otherwise) stores your programs and data files. Your PC needs a hard disk drive large enough to hold all your programs and data files. To determine the amount of disk space you need, add up the disk space requirements for all your programs (including the operating system), then triple that number for the total. In one way, hard disk drives are like file cabinets: you always seem to fill them up no matter how big they seemed at first. In other words, with hard drives, bigger truly is better! To learn more about hard disk drives, see Chapter 12.

Video Card Questions: Most current software supports the VGA video standard. You don't need to know what VGA stands for; just make sure your PC comes with a VGA-compatible monitor and video card (to find out what a video card is, see Chapter 10). Most manufacturers also offer Super-VGA displays. Super-VGA displays show more colors and have a finer level of detail than regular VGA displays, but they still are compatible with VGA.

Other Gadgets: Anything else you need? Some software requires a mouse—Windows and OS/2 programs are useless without one. Many entertainment programs work best with a joystick; if you need one, make sure your PC has a game port. Above all, make sure you have considered which options make using your software as easy as possible.

Last Step—Finding a PC with the "Right Stuff"

The purchase of a PC with the "right stuff" has been the plan all along. Now that you know your software needs, you can begin looking for a PC that meets those requirements, right? Not quite. Before you start looking, you'll want to know which PCs offer the best features for your money.

Suppose, for example, you decide you need a PC with 4M of RAM and a hard disk with 80M of space. You still don't know what kind of RAM to look for, or what specifications your hard drive should have. With just a little more information, you can be confident that you are getting the most PC for your hard-earned dollar.

You could read the rest of this book before you get your PC, but then you would probably know more computer stuff than you really want to. If you don't want to read this whole book first, just read the following short sections. The first sections provide purchase tips for items such as RAM, video cards and monitors, and hard disk drives common to all computer systems. The last three sections suggest configurations for DOS, Windows, and OS/2 PCs.

Don't worry if you don't understand everything in the following sections— that's why God made computer geeks. The important thing is to know which buzzwords and system specifications are important and which ones don't really matter.

General Things To Know About All PCs

Just as all cars have engines, transmissions, and wheels, computer designs have several key components in common. These computer components have their own terminology and specifications. The next few sections won't attempt to explain how these components work—you can read the other chapters later in the book if you're interested. These sections provide you with intelligent questions for salespeople that make you seem like a seasoned computer professional. The sections also tell you what to look for and what to avoid when shopping for your PC.

RAM (Random Access Memory)

RAM is the high-speed temporary memory where your computer keeps programs while it is using them. Two important questions about RAM should be asked when shopping for a PC.

1.   How much additional RAM can be added to the motherboard?

Make sure you can add extra RAM on the motherboard in case you need more RAM in the future. You also need to find out how much extra RAM costs, and in what increments it can be added to the PC. Avoid PCs that require *memory boards*, which are additional special hardware required to expand your PC's RAM. These boards are expensive and usually don't perform as well as motherboard-based RAM.

2.   How fast is the memory?

Memory speed is determined by how fast it responds to requests. RAM speed is measured in nanoseconds—a nanosecond is equal to one billionth of a second. Most newer PCs should have memory that is rated at 100 nanoseconds or better—the lower the number the better. High speed computers built around 386 and 486 processors, (see Chapter 9 for information on processors), however, should have RAM rated at a maximum of 70 nanoseconds.

NERDY DETAILS

A *nanosecond* (ns) is an incredibly small amount of time. 386 and 486 processors are so fast, however, that they can easily overwhelm even fast 70-nanosecond memory. To prevent the processor from having to spend too much time waiting, computer manufacturers include a "RAM cache" (pronounced like Johnny Cash) in their computers.

A RAM cache is a small amount of very fast memory (40ns), which sits between the processor and the main memory. The RAM cache keeps the most often used data handy for the processor. That way, the processor can get most of its requests from the speedy cache memory, instead of rooting through the main memory. The cache is smart too; it constantly updates the data it stores according to what the processor needs the most.

Hard Disk Drives

Hard disk drives store your programs and data permanently (more or less). When your computer prepares to use a program or data, it "loads" or copies the data into RAM from the hard drive. Many different types of hard drives exist, and many options are available—read about them in Chapter 12. Most people care about only three things when it comes to hard drives: speed, speed, and size.

1.   How fast is it?

Hard drives are measured in two different ways. The first is the access speed. *Access speed* measures how fast the hard drive physically finds data located on the hard disk. Your PC's hard drive access speeds shouldn't exceed 28ms (milliseconds or one thousandth of a second).

2.   How fast is it?

The second measurement is data transfer speed. *Data transfer speed* is measured in kilobits per second (kps). Your hard drive should rate at least 750kps; after the hard drive finds the data, it can move it to another location at 750 kilobits per second.

3.   How big is it?

A hard drive's capacity is measured in megabytes. Just in case anyone asks, a *megabyte* is approximately one million bytes (or exactly 1,048,576 bytes— maybe that little tidbit will put you over the top in Final Jeopardy some day). New software, especially Windows and OS/2 software, needs a lot of room. It is common for a program to need 10-15 megabytes of disk space just to store its program files. For this reason, you want a hard drive with plenty of room to store your programs.

The bottom line? Get the biggest, fastest hard drive you can afford. You'll appreciate the speed every time you use your PC. A slow hard drive can make using a PC frustrating.

Video Cards

Video cards perform the same function as TV tuners: they translate and then transmit signals from the guts of your PC to your monitor's screen. A monitor displays only information its video card sends it. When you are looking for your PC, make certain it comes with a VGA-compatible video system. There are differences, however, between VGA video systems. Here are a few questions to ask the "professionals."

1.   What resolutions can my video card produce?

Standard VGA cards work at 640×480 resolution; that is, 640 pixels wide and 480 pixels high. Many newer "Super VGA" video cards can work at 800×600 or 1024×768 resolutions. For Windows and OS/2, Super VGA cards are the way to go.

2.   How many colors can it display at one time?

Standard VGA cards can display up to 256 colors simultaneously in DOS and up to 16 colors under Windows or OS/2. Most users prefer video cards that can display 256 colors. Check to make sure your video card can display 256 colors at all resolution levels.

Monitors

Again, you should consider only VGA-compatible monitors. Your monitor is the single most used component of your PC—make sure you get one that is easy on the eyes. To ensure you are getting a good monitor, ask:

1.   Which resolutions can the monitor display?

The monitor should match the output from your VGA video card. The best choice is a "multisynchronous" (able to run at variable resolutions) monitor that can display at least 1024×768 resolution.

2.   What it the "dot pitch" of this monitor?

"Dot pitch" isn't some relative of the spit-ball; it refers to the size of the individual dots that make up each of your monitor's pixels. The smaller the dot pitch, the sharper the image. Your monitor should have a dot pitch of less than .31; .28 is more desirable. (For more information on dot pitch, see Chapter 10.) Stay away from monitors with a dot pitch of .41 or over, unless you don't mind staring at a fuzzy screen.

Specific Recommendations

You are now armed with enough questions to scare most computer sales-people, or at least get you some respect. There still are quite a few options to look for when you purchase a PC. The following tables list general system recommendations for DOS, Windows, and OS/2 systems. Each system is listed in good, better, best format. Compare these tables against the specification sheet for the PC you are considering. If you aren't certain what something means, either ask the sales rep or look it up in other parts of this book.

Again, don't worry if you don't understand all the terms; hopefully, the computer salesperson will know. This "shopping guide" ensures that you will find the best system for your needs and those of the software.

Picking a DOS System

Here's the skinny on systems that work well with DOS-based software.

Table 2.2
Get the Best DOS System You Can Afford

	Good	Better	Best
CPU/speed	386SX/16	386/33	Any 486
RAM	1M	2M	2M+
Hard Disk/speed	40M/<35ms	60M/<28ms	80M/<28ms
Video Card/colors	VGA/16 Colors	SuperVGA/256 Colors	Accelerated SuperVGA/256 Colors
Color VGA Monitor resolution	640×480	800×600	1024×768
Open Drive Bays	1 open	1 open	2 open and externally accessible
Open Slots	1 open slot	2 open slots	3+ open slots
Power Supply	150 watts	200 watts	250+watts

Use this chart to judge where your PC falls in the great spectrum of available PCs. You'll do fine with any of these systems, but go with the faster machines if you need more flexibility later.

"I Want Windows!"— Picking Out a Windows System

The process of choosing a Windows system is much the same as choosing a DOS system, except everything should be faster and better able to handle graphics. Here are the good, the better, and the best Windows machines.

Table 2.3
Get the Best Windows System You Can Afford

	Good	Better	Best
CPU/speed	386SX/25	486SX/33	486DX/33+
RAM	4M	6M	8M+
Hard Disk/ speed	80M/<28ms	120M/<18ms	240M/<15ms
Video Card/colors	VGA/16 Colors	SuperVGA/256 Colors	Accelerated SuperVGA/ 256 Colors
Color VGA Monitor Resolution	640x480	800x600	1024x768
Open Drive Bays	1 open	1 open and externally accessible	2 open and externally accessible
Open Slots	1 open slot	2 open slots	3+ open slots
Power Supply	150 watts	200 watts	250+watts

If you look closely, the only areas that changed from the DOS system are the speed of the processors, the amount of memory, and hard disk space.

If possible, get a system with a RAM cache and a video card with at least 512K video memory or preferably 1M video memory (another stupid specification).

TRICKS

Picking an OS/2 System—Making IBM Smile

OS/2 comes pre-installed on a number of different IBM machines. Before you purchase one, get someone to give you a demonstration on both the low-end PC and on the more powerful system.

Table 2.4
Get the Best OS/2 System You Can Afford

	Good	Better	Best
CPU/speed	386/33	486SX/33	486DX/33+
RAM	4M	6M	8M+
Hard Disk/ speed	80M/<28ms	120M/<18ms	240M/<15ms
Video Card/ colors	VGA/16 Colors	SuperVGA/256 Colors	Accelerated SuperVGA/ 256 Colors
Color VGA Monitor Resolution	640x480	800x600	1024x768
Open Drive Bays	1 open	1 open and externally accessible	2 open and externally accessible
Open Slots	1 open slot	2 open slots	3+ open slots
Power Supply	150 watts	200 watts	250+watts

Deja Vu? That's right. OS/2 needs almost the identical systems as Windows. The only difference is a slightly more powerful machine for the base unit. Any of these systems run OS/2 well.

NERDY
DETAILS

About every eighteen months, computer companies release computer chips at least twice as powerful as any before them. This aggressive forward push, combined with the heated competition among computer vendors, has caused PC prices to drop rapidly over the last couple of years. Now, 486SX-based computers cost the same as 386SX computers did only a short time ago (see Chapter 9 for information on processors), and the world's fastest PCs now cost less than the original IBM PC XT did years ago.

Get the most processing power you can for the money. Just realize that less than six months after you buy your PC, new PCs will be faster and cost less.

"Dear, What's the Credit Limit on the Visa?"

Now that you know what you want, it is time to find a place to buy your system. PCs are available from three major sources:

 Local computer dealers (check your yellow pages)

 Large chain or wholesale stores (You know, the ones that sell everything—3-gallon cans of red beans, computers, tires, washing machines, televisions, 50-pound boxes of soap . . .)

 Mail order vendors

You can find computer dealers and large chain and wholesale stores in your local phone book. To contact mail order companies for their latest prices, you need to purchase a couple of PC-related magazines. *PC Magazine* and *PC Shopper* are good choices. *PC Magazine* usually has only major mail order companies listed; *PC Shopper* lists just about every mail order company on the planet. Both of these magazines are on the shelves at bookstores and most grocery store magazine racks.

NERDY
DETAILS

Many computer vendors offer their computers through all three sources! For example, you can buy IBM PCs from a computer dealer, you can pick one up at the large chain or wholesale stores, or if you don't feel like leaving your house, you can call IBM and buy one direct.

I Don't Know, Where Do You Want To Go?

With so many different places to buy a PC, how do you decide where to go? When you speak with different computer vendors, you need to evaluate three major criteria:

 Price. What is the bottom line? How much is the PC going to cost, including shipping, taxes, and any other charges? Do you take small, unruly children as trade-ins?

NERDY
DETAILS

> Some companies lease their computers at attractive monthly rates. Don't let the monthly rate mislead you. To really compare price, ask them to quote exactly how much per month the lease will cost, with tax, and multiply this by the number of months. Next, add any deposits or "buyout" amounts necessary. The amount may be much larger than you expect. Before you lease, make sure you check out what your local bank has to offer. You may do better with a standard loan.

 Service. What will you do for me if something breaks? When computer companies talk about service, they usually are referring to warranty hardware service only. "Service" usually doesn't include answering your questions about how to use the thing, or how to solve problems with the software that shipped with the system.

 Support. What happens when I need help or don't understand how to use something? When companies talk about "support," they usually mean their willingness to help you understand how to use things (including software) that aren't broken.

STOP!

> Make sure you clarify what the computer vendor means by "service" and "support" before you buy a machine. It is much better to be surprised before your check clears, than after it's deposited.

You'll need to judge how each computer vendor stacks up in these three areas before you purchase a system. The right mix of price, service, and support can greatly reduce future frustrations.

NERDY DETAILS

"Low price, great service, free support—pick any two." This quote nicely sums up the dilemma you'll face when choosing where to purchase your PC.

Companies with the lowest prices and solid service usually can't afford to hire people to answer your support questions free. Companies offering free support (or any support at all) have to charge higher prices to offset the expense of having someone available to answer your questions.

Every PC vendor has strengths and weaknesses. Your job is to match your needs to the strengths of the vendor. This chapter lists typical strengths and weaknesses for different computer channels. The descriptions at least keep you from being surprised (or ripped off) when you start shopping for a PC.

Computer Dealers— "I'm Not a Salesperson, I'm a 'Consultant'"

This is how computer dealers typically rate in the price, service, and support categories:

 Price. Computer dealers usually are the most expensive source (although often not by much) from which to purchase a PC: they just don't have the huge buying power of the big chains or wholesale stores, plus their employees are typically more PC savvy and require higher pay.

 Service. Computer dealers usually have better trained sales, service, and support personnel. In addition, it is much easier to get your PC serviced by a local computer dealer than it is elsewhere. Prompt, efficient service, where and when you want it, is one of the reasons computer dealers stay in business. Plus, it's nice to have someone local you can intimidate in person when things aren't working quite right.

 Support. Computer dealers usually specialize in several applications; as a result, their support can be excellent. If the computer dealer specializes in the applications you need, their expertise and abilities to help you may be the only reason you'll need to do business with them.

Computer dealers are a good choice if they specialize in the software you need. They may be the only choice if your software needs are complex (such as computer-aided design), or if you are going to run your business's accounting system with your computer. When evaluating a computer dealer, make sure you are clear on the following points:

- If I buy the computer system here, is my support and service included? If not, how much does it cost? (If you have to pay for the support and service cost anyway, you may want to shop around for hardware.)

- If I buy my hardware elsewhere, am I charged more for service and support than if I buy the hardware here?

- Exactly how much service and support am I entitled to?

Mass Market Stores— "...And I Can Get My Tires Balanced Here Too?"

- **Price.** Mass market and wholesale stores usually have pricing only slightly higher than that of mail order companies. They also have begun to improve the quality level of the PCs they carry. The main benefits of these vendors are convenience and accessibility—you can see, touch, and test the PC before you buy it.

- **Service.** These stores usually rely on third-party service companies to provide warranty service, or they make you ship your PC back to the manufacturer for service. Third-party service companies are only as good as the local person they hired to do the service. Shipping a PC to the manufacturer for service is expensive because of shipping charges, and delays are as much as weeks before you get your PC back.

- **Support.** These stores may provide support, but it usually is limited to making the system functional—their support doesn't include software training. Besides, the same person who sells microwaves and stereos probably isn't anyone you want to rely on for software help.

Mass merchants and wholesale stores are a great place to buy a PC if you are going to use standard software such as word processors, spreadsheets, or graphics programs. These programs are simple enough that you can learn them on your own.

Mail Order—Is It Here Yet!?

 Price. Mail order firms usually have the best prices available and many offer 30-day money back guarantees. Mail order companies always seem to be first to implement innovative technologies and high-performance options. If price is your #1 consideration, then check out mail order companies.

 Service. Mail order firms have had to work hard to earn trust servicing customer's PCs. Some mail order companies rely on many of the same third-party service providers as mass merchant stores. Again, this service is only as good as the local service firm. Other mail order companies try to diagnose the hardware problem over the phone and then send you a replacement part. This is fine if you know how to take apart your PC and fix it yourself. It's not so good if you fear dissecting your PC. The last resort is to box the thing (hopefully you saved the boxes) and return it to the company. Count on waiting at least two weeks for the repair.

 Support. Support at mail order companies varies wildly. Some companies are willing to answer questions just like the mass merchants. Others may not support anything but the operating system that came with the PC.

NERDY
DETAILS

When you call for support, it can be a frustrating experience. Most often you are greeted by those mindless automatic answering machines. You know the kind—after you've patiently listed and responded to five minutes worth of stupid questions and pressed every key on your phone at least once, you hear a message say, "Everyone who works here is too busy to help you now. Please leave you name and phone number and we'll call you when we get a chance."

Rather than waste an hour in an emergency, you may want to call a company's help line before you purchase a PC, just to see what happens.

For your convenience, a few of the major mail order companies are listed in table 2.5.

Table 2.5
Trustworthy Mail Order Companies

Company	Phone number
Dell	800-433-8110
Digital Equipment Corp	800-332-4409
GateWay 2000	800-523-2000
Northgate	800-453-0188
Swan	800-645-7781
ZEOS	800-423-5891

GEEK

NERDY
DETAILS

Uncle Sam is calling!—pay taxes on all the stuff you bought! The editors wanted a big section indicating whether your PC purchase qualifies you for any tax deductions. I checked with a local tax expert (my wife, she's a CPA with tons of tax experience) and we are happy to report that yes, you can deduct your PC purchase—sometimes, maybe.

Turns out you need to read entire booklets that refer to other booklets that require still other forms just to see if you qualify for a tax deduction. The complexity and fear of being sued if this information is wrong forces the author to give this advice: check with your own accountant.

If you feel brave and want to read stuff even more boring than computer books, you can call the IRS at (800) 829-3676 and ask for publications #574 and #855. These publications at least get you started. The publishers, editors, and authors will not answer any tax questions—they are much worse than any PC questions.

CHAPTER
3

Some Assembly Required—Unpacking and Setting Up Your PC

"**S**ome assembly required"—normally those three words conjure up images of frustration and wasted time spent assembling something you swear was never meant to go together. Luckily, PCs are easier to assemble and set up than most children's toys. This chapter guides you through unpacking and setting up your PC. In this chapter you learn:

- The easiest way to unpack heavy boxes

- How to arrange your PC so that it is comfortable to use

- How to connect the snake's nest of cables without going crazy

- How to protect your computer from electrical surges and spikes

- What to do with all the paper, manuals, and boxes

- How to move your computer from one room to another or from one state to another

NERDY
DETAILS

Chapter 4 shows you how to start your PC (it's easy).

Ripping Open the Packages

PCs are really, really difficult to use if left in their boxes. The process of unpacking your PC is simple and requires no special tools. The only things you need are a copy of your invoice, a pen or pencil, a sharp kitchen knife (a short one!), and possibly a pair of scissors. Unpacking your PC is no more difficult than unpacking a television or stereo: you just have to open a few more boxes. This section helps you get your PC out of its box without hurting the PC or the box, or giving yourself a hernia.

Missing Anything You Paid For?

Before you begin tearing into your boxes, take a moment to make sure you have everything you paid for and that the descriptions on the boxes match what is printed on your invoice. While you are checking, make sure each item's serial number matches the serial number listed for that item on the invoice. Serial numbers usually are on the outside of the box, somewhere near the computer's model number and bar-code sticker.

If the serial numbers aren't on the outside of the box, make certain you remember to check them against the invoice after the boxes are opened. If the serial numbers don't match, call your computer vendor and ask for a corrected invoice. An invoice with mismatched serial numbers could cause problems if you ever need to have your PC serviced under warranty.

NERDY
DETAILS

Computers have three "names." The first is the actual product name. You may be familiar with PS/1 from IBM or Prolinea from Compaq. These names refer to a particular style of PC, but do not tell any specifics about how that PC is configured. The second name given to a PC is its model number. Model numbers denote how the PC is configured—its "standard equipment" list.

Finally, computer vendors use a serial number to provide a unique identity (like your Social Security card) for each model number for that particular kind of PC.

Best Way To Unpack Heavy Boxes—with Pictures!

When your PC arrives, you may be tempted to rip open the boxes and try to just pull your PC out of its box. More often than not, when you try to lift the PC out of the box in this manner, the box sticks to the packing material around the PC and you end up waving the whole thing around trying to separate the box from the PC. This makes for great slapstick comedy, but it is not the best way to unpack your PC.

To make unpacking your boxes as painless and safe as possible (for you and the PC), follow these simple steps (see fig. 3.1 for an illustration):

1. Using just the tip of your knife, cut the packing tape along the edges and down the center of the box. Be careful not to insert the knife too deeply (you don't want to scratch your PC).

2. Fold the four box flaps down flat against the side of the box, and holding them there, roll the box first onto its side, then very carefully, roll the box completely over so that the exposed portion is on the floor and the flaps are spread out around the box.

3. When the box is upside down, grasp it, and gently lift and rock it off the PC. You should have your PC, surrounded by its packing material, sitting safely on the floor.

Repeat these steps for the computer case (it's usually the biggest box), computer monitor, printer, and any other heavy boxes. After everything is out of the boxes, you can carefully remove all the packing material that surrounds your PC's pieces and parts.

Figure 3.1

Three (okay, four) simple steps to unpacking a PC.

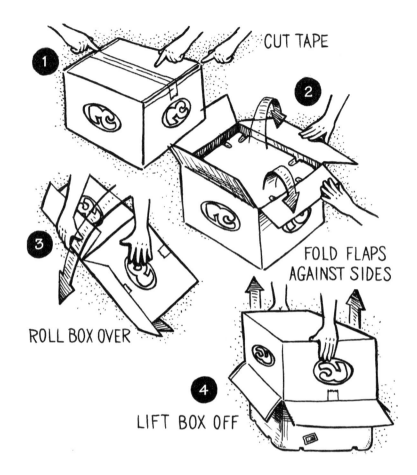

CUT TAPE

FOLD FLAPS AGAINST SIDES

ROLL BOX OVER

LIFT BOX OFF

More Unpacking—Getting Your Equipment Ready To Use

Computers and printers are packaged to survive the wild jungle of commercial shipping services. Remember the suitcase commercial with the gorilla? Computer manufacturers believe that all shipping companies treat their computers this way.

SAVE
THE DAY!

Insurance? What insurance? A PC is not a minor investment. For this reason, you should check your homeowner's or renter's insurance policy to see if your computer is covered. It's better to find out if you are covered now than wait until your PC is floating down the hall because your bathtub overflowed.

To prevent their computers and printers from being destroyed during shipping, manufacturers package them very securely in the box. Before you can use your computer or printer, you'll have to remove a bunch of packing material. In general, you can count on removing the following two items from your computer and printer:

 Disk Drive Protectors. Your PC probably shipped with cardboard or plastic drive protectors installed in the floppy disk drives. These drive protectors serve the same function as a boxer's mouthpiece (without the spit): they keep the internal parts of the disk drive from crunching into each other while the PC is being moved. On 5 1/4-inch disk drives, flip the lever on the front of the drive and pull out the protector. Occasionally, a 3 1/2-inch disk drive has a protector in it; to remove it, firmly push the drive button in and the protector pops out. Keep these drive protectors for use if you ever need to move or ship your computer.

 Print Head Restraints. Many printers have their printing mechanisms fastened down prior to shipping. They may be held by a piece of tape or some small piece of cardboard. It is important that you take this restraint out before you try to use your printer. See the setup instructions for your printer for instructions on how to remove its shipping restraint.

STOP!

Is that smoke I smell? If you plug in your printer and attempt to use it before you've removed all the shipping restraints, you can harm it. Make certain you followed the unpacking instructions that came with your printer before you turn it on.

The best way to make certain you've removed all the shipping restraints is to review carefully the "Read Me First" booklet that comes with your PC or printer. These are probably the only parts of your computer's documentation that you will use, so don't feel too bad about having to read through those few pages.

Arranging Your Computer

Setting up a PC is pretty much the same as arranging furniture in a new house or apartment: it's never just right the first time. A comfortably arranged computer is more enjoyable to use and has been known to improve game scores astronomically.

NERDY
DETAILS

Computer nerds and government health officials call computer arrangement "computer ergonomics." Ergonomics is the study of how to make equipment (machinery, cars, computers) easy, comfortable, and safe for humans. Historians aren't sure, but some think that ergonomics is named after the ancient Greek scientist Ergon.

General Setup Hints

When you are crawling around on the floor arranging your computer, you should keep a few general guidelines in mind. First, don't try to stand up while you are under the desk—concussions take the fun out of setting up your PC (not that it is fun—only nerds would think that). Next, make sure you remember two unquestionable computing principles:

Computers Always Place Third in Contests with Gravity and Hard Floors

Make certain whatever you put your computer on is sturdy enough to handle the weight of the computer. Complete computer systems often weigh over 50 pounds—enough to tip over smaller tables. If you are going to stand your PC on the floor, place it somewhere it won't be knocked over.

Nothing Ever Works Exactly Right the First Time

When arranging your PC, put everything in its place first, then connect the cables. That way you don't have to disconnect all the cables if or when you want to move something to a more comfortable location. In addition, do not wear your Sunday-best clothes; setting up your system requires crawling around, under, and behind your desk several times just to connect and route correctly all the cables and power cords.

TRICKS

While you are under your desk you may want to pick up all the tumbleweed-size dust-balls, old pens and pencils, and loose change. Any money you find helps defray the cost of your PC, even though it usually amounts to only 50 cents (no studies have determined the average amount, but stay tuned).

Specific Setup Hints

If this is your first PC, you may be wondering where to put each piece and part of your computer system. Relax, there are no set rules on how to set up a PC. The goal is to make it as comfortable and convenient to use as possible. You may have to fine-tune your system setup later. Hopefully, the following list of hints will help you set up your system successfully the first time.

Computer Case

People usually choose one of two ways to arrange their computer case—standing on its side or sitting flat on its feet. Either way you set it, make certain you can easily reach the power switch, floppy disk drives, the reset button, and any other buttons you want to play with. You also need to make certain the fan (located close to where the power cord connects) is not blocked in any way and that the PC is not sitting in front of a heating or cooling vent.

SAVE
THE DAY!

Computers use a fan to draw air through the system to help keep the computer at a constant temperature. Blocking the fan can cause the temperature to rise and potentially harm some internals. Make certain the fan isn't blocked by anything when you set up your PC.

Monitor

Try to set your monitor so that it is facing away from outdoor windows or other bright light. This makes it easier to read and prevents the afternoon sun from reflecting off your screen into your eyes. (Rock stars and Hollywood types who wear their sunglasses indoors can position the screen any way they like.) Your monitor should be positioned so that it is comfortable to read—try setting it so that the top of the screen is pretty much at eye level.

Keyboard

Obviously, you need to place your keyboard where you can reach it easily. Not so obvious is getting the keyboard set at the right height. To tell if your keyboard is at the right height, sit comfortably in front of your keyboard and relax your arms comfortably at your sides. Your keyboard should be level with your elbows. This ensures that the keyboard isn't too high or too low. For more on keyboards, see Chapter 11.

STOP!

An incorrectly placed keyboard and poor posture habits can lead to carpal tunnel syndrome (no, a carpal tunnel isn't an overgrown goldfish) or other related injuries resulting from excessive, repeated hand or wrist movements. These injuries can prevent you from typing or repeating the motions that caused the condition.

You can help prevent these types of injuries by positioning your keyboard correctly and adjusting your chair's height to keep your forearms level with the keyboard. Proper posture helps ensure that your hands and wrists are at the correct height. If your desk is too tall for "ergonomically-correct typing," (that's what the bigwigs say) look into under-table keyboard drawers—little platforms that pop out from under your desk.

Mice

You should position your mouse (ball-side down) at the same height as your keyboard. You can place the mouse on either side of the keyboard, depending on whether you are left- or right-handed; just make certain you have enough room to move it around. Mice work best on clean surfaces free of dust and food crumbs.

SAVE
THE DAY!

If you are left-handed, check to see if your software allows you to swap the functions of the buttons on your mouse. Button swapping is especially easy with Windows and OS/2.

Printers

When positioning your printer, the first thing to check is the length of your printer cable. You can't use your printer if you can't plug it in; make sure the cable reaches the back side of the computer case.

The kind of paper your printer uses determines the best way to arrange your printer. Printers use two different types of paper: single-sheet or continuous-feed paper or both. Single-sheet paper comes packaged just like typing paper and photocopy paper. Continuous-feed paper is made of individual sheets attached end to end and is fed into the printer in a continuous stream. (For more on printers and printing, see Chapter 14).

GEEK

NERDY
DETAILS

Most laser, ink-jet, and bubble jet printers work only with single sheet paper. These types of printers come with built-in sheet feeding devices that you can use to stack a bunch of paper in the printer so that one sheet can be pulled in at a time. You don't need to worry about making room for the paper with this kind of printer—its paper path is entirely self-contained.

If you plan to use continuous feed paper, be certain to leave room for the paper to move into and through the printer. Printers that use continuous form paper (most often dot-matrix printers) pull the paper through the back, front, or bottom of the printer. Figure out how you want to feed the paper and leave room for it either in front, behind, or underneath the printer.

Another consideration is to make sure the paper does not run into any obstructions—move all the cables and any other stuff out of the paper's way.

If you plan to use single sheet paper, place the printer where you can reach it easily. This makes it easier to load more paper, or to retrieve your printout before it falls out of the printer and behind your desk.

Modems

If you have an internal modem, hopefully it has already been installed for you. If not, check out Chapter 20 for tips on how to install one. If you have an external modem, you should place it where you can watch the modem's front-panel lights blink on and off and where you can reach the switch and the reset button.

Connecting the Cables

When you have all your computer pieces in place and you are comfortable with their arrangement, it's time to hook up all the cables. The process of hooking up cables is very straightforward. Just take your time, look at the different connectors, match them carefully, and you'll succeed the first time. When connecting the cables, remember "If it doesn't fit easily, chances are you're doing it wrong." If you get stuck and need more information on cables and connectors, go to Chapter 13.

A Quick Note on Cable Sex and Screws

A cable's connectors either have pins, or they have holes. Connectors with pins are called *male connectors* and connectors with holes are called *female connectors*. Some cables have both male and female connectors; others have two connectors of the same gender. This cable gender thing can be confusing; just make certain you are careful to double check the connectors before you try to mate them together. And no, hooking cables together and leaving them in a dark room will not result in cable babies.

While you are inspecting your cable's connectors to determine their sex, you'll probably notice that most cable connectors have small screws attached to them. These screws may have slotted or Phillips heads, or they may be thumb screws that you can tighten by hand. In any event, you don't have to tighten these screws for the cables to work properly. You can if you want, but it's not critical.

It's Alive!—Connecting the CPU Power Cable

Like Frankenstein, your computer needs a big jolt of electricity to wake up. Make certain your computer is off (flip the switch toward the 0 off symbol), then connect the power plug to the computer case. If you have ever used an extension cord, you'll have this part mastered. The computer's power cord always has a grounded three-prong plug on one end and usually a shielded three-prong plug on the other. Plug the normal end into your wall outlet and the other into the case. The power cord usually plugs into the case near the fan and the on/off switch.

STOP!

If your house doesn't have grounded, three-prong outlets you'll need to get an adapter with a grounding strap from your local hardware store. You may even want to call an electrician to check out the circuit. In any event, don't just cut off the round grounding prong on the plug and stick it in the outlet.

Hooking Up Your Monitor—No Antenna Required

VGA monitors have two cables: one is the power cord and the other is the video cable. Both cables usually are permanently attached to the back of the monitor. (The monitor's power cord also has a three-prong, grounded plug and plugs into your wall outlet.)

The VGA video cable is a 15-pin design. Video cable connectors are "D" shaped and can only be connected in one way. You'll find the receptacle for the video cable located either in one of the slots in the back of your PC, or along the bottom of the case near the keyboard connector (see fig. 3.2). Carefully line up the pins and press the cable into place.

Plugging In Your Keyboard

Keyboard cable connectors come in two different configurations: one is a larger 5-pin connector and the other is a smaller 6-pin connector. It doesn't matter which kind you have; they both work fine.

The keyboard cable usually connects to the back of the PC, although some companies are smart enough to put the cable on the front of the case. Both connectors have guide pins or ridges. Line up the connector properly and gently press it into the receptacle. If it doesn't go in easily, double check the alignment and try pressing a little more firmly.

Mouse Tails

Mice use three different types of connectors—a 9-pin serial, a 25-pin serial, or a smaller 6-pin connector. If you have a mouse with either the 9-pin or 25-pin serial connector, look for a port labeled COM1 on the back of your PC, line up the pins and press the cable in place. See Chapter 13 for information on ports.

Figure 3.2

VGA connectors and ports.

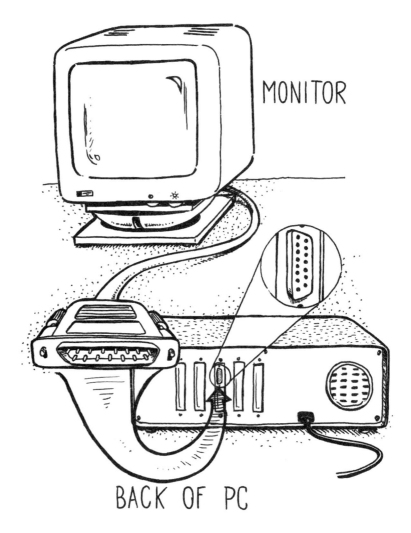

If you have the smaller, round connector (such as a 6-pin keyboard cable), plug it into its matching receptacle on the back of the PC. If you aren't certain which receptacle it fits into (sometimes there are two—one for the keyboard and one for the mouse), look above the 6-pin receptacles on the back of the PC for a label or icon depicting a keyboard or mouse.

Some mice manufacturers include all three types of connectors with their mice. With this kind of mouse (Microsoft's for
example) you'll find a small box close to one end of the mouse
cable that accepts any one of the three connectors. If you
have one of these mice, just check the back of your PC to see
where you can plug it in. First, check to see if you have a
separate mouse port that uses the small, round connector. If
not, check and see which size serial port you have. Serial ports
are male and have either 9 or 25 pins. Find the serial port
labeled COM1 and use the corresponding mouse connector.

Connecting Your Printer

Your printer also has two cables: a power cord and a data cable. The data
cable can be either a parallel or serial cable. Most new printers use a parallel
cable. Check the printer box or documentation to see if your printer is
parallel. If you can't find the answer in your documentation, or if you don't
want to read the manual (most of us don't), examine the backside of the
printer to see if the connector is parallel or serial. If you want to learn a lot
more about cables and ports, see Chapter 13.

GEEK

The most popular printer cable by a large margin is the parallel
cable. Parallel cables send information to the printer in
"parallel" and deliver eight pieces of information at a time.
Parallel cables are much faster than serial cables, but because
of their speed, parallel cables are limited to 15' in length. If the
cables are any longer than that, they begin to lose data before
it is sent to the printer.

Serial cables send data to the printer one piece (byte) at a
time in a constant stream. This sends data to the printer at a
slower rate, but at potentially greater distances (serial cables
can be up to 35 feet long, or the length of a '65 Sedan Deville
convertible).

Printer Power Cords— You Mean They're Not All the Same?!

Most printers use the same power cords as PCs. Some printers, however, use special power cords that have a small lumpy box in the middle of the cord. The lumpy box is a transformer and it modifies your household current to work with your printer. Power cords with transformers usually have a normal plug that goes into the wall and a strange connector that connects to your printer. Again, all you need to do is look at the connector and match it with the printer's power receptacle. When you have them lined up, press the power cord in place.

Connecting Printers with Parallel Cables

A parallel cable has a 25-pin male connector on the end that connects to the computer; on the other end is a connector with a bar running lengthwise through its center (see fig. 3.3). Once you have the ends figured out, match up the connectors and press them in place.

NERDY
DETAILS

> Parallel printers usually have diamond-shaped clips located on either side of the printer's parallel port. Squeeze these clips in the slot provided on the parallel cable.
>
> Some printers (usually more expensive laser printers) come with both parallel and serial connectors. You can change which connector is active either through an internal switch (on older printers) or through the printer's front panel menu. Most printers are set to parallel at the factory before they ship to dealers.

Serial Printers—One Little Bit at a Time

Just as you would expect, serial printers use serial cables to connect to your PC. Serial cables use either 9-pin or 25-pin connectors and often have 9-pin connectors on one end of the cable and 25-pin connectors on the other. Figure 3.4 isn't that exciting, but it does show the difference.

If you purchased your printer with a cable, hopefully the salesperson has already given you the right cable for your printer. The end of the cable with the female connector plugs into one of your PC's serial ports (most PCs have two serial ports); the male connector end plugs into your printer. If no cable came with your system, you'll need to purchase one. To get the right cable, you need to match up the connectors with both your PC and the printer.

TO COMPUTER

TO PRINTER

Figure 3.3

Parallel cables are the superhighways of data transfer.

Connecting a serial cable is only the first step toward making a serial printer work. The next step is to tell your system and your printer how to communicate with each other through your serial cable. See Chapter 14 for information on how to configure your system to use a serial cable.

Figure 3.4

Serial printers come in four different flavors.

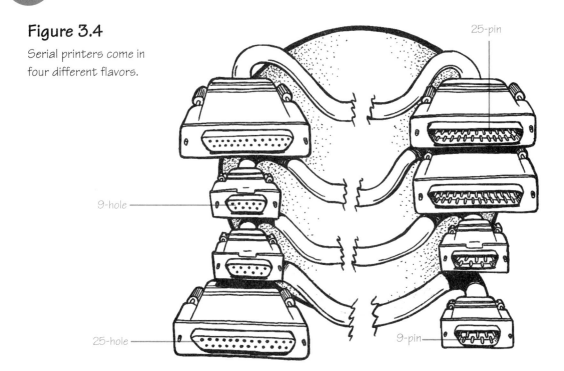

25-pin

9-hole

25-hole

9-pin

Hooking Up a Modem—
Much to the Phone Company's Delight!

There are two kinds of modems: internal and external. Over half of all modems sold today are internal and come pre-installed. Internal modems reside in one of your computer's expansion slots and are accessible from the back of your PC. External modems sit outside your PC and have some cool lights that blink on and off. The process of hooking up either type of modem is easy. If you have an external modem, start with Step 1. If you have an internal modem, skip to Step 3.

1. **Hook Up the Power.** Power cords for modems always have some sort of transformer (a little box, either built into the wall plug or in the middle of the cable), and usually a small round power connector. Plug the power cable into the wall and fit the other end of the power cord into the appropriate port on the back of the modem.

2. **Attach the Serial (not cereal) Cable.** Next, you need to connect the serial cable. The end of the cable with the female connector goes on your PC (normally, a 25-pin connector); the end with the male connector (usually a 9-pin connector) fits your modem.

3. **Connecting the Phone Line.** Your modem has two phone ports: one labeled "LINE" and another labeled "PHONE." Connect the phone cable from the wall to the "LINE" port on your modem. If you plan to use the same phone line for your modem and phone, attach one end of the phone line that came with your modem to the "PHONE" port and plug the other end into your phone. See figure 3.5 for a neat illustration you can show your friends.

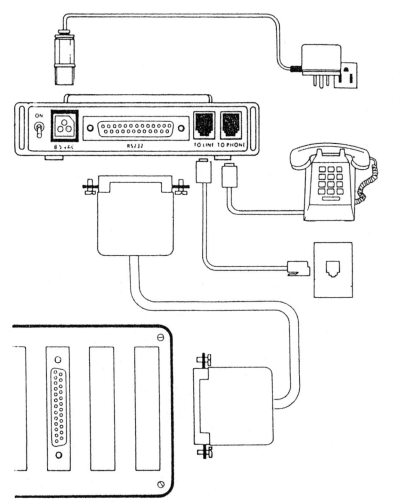

Figure 3.5

It may look complicated, but it's the same as an answering machine.

SAVE
THE DAY!

Click, Click, Click . . . Call-waiting interferes with your modem. When you use your modem, it constantly sends data in little bits across the phone line. The clicks made by call-waiting confuse your modem and result in an error message. If your modem gets too confused, it may hang up or lose data that is being transmitted. To turn off call-waiting temporarily before your use your modem, press *70 (or dial 1170 from your rotary phone). Call-waiting automatically resumes after your modem hangs up.

What If Some of My Cables Aren't Long Enough?

Some of your PC's data cables may be too short, depending on how you arranged your PC. The easiest (and cheapest) way out of this situation is to move things closer together. Another option is extensions that attach to your cables to make them longer. The most common extensions (called *extenders*) are for keyboard cables and video cables, but you can also get longer serial and parallel cables. Remember that one end of the extender cable needs a connector of the opposite gender to work.

Outlet Shortages, Dirty Power, and Other Shocking Things

Throughout this chapter, you've been plugging things into your wall outlets. Unfortunately, most homes don't have 520 outlets for all your computer stuff. In addition, you probably have four different power switches you need to reach before you can turn on the PC.

Computer companies make fancy extension cords that give you additional outlets, make your system easier to use, and protect your computer from power surges and brownouts. Consider picking up one of these doodads:

 Multistrips. Multistrips are extension cords with four or five outlets at the other end. The cool thing about multistrips is they let you turn your entire system on and off from one switch. The uncool thing about multistrips is they offer little or no electrical protection for your expensive PC components. Even multistrips with a little fuse thing don't offer any real protection.

Multistrips are fine for PC users who have reliable, clean, electrical power and who don't experience drops in power.

 Surge Suppressors. Think of a surge suppressor as a multistrip on steroids. They offer the same convenience as a multistrip, but also have built-in safeguards against power surges. Surge suppressors are designed to prevent a surge in electricity (from lightning, for example) from getting through to your computer system.

You should get a surge suppressor. If your lights flicker when your microwave or other big appliance turns on and off, get a surge suppressor rather than a multistrip.

SAVE
THE DAY!

How Much of This Paper and Junk Can I Ignore?

Now that your PC is unpacked, you undoubtedly have a pile of paper, manuals, advertisements, and other junk scattered all over the place. You may be tempted just to throw out the whole mess. Unfortunately some important things are mixed in this pile. Here is a list of what you can expect to find in this mess, and what you should do with them:

 Manuals. Save these. Every once in a while, a computer or software manufacturer actually puts something in a manual that you can use. Useful items include phone numbers for support or customer service and warranty information. Rumor has it that somewhere in all the pages is useful information for computer geeks who have the time to read the things. If you would rather not have the computer manuals take up a bunch of space on your desk or bookshelf, store them in the computer's box.

 Disks. You probably will receive a bunch of disks with your PC. You should save them all. One set of disks contains the operating system (DOS, Windows, or OS/2) installed on your PC. Another disk may have special setup software that you can use to improve the performance of your PC. Finally, if your PC came with a bunch of software pre-installed, all the disks for the software will be included.

All the disks are important; some are so important you should make backup copies. At a minimum, you should back up your operating system disks. See Chapter 5 for information on how to copy disks.

 Registration cards. Fill out and send these cards to the manufacturer. These cards identify you as a legal owner of software and ensure that you receive upgrade notices and any program fixes that the companies may issue.

Warranties. Keep a copy of the warranty with your invoice. Later, in Chapter 5, you can put together a configuration sheet that lists everything you have, where and when you got it, and any important phone numbers. This sheet is extremely helpful if you ever need to get your PC serviced.

Advertisements. A lot of companies are interested in hawking their products to new PC users, mostly because they think new buyers are gullible. Go ahead and browse through the advertisements—occasionally there is good deal. Just make certain you aren't buying software that has been replaced by a newer version of software or hardware.

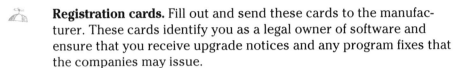

STOP!

Keep in mind that if you buy something from advertisements enclosed with your PC, you'll instantly land on the computer nerds mailing list, after which you will receive "valuable offers" for all types of truly useless stuff.

The boxes. Save the boxes because you will need them. If you ever move, or need to send the PC in for repair, you will appreciate keeping the original boxes and shipping material. If you don't have room for them, ask one of your friends or coworkers if he or she will store the boxes for you.

Moving Your Computer

Every once in a while, you'll need to move your computer. You should take certain precautions before you even move your computer across the room and other precautions if you plan to ship your computer across the city or country.

Short Moves

If you need to move your computer to another room or office (a window view?!), the biggest danger is simply dropping the computer. Make certain you have disconnected all the cables and bundled them neatly so that you don't trip over them when you are carrying the equipment. Insert the cardboard or plastic disk drive protectors into their respective disk drives. You are now ready to move your computer for a short distance.

STOP!

Never move your PC while it is running. The internals of a PC weren't designed to work while the machine is moving. You could lose data, or worse, trip over a cable and trash the whole system (and your leg).

Long Moves

Any time you need to ship your computer, even if it's to your car, you should back up your data. The process of backing up data is a pain, but it is much less of a pain than re-creating all the data on your system if it gets damaged. Check your DOS documentation or get *DOS for Non-Nerds* to learn how to back up your PC.

After you've backed up your data, carefully pack your computer in its original box using all the original padding and shipping materials. Replacements for packing materials can be a bit like solving a Rubik's Cube. If you need help, check the flaps on the top of the box; they often have repackaging instructions.

Make certain you use commercial packing tape to close your box. Normal masking tape isn't strong enough to keep the box closed and could result in your PC being damaged during transit.

SAVE
THE DAY!

If you have lost the plastic or cardboard disk drive protectors, use a blank floppy disk instead. A floppy disk works just as well as the original protectors. The disk probably can be used later if it doesn't get damaged during the move.

Feeling pretty smart? You should. You now know how to open boxes like a pro, set up a PC, why dirty electricity isn't cool, and you've learned way, way too much about cables. Hopefully, you'll never need to move your PC again and you can forget all of this stuff.

PART 2

Blast Off!

4. *Turning Your System On and Off—*
   Performing the Smoke Test

PERFORMING THE SMOKE TEST

CHAPTER
4

Turning Your System On and Off—Performing the Smoke Test!

H ere's the moment you've been waiting for. Your PC is all set up and it's time to kick in the power and see if everything works. Computer technicians call this the "smoke test," as in "Nothing is smoking, it must be okay." The process of turning your PC on and off is not difficult; you've been turning things on and off your entire life.

Useful things you'll learn if you read this chapter include:

- How to find the on/off switches and what the heck "0" and "|" mean

- Do I have to turn the printer on first?

- What your computer does as it "boots"

- Just what the heck "booting" is

- "I've just been "booted"—where am I?"

- How to "reboot"—both warm and cold types

- How to turn off your computer without polluting your hard drive, and...

- How to fix your computer when you screw up and pollute your hard drive anyway.

Read this chapter, and soon you will be a master of turning your PC on and off—just the thing you need to add to your resume in this age of intense global competition.

Finding the ON/OFF Switches— What Language Is OI?

The first thing to do is find the power switch. This may seem trivial, but power switches can be hard to find. Computer equipment designers try to hide the power switches where most users would never expect to look. They do this because they think it's fun to irritate you and also to prevent you from accidentally turning something off.

Why Did They Put It There?

Here are the most likely places to find the power switches for different parts of a PC:

 A computer's power switch is usually on the right side of the case near the back, or it's on the back of the case, close to where the power cord connects.

 Power switches on printers and monitors can be anywhere—they usually are well camouflaged. If you're stumped, see if its near the power cord.

 Some power switches are recessed into the front panel, and identified by the "0" and "I" symbols. These are the easiest to find.

STOP!

Before you power up your system, check two important things. First, be certain you have removed all the packing materials from the PC and the printer. Second, if your equipment has just been brought in from the cold, let it warm up to room temperature before you turn it on.

A really, really cold PC condenses moisture inside the case—water, computers, and electricity don't mix.

Does It Matter What I Turn On First?

Yes, sometimes, maybe. Occasionally, some components need to be turned on before others. As a general rule, turn on your computer last. First, power up your printer, modem, and CD-ROM (called "peripherals"). After everything else is on, start your PC.

SAVE
THE DAY!

Do I have to turn on everything? No—help curb the greenhouse effect and save yourself some electricity by powering up only those items you plan on using. Just remember that peripherals such as external CD-ROMs need to be on when your PC first starts.

You should turn on your peripherals first because your computer looks at a couple of special files (more on these later) when it starts. These files tell the system what kinds of peripherals are connected and how to talk to them. Next, the computer sends a wake-up call to all these peripherals. If the peripherals aren't on, they miss this wake-up call and the computer assumes they're gone and forgets they exist.

TRICKS

If your printer misses its wake-up call—if the printer isn't on when your PC starts—you can wake it up manually. Just press the "on-line" button on the printer so that the little light next to it goes on. Now you're ready to print.

One Switch Does It All!

You can avoid repeatedly groping around your computer's backside trying to find the power switch by using a multistrip or surge supressor (see Chapter 3). With a surge suppressor, when you've found all the switches, you can leave them on. You can turn everything on and off just by flipping the single master switch on the multistrip or surge supressor. Because your computer takes longer to come to its senses than the peripherals, your peripherals will be ready and waiting by the time the PC is awake and ready to make its "wake-up calls."

What Was That All About?— When Your PC "Boots"

After you turn your PC on it should display some text and numbers on-screen, make a few grinding noises, beep once or twice, and then start either DOS, Windows, or OS/2.

If all this stuff happened, congratulate yourself—you've just "booted" your PC. If this didn't happen, check out the "Something Doesn't Seem Right— Help!" section later in this chapter.

NERDY
DETAILS

Why do nerds speak of the process of starting a PC as "booting the PC"? Because the phrase "boot your PC" is more confusing that simply saying, "Start up your PC." Other people think that "boot" originally came from the Horatio Alger story in which the main character was told to "Lift yourself up by your bootstraps." Never mind that this is impossible unless you are in outer space. Aren't you sorry you asked?

Booting, Coffee, and Other Wake-Up Rituals

Think of "booting" as kicking your PC out of bed. Instead of hitting the snooze alarm and crawling back under the covers for more sleep, when your PC wakes up it always (unless it's broken or dead) goes through the same start-up routine.

Your PC is ready for work only after completing this routine, just like some people who need to gulp down their morning cup of coffee. If you watch your PC screen closely after you start it, you can see it race through a typical routine outlined in the following sections.

First, the BIOS—
Who Am I and What Am I Made Of?

When a computer wakes up (boots), it follows a list of instructions and then reads an inventory list to figure out how it is configured and which parts are supposed to be attached to the PC. The instructions are stored in a chip called the "ROM BIOS," and the inventory list is stored in a "CMOS" chip. These chips give your PC the information it needs to complete the "boot" process.

NERDY DETAILS

Two truly nerdy words you may encounter are ROM BIOS and CMOS. ROM BIOS stands for Read Only Memory Basic Input Output System. Read Only Memory (ROM) can only be read, not changed. The Basic Input Output System (BIOS) is the list of instructions your PC uses when it first wakes up. The ROM BIOS is a permanent list of instructions that your PC uses when it first wakes up.

CMOS stands for Complementary Metal-Oxide Semiconductor. The CMOS stores an inventory list of the guts of your PC. The CMOS can be updated through your PC's setup program to accept any changes to your PC. For example, you would need to update the inventory list stored in the CMOS if you changed video cards or installed more memory in your PC.

Second, Memory Tests—
Did Your PC Forget Something?

When you start your system, do you see the numbers race by (they look like the odometer of a very fast moving car)? That is your PC counting and testing its memory. While counting its memory, your PC may call some of the memory "base" and other memory "extended"—check out Chapter 9 for details.

Your PC checks its memory every time it starts up just to reassure itself that it won't forget anything while you're using it that day. This memory test is part of what computer nerds call the POST routine. *POST* stands for Power

On System Test. On some computers you can interrupt the memory test by hitting the space bar on your keyboard (as opposed to the space bar on someone else's keyboard).

Third, the Startup Files—Strange Disk Noises

The third thing your PC looks for is a set of special startup files. These files take over for the ROM BIOS and feed still more instructions to your PC.

Your PC first looks for these files in the floppy disk drives—that's why it makes a grinding noise while your PC starts. These files are most often found, however, on the hard disk drive.

NERDY DETAILS

What's so special about the startup files? On Windows- and DOS-based systems, your PC needs to find three files before it can finish its wake-up routine and be ready for work: IBMBIO.SYS, IBMDOS.COM, and COMMAND.COM.

The first two files are hidden files. You can't see them (or accidentally delete them) without using special DOS commands. The third file, COMMAND.COM, is the actual DOS program file. Don't delete it or rename it.

SAVE THE DAY!

Even veteran users occasionally erase their startup files, or mess them up in some way. The installation of some software packages can screw up your startup files so that they no longer work.

Screwed-up startup files can be an extremely irritating problem if you don't have an emergency boot disk. See Chapter 12 or 17 to see how to make your own emergency boot disk. (Emergency boot disks are so important we put them in the book twice!)

For more information on disks and disk drives, see Chapter 12.

Fourth, the Startup Beep!

Soon after your disk drives chug-a-lug and grind, your PC beeps. The beep occurs just to tell you everything is okay and your PC is ready to start its day. The beeps also let you know when things go wrong. On IBM PCs, for example, one long beep and one short beep means the PC's motherboard (see Chapter 9) has problems.

Fifth, Any Last Minute Instructions?
Two More Strange Files

The last two files your PC reads, if they are present, are CONFIG.SYS and AUTOEXEC.BAT. CONFIG.SYS contains instructions that DOS follows to fine-tune itself and to tell it how to work with peripherals that weren't listed in the CMOS. The AUTOEXEC.BAT file is simply a list of DOS commands you normally type at the keyboard. When these commands are placed in the AUTOEXEC.BAT file, the computer can play them back on its own—just like a tape recorder plays back the words you recorded.

SAVE
THE DAY!

Occasionally, you may want to interrupt the playback of your PC's AUTOEXEC.BAT file. Suppose, for example, the AUTOEXEC.BAT file normally starts Windows for you and for some reason, you don't want to go into Windows. You can stop the AUTOEXEC.BAT process by simultaneously pressing the Ctrl and C keys. These keys cause your computer to stop whatever it is doing and wait for your instructions.

After your PC completes these four steps it is ready to use. You have just been "booted" into either DOS, Windows, or OS/2.

This Ain't Kansas—
Where Did I Get Booted to?

Your computer has just finished booting, but where did it boot you to? (Excuse the sophisticated nerdy grammar.) Most PCs boot directly into DOS, Windows, or OS/2. The next sections show you how to tell where you have been booted and what to look for once you've arrived.

The C Prompt—"'C' What? I Don't See a Damn Thing Except C:\>"

Some PCs boot you right into DOS. You can tell you're in DOS if you see mostly a blank screen with a "C:\>" and a blinking line in the upper left hand corner of the screen. Check out figure 4.1 to see a standard DOS screen.

Figure 4.1

The extremely informative DOS screen.
Yeah, right.

Don't know what to do next? Don't feel bad; there's not much you can do with DOS alone. You need to find out the location of your programs (if any) on your computer. See Chapter 5 in this book for a brief overview of the most useful DOS commands.

If you're dying to do something with your computer right now, type **DIR** and press the Enter key. This command shows you the files stored on your disk drive. You may even see the AUTOEXEC.BAT and CONFIG.SYS files mentioned earlier. Feel better? Go to Chapter 5 if you can't wait to try some other commands.

On some DOS systems, you may have been booted into the MS-DOS Shell. Check out figure 4.2 to see if this is where you've landed. The MS-DOS Shell is DOS's built-in menu. This menu shows you how your files are stored on the hard disk and also lists some DOS commands in the bottom window.

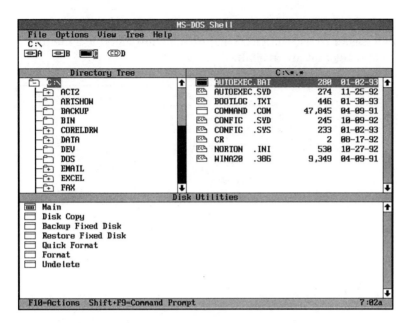

Figure 4.2

The "at least it's friendlier than DOS" DOS Shell.

The DOS Shell isn't much easier to use than DOS, which means you still need help learning how to move around in the PC and how to start your programs.

SAVE THE DAY!

Have you ever screamed "I need help with DOS!"? If your PC is DOS-only, and isn't using Windows, you're going to need help. The best help the author can recommend is to get *DOS for Non-Nerds* from New Riders Publishing. *DOS for Non-Nerds* tells you exactly what you need to know about DOS and ignores all the crud you don't need to know. An order card is in the back of this book.

It Doesn't Look Like DOS, But It's Not Windows or OS/2... What Is It?

Sometimes PCs are set up with an opening menu that may be a simple numbered list of applications (Press 1 for Word Processing, Press 2 for Graphics, or hold on the line for an operator), or it may be a menu that lets you use your arrow keys to highlight an item you want to use. Menus are

Chapter 4: Turning Your System On and Off—Performing the Smoke Test!

86

extremely common on network systems and in large companies. Either way, a menu system is easier to use than DOS. Figure 4.3 shows a typical menu screen with the choices that are available.

Figure 4.3

A menu provides a list of options—hold the onions!

```
                    A Super Simple Menu System

                    1. Word Processing

                    2. Spreadsheet

                    3. Database

                    4. Graphics

                    5. Attach to Network

                    6. Exit System


                    Press the number of the program
                    you want to use.



Enter Your Choice:
```

With many menu systems, it is possible to exit (accidentally) the menu, which dumps you back to the wonderful "C:\>" prompt. If your PC has a menu, find out from the person who set up your PC how to get back into the menu, just in case you make an unexpected visit to the lovely "C:\>" prompt. Write the command or procedure on a sticky note and stick in on your monitor.

SAVE
THE DAY!

You've lost your menu, you're stuck at the DOS prompt, and no one is around to help. Don't panic; you may be able to restart the menu by running the AUTOEXEC.BAT file your computer uses when it starts. To do so, type **\AUTOEXEC.BAT** (the backslash "\" is necessary) and press Enter. Some text should fly by, and (if you're lucky) bingo! your menu is back.

Windows—Much Cooler Than DOS

Most new computers have Windows preinstalled. If you're lucky, your PC has been configured to start Windows automatically. Figure 4.4 shows a typical Windows screen. Your Windows screen may look different because

Windows' appearance can be customized easily. You can change the colors and patterns, window sizes, and shapes—you can even "hang" pictures in the background.

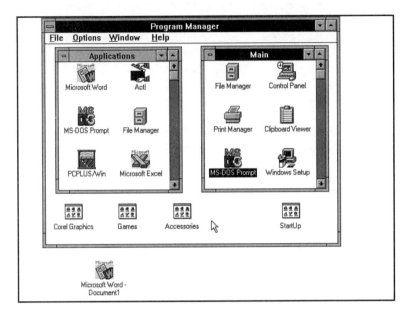

Figure 4.4

A "typical" Windows screen—yours may look different.

If your computer is supposed to come with Windows, but it didn't load automatically, try typing **WIN** and press the Enter key at the DOS prompt (C:\>—remember). If nothing happens, Windows probably hasn't been installed, or worse, you don't have the Windows program.

STOP!

If you find yourself staring at the DOS C:\> prompt, don't automatically assume you are out of Windows. Type **EXIT** and press Enter first. You might just pop back into Windows.

This is because you can start DOS without ever leaving Windows.

The best thing about Windows is Windows software. Unlike DOS programs, well-behaved Windows programs use commands similar to other well-behaved Windows programs. With Windows software, you can always find the **P**rint command under the **F**ile menu, and a **H**elp menu is always on the right side of the screen.

NERDY
DETAILS

CUA—Oh boy! Another acronym! Windows software incorporates a technique called Common User Access (CUA). This cryptic term simply means that different Windows software packages use similar menus and work in consistent ways—just like all cars have a steering wheel and gas and brake pedals. The best part about CUA is that the commands you learned in one program often work the same way in other programs.

For more information on Windows, see Chapter 6. This section includes just enough information to get you started with Windows, but not enough to make you dangerous.

SAVE
THE DAY!

Somebody Help Me With These Windows! Yes, Windows is easier to learn than DOS. Climbing a 30' cliff also is easier than climbing a 60' cliff. Even with Windows, new users need to grab an occasional safety rope. The best rope available is *Windows for Non-Nerds* (New Riders Publishing).

Windows for Non-Nerds tells you exactly what to hang onto and how to avoid crashing. See the back of the book for information on how to get your copy of *Windows for Non-Nerds*.

Oh Ess Two—IBM's OS/2

Maybe OS/2 appears after your PC boots. If you have OS/2, your screen should look like the one in figure 4.5. OS/2 is the first type of software in a whole new generation of high-powered operating systems.

OS/2 combines the ease-of-use of Windows with the capabilities of today's more powerful hardware. Think of OS/2 as Windows on steroids: larger, faster, more powerful, but still legal. OS/2 doesn't care what kind of software you have; it can use DOS, Windows, or OS/2 software with equal ease. Software written specifically for OS/2, however, can more easily take advantage of OS/2's advanced features.

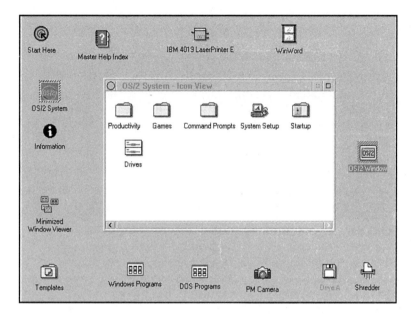

Figure 4.5

The IBM OS/2 screen—
Windows on steroids.

OS/2's main advantage is that it is a 32-bit operating system; Windows still is a 16-bit operating system. That means OS/2 works with 32-bit chunks of information at the same speed that Windows works with 16-bit chunks of information. The movement of bigger chunks of information can make OS/2 faster than Windows for some applications.

NERDY
DETAILS

OS/2 won't be alone in the 32-bit world for very long. Microsoft, the maker of Windows, is preparing Windows NT for release some time in the summer of '93. Microsoft Windows NT is an advanced 32-bit version of Windows that offers the familiarity of Windows with all the power of OS/2.

OS/2's power has a cost. OS/2 requires more disk space and more memory than does Windows. OS/2 also needs a faster computer to achieve performance similar to Windows. All in all, you won't go wrong using either OS/2 or Windows.

Something Doesn't Seem Right— Help!

Nobody's perfect, and not all PC systems start up perfectly the first time. Most PC startup problems aren't serious and can be fixed easily. Here is a list of the most common symptoms and how to fix them:

 Nothing happened when I flipped the switches! Check all your power cables to make sure they are plugged in securely. Next, make sure everything is plugged into the wall outlet. If you are using a multistrip or surge supressor, check its fuse or reset button.

 The lights are on, but no one is home! If everything is buzzing and humming and you can't see anything on the monitor, open your eyes. If that doesn't help, check to see if the monitor is plugged in, and that the monitor is actually on (the tiny light on the front of the monitor should be shining). Next, check to see if your video cable is attached (see Chapter 3 for help with video cables). Finally, try spinning the little contrast and brightness knobs on your monitor.

 Non-System disk or disk error. Replace and press any key when ready. If you see this message, you either forgot to take out the disk protector from a new PC, or a floppy disk was left in the floppy disk drive. Remove the disk or disk protector and press the Enter key.

 Keyboard Error. Your keyboard cable probably came loose. Make certain your keyboard is plugged in.

 CMOS Setup Error.... Oops. This one you can't fix unless you learn a lot more than you probably want to about PCs. If you see this error, you'll need professional help (for your PC).

 My monitor is spinning and my disk drive is oozing blood. Run. Fast. Then call Stephen King. Maybe you can sell the book rights to your PC's story.

If nothing in this list helps, try turning everything off and back on again. If that doesn't cure the problem, turn to Chapters 17 and 18 for additional troubleshooting information and where to go for help.

New Shoes—Rebooting the System

Every once in a while your PC will become thoroughly confused and quit working. It will just sit there with the letter you spent all morning crafting to perfection, and nothing will happen. After you pound on the keyboard and try desperately to save your work, the PC begins to beep whenever you hit a key. At this point, your PC has a terminal case of amnesia—any data you didn't save are goners.

PCs get amnesia from a variety of sources. Maybe there was an electrical surge, or one of your programs crashed. If you are on a network, maybe some clod started fiddling with the network cable and crashed your system. Because these things happen, save your work often.

SAVE
THE DAY!

Always, always, always save your work. Some software packages even have an "autosave" feature that saves your work every few minutes. Check to see if your software has an autosave feature. However you do it, save your work often.

No matter how it happened, when your PC is locked up with a terminal case of amnesia, it is time to reboot your system. Rebooting returns your PC to its senses, although it won't return any unsaved data. Reboot your system in one of two ways.

A "Warm" Boot—Try This Method First

Press the Ctrl, Alt, and Delete keys all at once to make your computer repeat most of its normal wake-up routine. The only things you won't see when the letters start to fly is the BIOS message or the memory count. A "warm boot" is easier on your PC and is a slightly more polite way of letting your PC know you're not happy and that it needs to get its act together.

The Dreaded RESET Button— Use This Method Last

The reset button makes your computer think it has been turned off and then back on (computer geeks call this a "cold-boot"). The reset button is a sure way to get your PC's attention.

STOP!

The Ctrl-Alt-Delete keys and the reset button destroy all the data that you haven't saved. Some believe that's why PC manufacturers chose the Crtl, Alt, Delete keys and required that you press them all at the same time. To press these keys requires either two hands or some serious finger contortions; you're not likely to press them by accident.

No one knows what computer designers were thinking (if they were thinking) when the deadly reset button was placed on the front of the PC next to the useless Turbo button.

I've Had Enough Fun for One Day— Turn This Thing Off

When you're done working (or playing) on your PC, it's time to turn it off. Before you do, make certain you have:

1. Saved all your data. If the PC is turned off while unsaved data is on-screen, the data will be erased.

2. Exit all applications—including Windows and OS/2.

3. Shut the thing off.

Follow these three simple steps to ensure you don't lose any data and you don't confuse any of your programs.

NERDY DETAILS

Computer geeks constantly debate whether it's better to shut your computer off or just to leave it on. That's because they have nothing better to do. There are even some geeks who get paid to argue about that stuff.

To spare you the irritation of reading all the arguments, here's the real scoop, minus the crud: always turn your monitor and peripherals off when you are done using them for the day.

Turn your PC off only when you are done using it for the day. Leave it on when you go to lunch, or if you will only be away from the computer for a short while.

Oops. I Turned It Off with Programs Still Running

Ouch! Assuming you didn't need any data on-screen, the only harm you've done is to pollute your system with some file fragments. To forget once or twice is no big deal, but forgetting a whole bunch of times can leave enough file fragments on your system to make it quit working properly. Keep your PC clean; shut down your system properly.

Okay, I've Been Polluting My System—Help!

Unlike toxic waste dumps, cleaning up your system is easy and doesn't require any gas masks, funky white suits, or knee-high boots. Here is a good way to unpollute your hard drive, depending on the operating system you use:

- **DOS Systems.** From the C:\> prompt, type **CHKDSK /F** and press **N** when DOS asks if you want to save the fragments to a file.

- **Windows Systems.** Exit Windows by saving your data and closing all your applications. Exit Windows. Now follow the instructions listed for DOS systems (the preceding bullet). When you finish, type **WIN** to restart Windows.

- **OS/2.** Follow the same procedure as that for Windows, except if you are using the OS/2 High Performance File System.

Wow. Now you're an expert at turning your system on and off and you can amaze your coworkers and friends by casually mentioning, "Yeah, I'm waiting for my PC to finish reading its CMOS." One caution: too many brushoffs like that and they'll either think you're a PC Nerd or you'll be in charge of the company network.

PART 3

Software— Getting Things Done

A DOS Primer,
or "The Joy of DOS"

DOS can be simple. DOS can be simple. Keep saying that to yourself, over and over again. Doing so will make you really believe DOS can be simple—or it will make your friends wonder if you've joined some new religious cult.

However, even though DOS can be simple, DOS is never very helpful. Tinkering around with DOS makes it clear that DOS doesn't provide any hints on how or what to do next. If you were brave enough to browse through the 400-page DOS manual, you probably wondered how you could ever memorize all the DOS commands. You can stop wondering. Most of those commands are useless to normal people, or only need to be used once.

This chapter gets you started on the right track, and it may be all the DOS knowledge you'll ever need (or want, for that matter!). This chapter presents the following DOS essentials—general DOS things you should know:

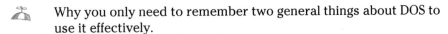

   Why you only need to remember two general things about DOS to use it effectively.

   Which 8 of the nearly 100 DOS commands are useful on a day-to-day basis.

   How a handful of DOS commands that seem to have been specifically designed to trash your computer can be avoided.

General DOS Thing #1:
How DOS Makes You Name Your Files

Just like most people (except Cher, Madonna, and Sting), files on DOS systems all must have first and last names. The first names can be up to eight characters long. The last names, called the *extension* by DOS experts, are limited to three characters.

The first name is always separated from the last name by a period (.). DOS or your software almost always chooses the three-character last name for you—all you have to make up is the first name.

Giving Your Files a First Name:
"What's in a Name?"

Name your files a first name that helps you to remember days, weeks, or months later what is in the file. (If it's years later, you probably should have saved the file to a floppy disk long ago so as not to clutter up your hard drive.)

Suppose you just finished writing a brilliant report that details the first-quarter financial results of your company. How do you name the file so you can tell what it is later if you only have eight characters to work with? Simple: abbreviate like mad! If you want to use all eight allowable characters, you may call the file FRSTQRTR.DOC, or FINANCE1.DOC. (Remember, the program adds the period and the last name.) If you prefer shorter names, you could name the file QTR1.DOC or 1STQTR.DOC—using the number one to remind you that this file has stuff about the first quarter.

STOP!

DOS doesn't allow you to use the following characters in a file name:

. , " ; = | + = * [ ] : / \ < >

These characters are reserved by DOS for other features, or just for the heck of it. Just don't use them in your files' first or last names.

TRICKS

Most computer users end up with more files and file names than anyone can keep track of. Help keep yourself organized (and impress your boss) by printing the file's name right on the document itself. This little trick allows you to find the data file easily for every document you print. Now when someone asks you to make copies or changes to a memo you've already saved, you can ask them exactly which of the 1,000 memos on your computer they are talking about!

What a Last Name Tells You

You don't have to worry about thinking up a file's last name. The program that created the file usually assigns the last name for you. However, even though you don't get to choose your own, the file's last name does tell you a lot about a file.

Those last three characters either tell you where the file came from (what application created it) or what type of file it is. Table 5.1 shows you many of the common file names, where they come from, and what their file type is.

Table 5.1
Some Common Last Names and What They Tell You

Last Name (or Extension)	What It Says About the File
BAT	This is a "batch" file. Batch files "play back" the DOS commands listed in them.
COM	"COM" files are program files.
DBF	"DBF" files are database files that are compatible with Borland's dBASE program.
DOC	"DOC" files are usually word processing files— unless you're using WordPerfect (see .WP4).
EXE	"EXE" files are also program files.

continues

**Table 5.1
Continued**

Last Name (or Extension)	What It Says About the File
SKI	File names ending in "SKI" usually originated in Poland.
SYS	"SYS" files are system configuration files. CONFIG.SYS is a common SYS file.
TXT	"TXT" files are plain text files—they contain unformatted information that can be understood by all programs, even DOS.
WKS, WK1, WK2, WK3	These are all Lotus 1-2-3 spreadsheet files.
WP4, WP5	These are WordPerfect files.
XLS	The spreadsheet Microsoft Excel saves its files with this last name.

As you get more familiar with your computer and software, you'll notice that different programs save their program files with different last names. These different last names make it easier to find files and help you to recall which software package you used to make them.

General DOS Thing #2: How DOS Stores Files

DOS stores files much the same way you do, but instead of shoe boxes in the closet, DOS uses a strict filing system. This filing system uses storage areas called *directories*. A directory is nothing more than an expandable file folder that can hold other expandable file folders. These file folders "hold" your data files.

Just like your files, each of these file directories has a name. These directory names combine to form a kind of home address for the files stored in them. All of the different directories are stored under one master directory. This directory is called the *root directory*.

The syntax (the way in which commands are typed) for DOS commands doesn't make any sense at first, but it becomes more clear once you understand all this directory lingo. The syntax is this:

```
C:\DATA\FILENAME.EXT
```

The `C:\` part is the master folder (imagine a big folder). This master folder is called the root directory; all other folders are stored in this folder. *DATA* is a smaller folder (a subdirectory); the file FILENAME.EXT is a file inside the folder. The .EXT stuff is called the extension. Each file has a name and an extension. All Excel spreadsheets have an .XLS extension; letters and other documents created in Word for DOS have a .DOC extension.

DOS uses the backslash (\) to separate folder and file names from each other. A file that is stored on a floppy disk might appear as such:

```
A:\DATA\OLD\OLDFILE.DOC
```

Notice that this file name resembles the file name a few paragraphs before. Notice, however, that this file happens to be spread inside still another folder. You have to open three folders (A:\, DATA, and OLD) to get to this file!

The file is stored three directories (remember a directory is just DOS's name for folders) from the top. The row of folder names separated by the backslash (\) makes up the file's *address*—where the file is stored. The address is often referred to as the *path*. In other words, you need to go through all the outer folders before you get to the folder that holds your file. Look at one more example.

This time, instead of storing your file on a floppy disk, store the file on the hard drive. The path to the file might be this:

```
C:\DATA\NEW\NEWFILE.DOC
```

In this case, the path begins with the letter *C* rather than the letter *A*.

Pat yourself on the back. You now know how files are named and stored, and that each file has a path (or address) that list which series of directories you have to open to get to the file. Simple, right?!

The Big Eight DOS Commands

DOS has over 90 commands; that's the bad news. The good news is that DOS, like high school math, assumes you'll need to know a lot of junk that you'll never use in the real world. With DOS, you only need to learn eight commands to be a productive DOS user. The rest of the commands are like the quadratic formula—not too terribly useful in day-to-day life.

Combine these eight commands with what you know about file names and directories, and you are now a "street smart" DOS user. You may not know everything there is to know about DOS, but you know the basics. If you want to know more about DOS, check out *DOS for Non-Nerds* (New Riders Publishing)—which helps you learn more about DOS, but not so much that people will think you are a DOS geek. See the coupon at the back of this book to get your very own copy of *DOS for Non-Nerds* (subject to certain state and regional restrictions).

The DOS Prompt—Just What the Heck Is It?

If you've bothered reading any of your software manuals, you've probably been asked to type something at the *DOS prompt*. But, like most software manuals, they never told you what this prompt is or what it looks like. The DOS prompt is nothing more than DOS's way of waiting or "prompting" you for instructions. Table 5.2 shows you the most common DOS prompts.

Table 5.2
Common DOS Prompts

What You See	What It Tells You
C>	Only that you're currently somewhere on drive C.
C:\>	You're in the first file directory folder on drive C.
A:\>	You're in the first file directory folder on drive A.
C:\DOS>	You're in the DOS directory folder on drive C.

Note that the DOS prompt always starts with a disk drive letter. This is the drive (and directory folder, if listed) that will be affected by any DOS commands you enter.

TRICKS

DOS can help you remember which directory you have opened.
Type **PROMPT PG** and press Enter. Now when you change
directories, the DOS prompt will show you where you are! Neat,
huh?

Finding Your Files

DOS stores (okay, sometimes it hides) your files within directories, and
because directories are stored in still other directories, finding your files can
be a challenge. That's where the DIR command comes in handy.

Typing DIR and pressing Enter lists all the files in your current folder on the
screen. Figure 5.1 illustrates what happens after you type the DIR command.

```
C:\PC>dir

 Volume in drive C has no label
 Volume Serial Number is 1932-4F05
 Directory of C:\PC

 .             <DIR>      02-22-93   10:54a
 ..            <DIR>      02-22-93   10:54a
FORMAT   COM   33087 09-01-92    6:01a
KEYB     COM   14986 09-01-92    6:01a
SYS      COM   13440 09-01-92    6:01a
UNFORMAT COM   18560 09-01-92    6:01a
CHOICE   COM    1733 09-01-92    6:01a
HELP     COM     413 09-01-92    6:01a
EDIT     COM     413 09-01-92    6:01a
TREE     COM    6901 09-01-92    6:01a
LOADFIX  COM    1131 09-01-92    6:01a
VSAFE    COM   62336 09-01-92    6:01a
COMMAND  COM   52273 09-01-92    6:01a
        13 file(s)     205273 bytes
                     24887296 bytes free

C:\PC>
```

Figure 5.1

What happens when you
use the DIR command.

There are dozens of tricks to using the DIR command. All you need to do is
give the DIR command a little added encouragement, and it can do all sorts
of neat stuff! You add these extra instructions with the forward slash (/) and
the letter of the instruction you want the DIR command to follow. Table 5.3
lists the two simplest ways to use the DIR command and a couple of the
most common extra instructions using the forward slash (/).

Table 5.3
Common Uses of the DIR Command

What You Type	What Happens
DIR	All files in the current directory are listed.
DIR A:	Shows you all the files on a floppy disk in drive A.
DIR /?	DOS shows you a help screen of how to use the DIR command (sorry, DOS 5 and newer versions only).
DIR /P	All files in the current directory are listed one screenful or "page" at a time—this keeps the files from racing off the screen before you can read them.
DIR /W	All the files in the current directory folder are listed in four columns.
DIR *FILENAME.TXT*	DOS looks for that specific filename in the current directory.
DIR *FILENAME.TXT* /S /P	DOS looks for that specific file in all directories beneath the current directory and lists them one screen at a time.

Look at the last example in table 5.3. You can combine more than one instruction to make DOS do exactly (or close to, anyway) what you want it to do. Or, for example, you could combine the /W and /P instructions to list files in four columns *and* keep them from scrolling off the screen.

Wild Cards—I Forgot the Full Name!

You can use DOS's wild card character when searching for files. A *wild card* is a symbol that represents all characters. DOS's wild card character is the asterisk (*, you'll find it above the number 8 on your keyboard). Table 5.4 outlines some uses of DOS's wild card character.

Table 5.4
Get Wild with DOS's Wild Card Character

What You Type	What Is Supposed To Happen
DIR *.TXT	Searches the current directory for every file that ends in TXT.
DIR REP*.*	Searches the current directory for all files that start with the letters REP. It may find REPORT.TXT, or REPLY.DOC.
DIR REP*.* /S	Will find all files in the current directory, or any directory contained within the current directory, that start with the characters REP.
COPY REP.* C:\DATA	Copies all files in the current directory folder with the first name REP to the C:\DATA directory folder.
DEL REP*.*	Deletes all files in the current directory folder whose first three letters start with REP.

SAVE
THE DAY!

If you have DOS 5 or a later version, you can get help using any DOS command by typing /? after a command and then pressing Enter. This will give you a help screen that shows your command options. DOS isn't completely unfriendly, just mostly unfriendly!

Cleaning Your Screen

Filling your screen with file names is fun, but sooner or later you'll get tired of the clutter and want to clear everything off your screen.

DOS uses the CLS (rough abbreviation for CLear Screen) command to clear the screen. Just type **CLS** at the DOS prompt and press Enter. Pretty neat, don't you think? Too bad straightening up the garage isn't so simple!

There aren't any options for CLS. It only does one thing—clear your screen. Don't you wish all of DOS was this simple and reliable?

Storing Your Files

Because DOS stores all your files in directory folders, you'll want to know how to make and delete your own folders. Keep reading to find out how. Once you know how to create your own folders, you can organize (or disorganize) your files any way you want.

MD & RD—DOS's Way of Making and Removing Directories

Using the MD (Make Directory) command makes a directory folder. OK, what do you think RD stands for? Good guess! The RD command removes or deletes a directory folder.

Table 5.5 shows you how the MD and RD commands are supposed to work.

Table 5.5
Making and Trashing Directory Folders in DOS

What You Type	What DOS Does
MD REPORTS	DOS makes a directory folder named REPORTS.
MD Rumpelstiltzkin	DOS makes a directory folder called RUMPELST—remember, DOS limits you to eight characters per file.
RD REPORTS	If there is nothing in the directory folder, DOS will remove the folder. If there are files in the directory, DOS will ask you if you want to erase them. If you type **Y**, DOS will trash your files and your directory folder. At least it asked first.

STOP!

If you try to delete a directory that still has files in it, DOS will warn you with the following message:

```
All files in directory will be deleted!
Are you sure (Y/N)?
```

If you reply Y, all files in that directory will really be deleted. Before you press N, check to make certain you can live without all the files in the directory you're about to remove.

Of course, it helps to delete a directory only after you have placed yourself outside that directory. Just like demolition experts who don't stand inside the building they are about to destroy, DOS makes you get out of the folder you are trying to remove. The quickest way to get out of the folder, without getting lost, is to type CD .—that will take you one folder "up" and enable you to remove the directory

Use directory folders to help organize your data and programs. You may want, for example, to make a LETTERS folder to store all or your letters, or a TODO folder in which you store current project files.

You can organize and use DOS's directory folders any way you like, but don't just store everything in one file folder. Doing so will confuse DOS and make it very hard for you to find the file you need.

Moving from Folder to Folder to Folder

You use the DOS CD (Change Directory) command to move from one folder to another. All you need to do is type **CD**, the directory folder address where you want to go, and then press Enter. DOS then moves you directly to that folder. Table 5.6 demonstrates how to use the DOS CD command.

Table 5.6
Moving from One Directory Folder to Another

What You Type	What DOS Is Supposed To Do
CD	This tells you which directory folder you are currently in.
CD\	This changes you to the root directory—the master folder directory.
CD\DATA\OLD	This will change you to the \DATA\OLD directory folder.

Practice changing directories a few times. You'll get the hang of it quickly, and it will help you understand how the directory folders on your computer are organized.

Copying Files—DOS's Photocopy Option

Copying files in DOS is just like making a photocopy of a letter. You even use a command name, COPY, that makes sense! What will these DOS geniuses think of next!

The DOS COPY command has three parts: the command itself (COPY), the name of the file (or directory folder) you want to copy, and the destination address where you want the data copied to. Here is an example of the COPY command:

```
C:\>COPY C:\DOS\FORMAT.COM C:\
```

The C:\> is the ever-present DOS prompt. The COPY command comes first—make sure a space comes after this command. The full "path" of the file you want to copy is C:\DOS\FORMAT.COM; the destination (the address) of the newly copied file is C:\. If you are in the directory folder where the file you want to copy is stored, then you only need to enter the file's name, not its full address when copying it. One other cool thing: the same wild cards that worked with the DIR command also work with the COPY command!

Table 5.7 shows you other examples of the COPY command.

Table 5.7
Photocopying Your Data Files

Typing This stuff	Makes DOS Do This
COPY *.TXT A:	Copies all files in the current folder with a last name of TXT to a floppy in drive A.
COPY C:\DATA\DATA.DOC C:\DATA\OLD	This copies the DATA.DOC file into the OLD directory folder.
COPY A:*.*	This copies everything in the first directory folder on drive A to whatever file directory you are currently in.

Copying files takes a little practice. Don't get frustrated if you make a few mistakes—everyone does!

Erasing Files—DEL, DELETE, and ERASE

All computer users eventually collect some files that they don't need anymore. The computer geeks who invented DOS must have had tons of old, useless files because they included three different commands that delete files in DOS. You can use DELETE, DEL (the short version of DELETE), or ERASE. All three commands work exactly the same way.

Because DEL has fewer characters to type, that is the one most people use. If you like to type extra characters, go ahead and use DELETE or ERASE.

Table 5.8 shows you how to get rid of unwanted files.

Table 5.8
DEL: The DOS Exterminator

What To Type	What DOS Does
DEL OLDFILE.TXT	This deletes a file called OLDFILE.TXT.
DEL *.TXT	This deletes all files ending in TXT in the current folder.
DEL *.*	This deletes EVERY file in the current directory.
DEL C:\DATA\JUNK.DOC	This deletes a file called JUNK.DOC in the DATA directory folder.

SAVE
THE DAY!

Every PC user eventually deletes something that on second thought should never have been hosed. If you have DOS 5 or newer, these files aren't necessarily gone forever—you may be able to UNDELETE files that have been accidentally deleted! While we're at it, can we undelete these last couple of years and start over?

continues

continued

To undelete files, simply type **UNDELETE** plus the name of the file you want to get back. If you don't remember the name, you can use DOS's wild card feature (UNDELETE *.*) to return every file from the great DOS scrap heap in the current directory.

If DOS can save the file, it will ask you if you really want to save the file (No, I typed undelete for fun!), and then it will ask you to type in the first character of the file. If you can't remember the first letter, enter any character you want—DOS will still undelete the file, it will just have a different name now!

Preparing Disks So They Can Store Files

Every DOS user uses floppy disks. Before floppy disks can store data, they need to be formatted. Again, in a flash of insight, the makers of DOS called the command used to format floppies FORMAT. Amazing. Two commands that do what they say.

STOP!

Before you format a disk, check (using the DIR command) to see if there are any files on the disk worth saving. Copy these files to your hard drive or another floppy—formatting will erase all the files on a floppy.

Formatting 3.5" Floppy Disks

To format a normal 3.5" floppy, first stick a floppy in the disk drive. Next, from the DOS prompt, type **FORMAT A:** and press Enter. Type **FORMAT B:** if you've put the floppy in the drive B.

You may want to format an older, low-density 3.5" disk (see Chapter 11 for more information). You need to type extra instructions at the DOS prompt. To format a low-density 3.5" disk, type **FORMAT A: /F:720** and press Enter.

DOS will ask you if you want to name your disk (DOS calls it a VOLUME— why I don't know). If you want to, enter a name and press Enter. Next, DOS will ask if you want to format another disk. If you do, press Y; if not, press N.

Formatting 5.25" Floppy Disks

To format a normal 5.25" floppy, first stick a floppy in the disk drive. Next, from the DOS prompt, type **FORMAT A:** and press Enter. Type **FORMAT B:** if you've put the floppy in drive B.

You may want to format an older, low-density 5.25" disk (see Chapter 11 for more information). You need to type extra instructions at the DOS prompt. To format a low-density 5.25" disk, type **FORMAT A: /F:360** and press Enter.

DOS will ask you if you want to name your disk. If you want to, enter a name and press Enter. Next, DOS will ask if you want to format another disk. If you do, press Y, if not; press N. Simple as formatting 3.5" floppies!

STOP!

Never format drive C, D, or anything higher. These are your hard drives and formatting them will really ruin your day, not to mention all of the data and programs on your computer. Only use the format command for drives A and B!

To learn more about floppy disks and floppy disk drives, see Chapter 11.

The Four Deadly Commands

There are four commands that can really trash your system. These commands are either useless for most users or only need to be used once when your PC was set up. Those files, and what they can screw up, are listed in table 5.9.

Table 5.9
The Four Deadly Commands

Command Name	What It Does
DEBUG	DEBUG is used to change the guts of program files. The problem is that even the smallest change can cause the program to crash. Leave DEBUG to the DOS geeks.

continues

Table 5.9
Continued

Command Name	What It Does
FDISK	FDISK is used at the computer factory to prepare your hard drive for formatting. Using FDISK after your hard drive is already formatted is an easy way to lose all your programs and data.
FORMAT C:	FORMAT C:—never type this command. This will erase everything on your hard drive and will likely ruin your day.
RECOVER	RECOVER sounds like it might be a helpful command. It's not. RECOVER turns the files on your hard drive into a useless mess. In fact, go ahead and erase this command (it's in the C:\DOS directory).

Now you know which commands to use and which not to use.

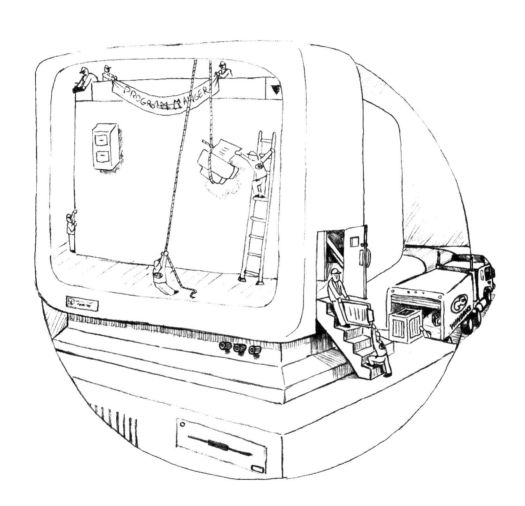

CHAPTER
6

Do You Do Windows?

S eventeen million users can't be wrong! When Microsoft Corporation introduced Windows, the developers (and the Marketing Department) were convinced they found the answer to make using PCs as easy as programming your VCR. Were they right? Well, kind of. During the first few years of the program's existence, not too many computer users were convinced that Windows made PC computing as easy as pie.

Microsoft finally got the attention of computer users when they introduced version 3 of Windows. If you have a computer with Windows, or if you're considering buying the program or a computer with it, this chapter introduces Windows and shows you how to use it. You see Windows up close and personal by learning how to:

 Understand this whole Windows analogy thing

 Examine the parts of a window (... and this—"clink" "clink"—is the see-through part...)

 Examine menus (the computer kind)

 Examine dialog box elements

What Is Windows?

In simple terms, Windows is, first, an easy way of using DOS and, second, a way of making many different programs similar. No matter whether you're using a program to create the community newsletter or to keep track of your personal finances, Windows programs look similar, and the way you use them is similar.

What makes Windows programs similar? The Windows GUI (pronounced gooey, as in "gooey chocolate") does. Think of Windows as the chocolate coating for bitter-tasting DOS pills—Windows makes PCs easier to use. In nerdy terms, though, GUI stands for *graphical user interface* because Windows is a graphical way of using commands and manipulating programs. True "Windows" programs have many similarities; for instance, you don't need to learn a completely new way of running a program every time you pick up a new one.

NERDY
DETAILS

The Windows environment enables you to continue using your DOS programs. A DOS application that runs under the Windows environment is said to run within a "DOS window." Windows 3.1 enables DOS programs to use graphics mode and text mode when running in a window. DOS programs can run in a window only in 386-enhanced mode.

If you're used to using DOS and DOS programs, get ready for a different way of using computer programs. Instead of entering commands at a prompt, you manipulate symbols on the screen. (These symbols can be manipulated by using the keyboard or the mouse.)

What the $#@% Is a Window!?

Even though the folks at Microsoft were pretty smart about developing Windows, they weren't too smart about explaining it. The developers of Windows use mixed metaphors when explaining the program. First, they want you to think of the program as a Window. Then they throw in a metaphor of a work desk (the *desktop*) to refer to the entire Windows environment.

A *window* is a rectangular area on-screen that displays information from a program. You can expand a Window to cover the screen—*maximizing* the window. Or you can reduce the window to an icon—*minimizing* the window. To restore the icon to a window, double-click on it. Figure 6.1 shows several common Windows applications as windows (Clock and Notepad) and as icons (Program Manager and File Manager).

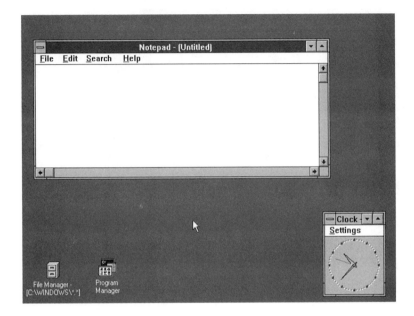

Figure 6.1

Program windows and icons on the desktop.

Technically, the desktop is the screen background for Windows, but the term also means all the things you see when you look at the Windows screen (like the items on an office desktop). Each new task, such as writing a letter or drawing a chart, is run within individual display areas called *windows*.

Mouse Actions

If you have used DOS programs, one of the biggest differences of Windows is the use of the plastic thing with the ball in the middle (a *mouse*) that sits near your keyboard. When you move the mouse or press the buttons on the mouse, something definitely happens in a Windows program (for example, you might delete something and never see it again).

The location of the mouse is represented on-screen by the *pointer*. The standard pointer is the arrow, as shown in figure 6.2. The pointer and the mouse move together. By sliding the mouse away from you, you move the pointer up on the display (unless you're underwater working upside down). Pulling the mouse toward you moves the pointer down on the display. Side-to-side motions move the pointer to the left and right on the display.

Figure 6.2

The location of the mouse, represented by the arrow pointer.

Mouse actions are performed by using the mouse buttons. In Windows the left mouse button is the *select button*. Depressing and releasing the mouse button is referred to as *clicking* the button. In most situations, clicking the mouse button while the pointer is over an object selects that object.

TRICKS

Some actions are quicker to perform by using the keyboard. When you use a DOS program in a window and you want to switch to full-screen mode, for example, press Alt-Enter. To perform the same action by using the mouse, you must select the program's control button and select the Maximize command.

If you start using Windows, you will come across the term *drag and drop*. The term doesn't refer to the way you carry your garbage out at night; it's the way you change the position of an item on-screen by dragging the item to a new location. To drag an item, position the pointer over the item, press the mouse button, move the mouse to the new location (while still holding down the mouse button), and then release the mouse button.

The final mouse action is *double-clicking*; double-clicking requires positioning the pointer over the item and clicking the mouse button twice within a specified period of time.

The Pointer

The pointer used in Windows often changes to indicate the type of action being performed. Figure 6.3 shows several common Windows pointers.

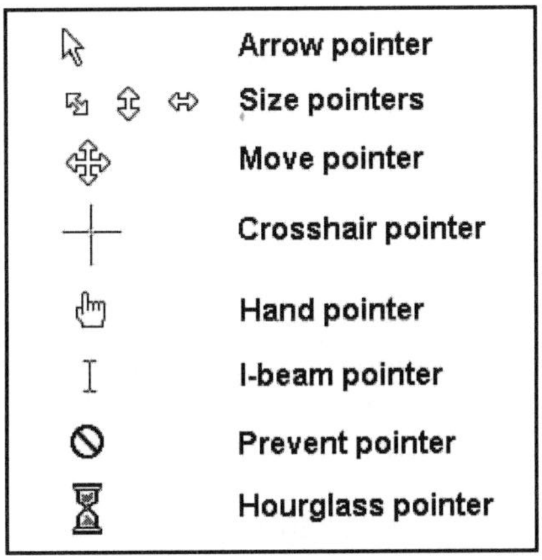

⬉	Arrow pointer
⬔ ⬍ ⬌	Size pointers
✥	Move pointer
+	Crosshair pointer
☝	Hand pointer
I	I-beam pointer
⃠	Prevent pointer
⧗	Hourglass pointer

Figure 6.3

The pointer changes indicating Windows' current function.

When resizing an object, the pointer changes to a multiheaded arrow. When moving an object, the pointer changes to a ghost of the object. (A *ghost*, within Windows, is an object that is represented with a light gray outline or a special picture.)

One of the most common (and least loved) pointers is the hourglass, which appears when Windows performs a task that requires you to wait. Although it is annoying to have to wait, the hourglass lets you know the system still is functioning.

When working with text within Windows, the standard pointer is replaced with a flashing dark vertical bar called the *insertion point* (see fig. 6.3). This bar indicates the location in which new text is inserted when you start typing.

Only Nerds Would Love Windows Icons

When you first use Windows, you'll see many small pictures (*icons*) that represent files or actions. If you want to manipulate an icon (makes you feel in control!), move the mouse to position the pointer on the icon, click (to select the icon), double-click (to activate the associated program), or drag (to move the icon).

STOP!

Windows programs continue to run even when you shrink them down into an icon. If you click on the down arrow in the upper right hand corner of a program, the program shrinks into an icon. The program is still "on" (it's running) even as an icon. If you turn off your computer or exit Windows before you save your work, you can lose your changes.

Mom, Dad, and Kid Windows

When you begin an application, such as a word processor, a window opens. This window is the *parent window* or *application window*. When you want to do something, such as write a letter, you open another window to do your work. This window is called a *child window* or *document window*. If you get tired of writing your letter and want to turn to the secret spy-thriller novel you've been writing, you can open another *child window* in front of the letter.

You can stack a bunch of parent and child windows on top of each other or place them side by side. You can resize windows to display as little or as much of the information as you want. You can change the position or size of the window without changing its content.

Examining the Parts of a Window

All windows within the Windows environment have the same basic set of components (see fig. 6.4). You use these components to manipulate the window's view and its position relative to other windows.

Control Button   Title Bar   Minimize Button

Menu
Bar

Maximize
Button

Window
Border

Scroll
Bars

Figure 6.4

Basic window
elements (no need
to memorize these).

The Title Bar

Every window has a title bar across the top that contains the name of the
application (Clock or Microsoft Excel, for example). If a document is open
and maximized, the document's name also appears in the title bar.

SAVE
THE DAY!

The title bar also is used to indicate the active window. If your
desktop is cluttered with a lot of open windows, you can easily
tell which window is active—its title bar looks different. In
Windows' default colors, the active title bar is a medium blue
and other title bars are white.

GEEK

NERDY
DETAILS

You can easily change colors of most Windows components by
clicking on the Color icon in the Control Panel.

Aside from providing information about the program and current document,
the title bar can be used to move and change the size of the window. To
move a window that is not maximized or full-screen, for example, select the
title bar by clicking on it with the mouse and holding down the mouse
button, and then drag the window to the desired location.

The title bar has a second function. When you double-click on the title bar, the size of the window toggles between the maximized (full-screen) and the windowed states. You can also maximize a window by clicking on the button on the far right of the title bar, as the next section explains.

Buttons That Shrink and Enlarge Windows

Application windows have two buttons in the upper right corner. You use these buttons to control the way the application is displayed—as an icon, a window, or maximized. Most document windows contain only the button on the far right, called the *Maximize button*. The second button on application windows (the leftmost of the two) is called the *Minimize button*. By clicking on the Minimize button, you reduce the application to an icon.

Window Borders—Resizing

The border around each window enables you to change the size and shape of the window. If you grab the side of the window, you can change only the position of that side. By grabbing a corner, you change the position of both neighboring sides. When you place the mouse on the border or corner, the mouse pointer changes into a double-headed arrow, enabling you to drag the window border to enlarge or shrink the window. The type of arrow indicates the way the window can be resized.

NERDY
DETAILS

Whenever you move the pointer to the edge of a "window," the pointer changes shape so that you can resize the window. The arrows you see include:

Type of arrow	Resize the Window
Vertical arrow	Resize vertically
Horizontal arrow	Resize horizontally
Diagonal arrow	Resize diagonally

NERDY
DETAILS

The lower right corner of most windows is an empty square. This square, often called the *Resizing button*, also can be used to change the size of the window. Because it is larger than the window border, the Resize button is much easier to grab.

Scroll Bars—Changing the View

If a program contains more information than can fit in a window, scroll bars appear along the right and bottom sides of the window. Scroll bars do not appear if the window is big enough to display everything in it.

The scroll bar along the bottom shifts the view across the document; the scroll bar along the right side moves up and down through the document. If the document is too large in only one direction, only one scroll bar appears.

TRICKS

Each scroll bar contains a raised box, referred to as a thumbtrack. When you move the thumbtrack with the mouse, you scroll quickly to different locations in a document. If you know that the text you are looking for is two thirds of the way down your document, for example, you can drag the thumbtrack to a position two thirds down the scroll bar. When you release the mouse button, the view jumps to the new location.

You can move the view down the document to display the next full window of information by clicking in the scrolling region below the scroll box.

The Control Menu—Managing a Program

On the far left of the title bar is another button (looks like a hyphen), which activates the Control menu. The Control menu is a special menu that is a part of both icons and windows. You can click on the Control menu button of a Windows application to display the Control menu, as shown in figure 6.5. The same Control menu is displayed by clicking on a program icon on the Windows desktop. The Control menu even is available when an application is running full-screen. To display the Control menu for a maximized window, press Alt-spacebar.

Figure 6.5

All Windows applications have the same items on the Control menu.

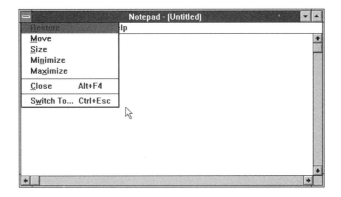

If you are working on a file (that is, writing a letter, changing a spreadsheet, or drawing a picture), another Control menu button appears below the Control menu button (see fig. 6.6). This button looks like a small hyphen. The smaller Control menu button has a few options specific to the program you are using.

Figure 6.6

Application and document Control menu buttons are slightly different.

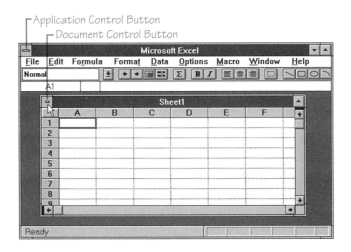

Windows Menus Aren't That Enticing If You're Hungry

Every Windows program, even a simple application program like Clock, has a menu bar. The menu bar is always located directly below the title bar and is a complete collection of all the commands you can use (see fig. 6.7). By selecting a menu name (File, Edit, View, Help, or whatever you see up there) from the menu bar, you can view a list of commands that drop down from the menu bar. The menu bars of Word for Windows and Excel are shown in figure 6.7.

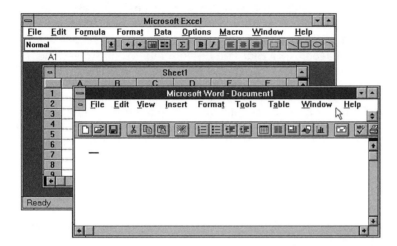

Figure 6.7

Menu bars for Excel and Word for Windows.

Selecting a Menu Item

Even if this Windows program thing still seems confusing, you definitely won't have trouble opening a menu. Windows' developers went way over-board in the number of ways you can open a menu. Here are a few ways to get to the menus at the top of every application:

1. **Click till you're sick.** Click on the menu bar to display a menu, then click on a menu item to perform an action (let's eat!). To exit the menu without doing anything click anywhere outside the menu.

2. **You've been draggin' all day.** Another way to choose a menu option is to point to the menu name, press the mouse button to display the menu, drag the pointer down the menu until the desired menu item is highlighted, and then release the mouse button.

3. **When you're in a hurry (accelerator keys).** Windows menu names on the menu bar contain one underlined character that can be used to select that menu. These characters are referred to as *accelerator keys*. Press Alt (or F10) to activate the menu bar, and then press the letter associated with the desired menu to open it. The File menu, for

example, can be activated by pressing Alt-F. When the menu displays, type the underlined key associated with the command you want to use. When the **F**ile menu displays, for example, press O to select the **O**pen command.

4. **When you're in a big hurry (the speedy Alt key).** You also can select the **F**ile menu by holding down the Alt key and then pressing F (Alt-F). The menu bar is activated when the Alt key is pressed, not when it is released. Note that you do not have to wait to see the menu before you choose the next letter.

5. **Shortcut keys are confusing, but even faster.** Most commands have a shortcut key combination you can use to execute the command without even opening the menu. These confusing combinations (for example, Ctrl-Shift-F12, Alt-F4, Shift-Numpad-5) are called *shortcut keys*. Although you need to memorize these (no, not that!), shortcut keys save heaps of time. In the menu shown in figure 6.8, notice the shortcut keys appear right next to the command.

Figure 6.8

The **E**dit menu has several shortcut keys.

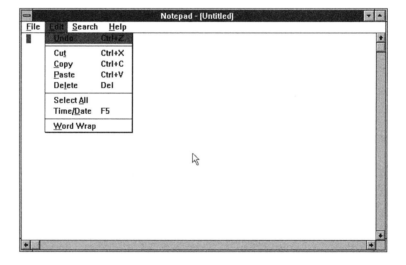

A major advantage of the standard Windows interface is that the same shortcut keys work in most Windows programs.

NERDY
DETAILS

6. **The arrow keys (for seasoned nerds who still do not have a mouse).** The arrow keys also can be used to select menus and menu items. The menu bar first must be activated by pressing Alt or F10. Then, use the arrow keys to move around. Press Esc to close an open menu or to cancel the activation of the menu bar, if no menu is displayed.

Dimmed Options Save Dimwits from Disaster

Windows is a "smart" program: Windows programs generally do not enable you to select an option that is inappropriate or unavailable. Thus, if a menu item is inappropriate or unavailable, Windows automatically changes the color of the menu item to gray (by default). If you try to choose the unavailable menu item, the program ignores your request.

Items with a Solid Arrow (>) Mean More Choices

Some menu items have submenus. A solid arrow to the right of a menu item indicates a second menu displays when you choose that item. This type of menu is called a *cascading* menu.

Cascading menus present a series of options or offer a new level of menu choices. If the menu presents a series of options, selecting the value sets the menu item equal to that value. If the cascading menu presents a series of menu items, selecting one of those items is the same as selecting an item from a first-level menu (a pull-down menu from the menu bar).

Items with Check Marks

In some programs, a menu bar selection is actually a list of options that can be either on or off. If an option is turned on, it has a check mark beside it; if it is turned off, it is not checked. Figure 6.9 shows two checked-off options of the File Manager menu.

Menu Commands with an Ellipsis (...)

The *ellipsis* symbol (three periods) means "continued." An item on a Windows menu that is followed by an ellipsis means a dialog box appears when you choose the menu item. A dialog box asks for additional information from the user before anything happens.

Figure 6.9

The Save Settings on Exit and Status Bar options are active within File Manager.

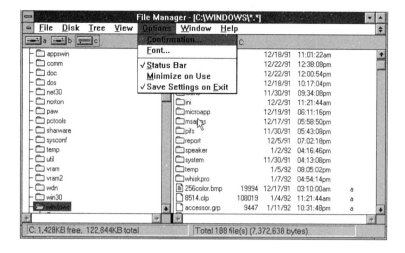

You Want Choices? Dialog Boxes Sometimes Have Too Many

Dialog boxes come in many sizes and "flavors," but they all have one thing in common: they gather and contain information that relates to the current action. Although each dialog box is different, every one is composed of a combination of specific items. Figure 6.10 shows a dialog box containing a number of standard controls.

Figure 6.10

A typical dialog box.

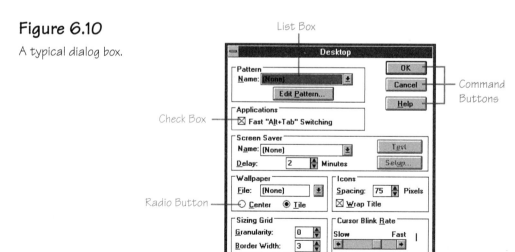

You Want Choices? Dialog Boxes Sometimes Have Too Many

129

Text Boxes

A *text box* (sometimes referred to as an edit box) is a rectangular box that accepts input from the keyboard. In most text boxes, any existing text is highlighted automatically and is deleted when you begin typing. You also can use the mouse (or the arrow keys) to move to a specific point within the text and insert new text. Backspace and Del can remove single characters or blocks of characters when highlighted with the mouse.

List Boxes

A *list box* shows choices, often sorted alphabetically. You can scroll up and down the list by using vertical scroll bars, such as those used to navigate a window's screen display. When the desired item is displayed in the list box, click on it with the mouse. If you double-click on an item in the list, the program selects the item and closes the dialog box.

If you do not have a mouse, get one; dialog boxes are a lot easier to use. If someone stole your piggy bank and a mouse is not financially possible, use Alt and the accelerator key or press Tab and the up and down arrow keys to make your selection. When the selection has the gray outline, press spacebar to highlight it or press Enter to select the item and close the dialog box in a single step. You also can use PgUp and PgDn to move through the list more quickly.

Pull-down Lists

A list box takes a large amount of space inside a dialog box. In the File Name list box in the Open dialog box in the File menu, for example, room for eight file names exists. A *pull-down list* is a space-efficient way of combining a text box and a list box, which allows several lists to be included in a single dialog box, as shown in figure 6.11.

Radio Buttons

Radio buttons (also called *option buttons*) in a dialog box are always grouped so that only one button in each group can be selected at a time. (When you select a button in a group, any other button that was selected is turned off.) These round little buttons are referred to as radio buttons because they resemble tuning knobs of an old-fashioned radio.

Figure 6.11

Pull-down lists in
the Desktop dialog
box.

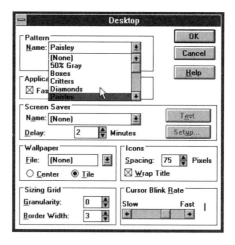

Check Boxes

A *check box* works the same way that you check a box on an order form:
click on the mouse to check the box. When the box is checked, it is considered on or true; when it is empty, it is considered off or false. The Word for
Windows Print Options dialog box, shown in figure 6.12, has several check
box items, including **R**everse Print Order, **D**raft, and **U**pdate Fields.

Figure 6.12

Any combination of
check boxes can be
selected.

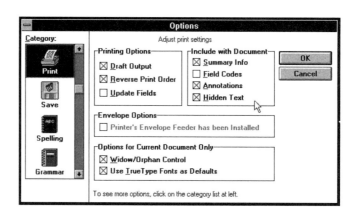

Click on an empty box to check it, and click on a checked box to clear it.
Most check boxes can be accessed by using an accelerator key. If you use
the keyboard, press the spacebar to change the status of a check box from
checked to cleared (or from cleared to checked).

You Want Choices? Dialog Boxes Sometimes Have Too Many

131

Command Buttons

The *command buttons* on a dialog box are used after you complete all necessary information. Two command buttons included on almost every dialog box are OK and Cancel. By clicking on OK, you tell Windows to proceed with your selections; clicking on Cancel tells Windows that you want to exit and cancel the command.

The keyboard equivalent of Cancel is always the Esc key. Enter is a key equivalent for the *default* command button. (The default is the item selected before you make any changes.) In most dialog boxes, the OK button is the default and pressing Enter accepts the changes.

When you use the keyboard and move to a command button, the outer edge of the button becomes darker, meaning that the button is selected. You can activate the current button by pressing Enter.

Windows May Be Confusing, But at Least It's Consistent—File, Edit, Help

In addition to the Control menu, three menu names appear within the menu bar of most applications: File, Edit, and Help. The resulting pull-down menus also are consistent from one program to another. This consistency is a powerful time-saver when you learn a new Windows program.

The File Menu

Several commands always are found on the File menu. The last command on the File menu, for example, always is Exit and the first three File commands usually are New, Open, and Close.The next pair of commands found on most File menus are those used to save a file—Save and Save As. Not only are the commands the same, but the accelerator keys and shortcut keys (if any) are the same between programs. The other command commonly found on the File menu is the Print command. Depending on the program, a single Print command or a collection of printing menu items may be found here (such as Print, Printer Setup, and Print Preview).

The Edit Menu

The Edit menu contains commands for moving data between a program and the Windows Clipboard, as well as a few other helpful things.

NERDY
DETAILS

The clipboard is a common storage area for data. Data is copied to the clipboard, then pasted from the clipboard into the same program or a different program.

The Edit menu for most Windows programs contains the Undo, Cut, Copy, Paste, and Delete commands. These common commands make your typewriter obsolete—Edit commands enable you to move text and pictures around before you print anything. The only option on a typewriter is the correcting key (but typewriters cost about 1,000 bucks less, or the cost of a round trip to the South Pacific).

The Cut command removes the selected data (you must select the data prior to cutting it) from the program's window and places it in the clipboard. The Copy command copies selected data from the program to the clipboard. The Paste command pastes (copies) data from the clipboard into the program's window. The Delete command deletes selected data from the program's window, but does not place the deleted data in the clipboard. The Undo command reverses (undoes) a previous edit command.

The Help Menu

Although Windows' User's Guide is a helpful manual, you might find it inconvenient to stop work to look up something. You can get on-line help whenever you need it by selecting the Help command from the menu bar of your program. Although some Windows programs still provide their own individual help systems, more and more programs are taking advantage of the Windows Help utility.

Hopefully, all these new terms won't scare you away from Windows. Windows really is easier to use than DOS, and you don't have to learn any nerdy commands. Windows makes PCs more fun to use, even though a description of it may put you to sleep. Hello?

I've Had Enough! How Do I Get Out?

133

I've Had Enough! How Do I Get Out?

You can exit Windows in one of four ways: by selecting the
E**x**it command on the **F**ile menu; by pressing Alt,F,X; by
pressing Alt-F4, or by double-clicking on the Control
menu button. As you can see, Windows is easy to get
out of, even if you're not into it.

CHAPTER
7

OS/2 Made as Simple as Possible (Give Us a Break—It's a Big Program)

S o what is OS/2? It's a complicated operating system from IBM (but you can learn it). There, now you know!

About OS/2

OS/2 is IBM's premier operating system for PCs. It provides a lot:

- A powerful and intuitive (psychic) Workplace Shell. Watch out—it may read your mind.

- It can multitask, which means that it can walk and chew gum at the same time.

- It's compatible (lovey-dovey) with all DOS and Windows programs. If you are using OS/2 2.0, you can run programs written for Windows 3.0. If you are using OS/2 2.1, you can also run programs written for Windows 3.1.

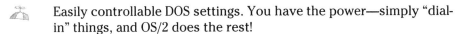

- Easily controllable DOS settings. You have the power—simply "dial-in" things, and OS/2 does the rest!

- Back to kindergarten—you can cut and paste between OS/2, Windows, and DOS programs.

- The really important stuff. There are a whole bunch of games and productivity programs (called "applets") thrown in with it.

Where Do I Start?

Well... let's get going by starting up the computer with OS/2. Because OS/2 is already installed on your machine, just turn your computer on. Easy, isn't it? After OS/2 goes through its startup process, you should see an opening screen that shows the Desktop, as shown in figure 7.1.

Figure 7.1

The OS/2 Desktop.

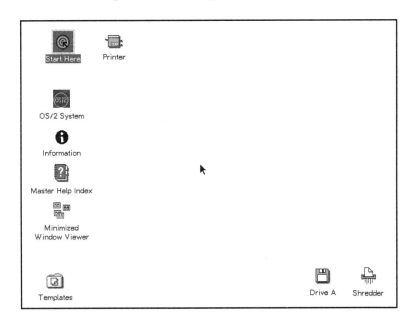

The blank area of the screen ("top of the desk") is called the *desktop*. On your desktop, you can see your main tools, such as the shredder icon that is used to erase files (or really incriminating dirty pictures), the printer icon that you'll use to print, plus some other stuff that we'll get into later.

An *icon* is a little picture that represents something. In OS/2, icons represent things like folders, files, and programs.

NERDY
DETAILS

All of your folders, files, and programs are somewhere on your desktop. Sometimes they will be arranged inside of other folders, so you can keep your desktop nice and neat. Or, you can keep your desktop really messy so that only you will be able to find anything (even if you usually have to use a Dustbuster).

Before you do anything else, find the little black pointer on your screen. In figure 7.1, it's right in the middle of the screen. Move your mouse around and notice how the mouse pointer on the screen follows it.

Now, find the icon in the upper left corner of the screen called Start Here. The picture shows a little bullseye with a mouse pointer right smack dab in the middle of it. In figure 7.1, this object is highlighted. Follow these steps:

1. Move your mouse so that the very tip of the mouse pointer on the screen points at the middle of the bullseye.

2. "Click" the left mouse button once. To do a click, simply press the mouse button down until you hear and feel it click, and then release it immediately. In practice, this is just like typing a key on the keyboard and takes all of a tenth of a second to do.

When you click on the object, you'll see it darken so that it looks just like figure 7.1. What you just did *selected* the object—you told OS/2 that you wanted to do something with it.

3. Now it gets really tricky (Not!). You want to tell OS/2 that you want to open up that object, and that is usually done with a *double-click*, where you do two quick clicks together as fast as you can. They should happen as fast as you can say "Click click." (And don't come running to me if your spouse looks at you funny when you start saying "click click" while doing this.)

Now you'll see the Start Here object open up on your screen. Your screen should look like figure 7.2.

Figure 7.2

The Start Here
program.

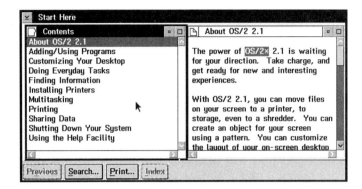

Leave the Start Here program on your desktop. You'll learn how to close it at the end of this section.

WIMP

Before you get mad at me, no one's calling *you* a wimp! WIMP stands for the components of computers that are graphically-based (pictures, to you and me): Windows, Icons, Menus, and Pointers. Figure 7.3 shows you these objects.

Figure 7.3

WIMP objects.

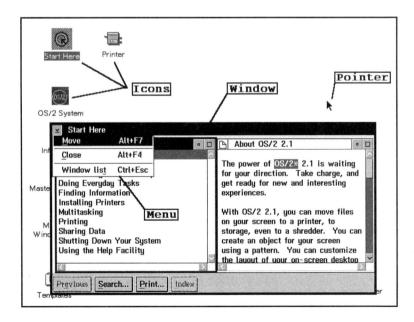

Windows

When you open up a program, or *run* it, it opens up into a window, as shown in figure 7.3. Each *window* that is open on your desktop represents a running program. Some programs might have multiple windows, but most only use one.

Icons

Icons are the little pictures you see on your screen, like the printer icon or the shredder icon. An icon represents some object in your computer, like a program, folder, or data file. With OS/2 you can even edit your icons and make them look like whatever you want.

Menus

Each window has at least one menu, called the *control menu*, which is shown in figure 7.3 (for all you control freaks). Other programs might also have additional menus that are usually called **F**ile or **E**dit (to file or edit things).

Each menu has *hot keys* on it. Hot keys are always the underlined letter in the menu. You can *pull-down* a menu in a window by holding down the Alt key and pressing the underlined letter. For example, if a program has a menu called **F**ile, you can press Alt-F to pull down the menu.

Each menu also has hot keys for each choice. For instance, in figure 7.3, notice how the **C**lose menu item has an underline under the letter C. That means that, after you've pulled down the menu, you can just type **C** on the keyboard instead of having to use your mouse.

Pointers

This one is pretty obvious. The pointer is the little arrow on your screen that is moved with your mouse. It lets you "point" to various parts of the screen to accomplish whatever you're trying to do.

Objects

Each icon, or picture, that you see on the Workplace Shell (WPS) screen is an *object*. Nothing complicated here. As you would expect, each object is simply a "thing" that can be erased, copied, moved, or otherwise messed with.

NERDY
DETAILS

The WPS is said to be *object-oriented*. This refers both to the way in which it lets you work with the objects, as well as the methods that are used to write programs that work closely with the WPS.

Okay class, let's review the standard objects on the OS/2 desktop, along with a description of each one and, if it's a folder, what's in it. The desktop is shown in figure 7.4.

Figure 7.4

The standard
WorkPlace Shell
Desktop.

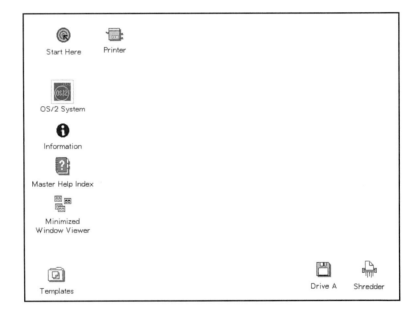

Each object has its *object type* listed in parentheses after its name. Starting in the lower left-hand corner and working clockwise, the objects you see in figure 7.4 (and hopefully your own desktop!) are:

 Templates (folder). If the Templates folder is opened, you will see a number of *templates* that you can use to create new objects on the desktop. For instance, if you want to create a new folder on the desktop, all you have to do is open up the Templates folder, find the Folder template, and drag it onto the desktop. Presto! A new folder! (You'll learn about more nifty templates later in this chapter.)

Minimized Window Viewer (folder). When you open programs and windows, you will learn how to *minimize* them (make them teeny tiny). A minimized program continues to run and to process data, but takes up no space on the desktop. (Don't you wish you could do this with all your stuff at home?) When an object is minimized, it retires to this folder. You can open up this folder to see all of your minimized objects, and double-click on them to bring them back up onto the desktop.

Master Help Index (program object). The Master Help Index opens up into a large book that contains most of the documentation for OS/2. In it you will find many, many descriptions about how to do different things in OS/2. It is chockfull of nerdy details, but you may have to look something up, God forbid! And you don't even need to worry about losing it or leaving it at the office!

Information (folder). The Information icon represents a folder that can be opened up to show you some more objects that contain OS/2 documentation. The objects inside Information are mostly represented as book icons, and use the OS/2 Help System when you open them.

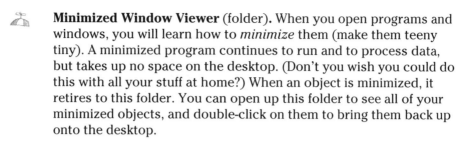

OS/2 System (folder). Inside the OS/2 System folder you will find quite a lot of things. You can find the folders that contain the system settings, the folders that contain the productivity programs, and the Drives object (a special object to manage your files). But wait! You also get your hands on the games that come with OS/2. Stop playing now and pay attention!

Start Here (program). We already talked about this one.

Printer (printer). Funnily enough, you use the Printer object to manage the printer. (See how easy this is?) You can see what stuff is waiting to be printed, view the waiting printer jobs, delete them, or hold them indefinitely.

Shredder (shredder). The Shredder object has only one purpose: to delete other objects (as Ollie North has proven). You'll learn how to use it later on in this chapter.

Drive A (drives). This object represents the A: drive on your computer—the first floppy diskette drive. You use this object to manage files on your floppy disk.

Three Blind Mice

Now that you know about the objects on the desktop, you should know how to get from one to another with that sensitive, temperamental little creature, the mouse. After you've mastered the basics of "mousing around," we'll be all set to roll up our sleeves and start messing around with the Workplace Shell.

TRICKS

Purchasing a pad to use with your mouse is a good idea. While you often can get by just using the mouse on your desk, or on a stack of paper or something, the pad really does make it easier to work with the mouse, and also cuts down wear on the bottom of the mouse. If you don't have one, get one. They sell for about $5-10 in almost all computer stores. You can even get nifty ones with pictures on them! I've even bought some that have that stuff that changes color from skin temperature, like a "mood ring." Groovy, man!

NERDY
DETAILS

The mouse pointer benefits from something called *mouse acceleration*. No, this doesn't happen when you pour coffee into your mouse. Instead, you might notice that when you move the mouse quickly, the pointer covers more space than when you move it slowly. This makes the mouse more controllable.

Clicking

If there's one thing you'll be doing a lot of with the WPS, it's clicking your mouse buttons. A click is simply a quick press and release of one of the mouse buttons.

Double-Clicking

Somewhat rarer than the fabled click, a *double-click* is when you press one of the mouse buttons twice in rapid succession. A double-click always means: Select the object, and open it up (although you may feel like doing some flamenco).

Dragging

A *drag* is when you click mouse button 2 on some object, and, while you hold the mouse button down, move the object to some another place. If you have a long way to travel, you can even pick up the mouse while you're dragging, move it back to get some more room on the mouse pad, and then set it down and continue dragging. There are also a couple of places where you'll drag with mouse button 1; we'll cover those later in this chapter.

Operation: Rearrange Desktop!

Now that you understand objects, and you can steer the mouse, let's do something!

We'll start by rearranging your desktop—because it's a good way to practice, and I like the desktop arranged differently. After we're done, you can rearrange it however you want. For now, though, I'm the author and you're the reader, so do it my way.

Moving Objects

First, let's move the Drive A object from its spot next to the Shredder to the upper right hand corner of the screen. Putting objects that you routinely drag other objects into, like the Drive A object, next to the Shredder is a really bad idea. For example, say you were moving some objects from the computer onto a floppy diskette, and you dragged a little wrong, and instead of dragging them to the Drive A object, you accidentally dropped them in the Shredder? Whammo! No more files!

To move the Drive A object, move your pointer so that it's directly over the object, and then press and hold down mouse button 2 (the right one, normally). While you're holding down the mouse button, drag it up to the upper right hand corner of the desktop. When it's where you want it, let go of the mouse button to drop it into its new home.

Figure 7.5 shows the beginning of the drag; figure 7.6 shows how it looks when you're done.

Figure 7.5

Dragging the Drive A Object.

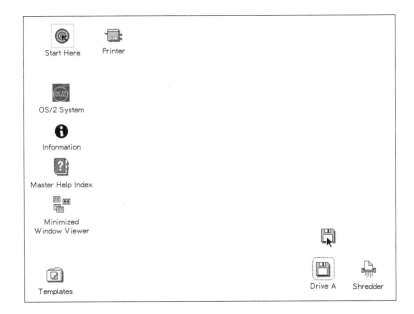

Figure 7.6

The Drive A Object in its new home.

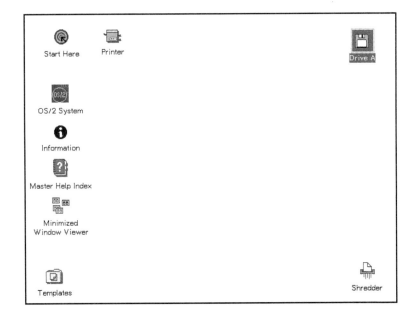

Copying Objects

To copy an object, do this:

1.   Hold down the Control key on the keyboard.

2.   Using the mouse, move the object just like you normally would (by dragging it with mouse button 2 held down).

While you're dragging it, you'll see that the icon is a different color than it normally is. It isn't blushing, it's showing that you're about to copy the object. When you've dragged it a little bit away from the original, let go of the mouse button and then the Ctrl key (mouse button first!).

Deleting Objects

To delete an object, just drag the object and drop it into the Shredder.

STOP!

Deleting an object with the WPS doesn't necessarily just delete that one object. In the case of a folder, it deletes anything inside of it! No matter how many levels deep! For this reason, make extra double sure that you haven't left anything important in a folder that you're about to delete, or it's bye-bye to whatever is (was) in there.

You're probably thinking to yourself: "What a useful tool for some former White House residents!" You're right!

Dragging and Dropping

Now move the Start Here program object into the Information Folder. The easiest way is to start moving the Start Here object just like you were moving the Drive A object, except that you will move it until it's right on top of the Information folder. You'll know when you've got it right when a box surrounds the Information folder, which indicates that you're about to drop it there. Let go of the mouse button, and after a brief pause (while OS/2 re-arranges things internally), you'll see the Start Here object disappear!

To confirm that you dropped it in the right place, double-click on the Information object. You should see the Start Here object among the other objects, all happy with its new friends, as in figure 7.7.

Figure 7.7

A party of Information objects.

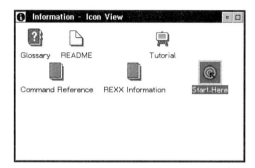

Notice that the Information object's icon on the desktop became shaded (also referred to as being "cross-hatched"). This is OS/2's way of telling you that the object is open. Of course, you can tell it's open, but in other cases it may not be quite so obvious, so this is useful information.

Closing an Object

You learned at the beginning of this chapter how you could close an object by pulling down its control menu and choosing the **C**lose option from the menu. Now you'll learn a shortcut.

If you double-click on an object's control menu, that object will close automatically. Go ahead and use this method to close the Information window, which is open on your desktop.

Notice that the shading on the Information object disappears once the object is closed. Neat, huh?

Desktop Changes—Finishing Up

Because we always want to leave our campsites in better shape than when we found them, do this:

 Move the Templates folder so that it is just above the Shredder object. Because you never drag anything into the Templates folder, it's safe to put it near the Shredder. (Don't drop it into the Shredder by accident!!)

Neaten up the position of the Printer by moving it to the upper left corner of the desktop. Or you can express your individuality by leaving it right where it is. Whatever makes you happy on this one.

When you're done with these changes, your desktop should look like figure 7.8.

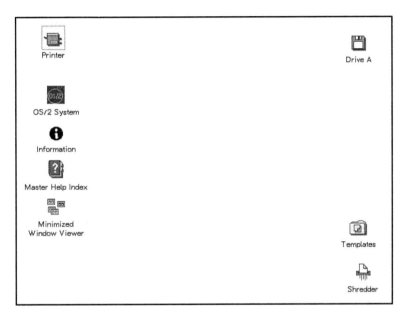

Figure 7.8

The rearranged desktop.

Menus: They Pop Up Everywhere

Every object on the desktop has a *pop-up menu* (sometimes called an *object menu*). The pop-up menu lets you choose from the available options for that particular object. Different object types will have different menu options, depending on what actions are allowed for that object.

But We Don't Do Windows

As you have seen, the Workplace Shell uses a lot of windows to display folders, programs, and the like. There are some finer points to working with these windows. This section will show you how to use and take advantage of windows.

Opening a Window

There are two different ways to open a window: the double-click and the object's pop-up menu. To open a folder (which, when you get right down to it, is just another window), you can activate the pop-up menu, and then choose **O**pen.

Let's play around with the Information folder on your desktop. Open it up by clicking mouse button 2 on the Information icon (to bring up the menu), and then click on **O**pen from the pop-up menu. The result should look like figure 7.9.

Figure 7.9

The opened Information folder.

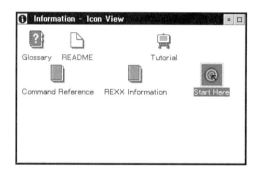

Changing the Window's Size

If you very carefully move your mouse pointer over the borders of the window, you'll notice that the mouse pointer changes shape when it is immediately over the border. When the pointer changes shape, you can press and hold down mouse button 2 and resize the window. This is much easier than doing it the other way!

Also, if you "grab" the corners of the window, you can resize in two dimensions at the same time.

Moving the Window

There are two ways to move windows about on the desktop. First, you can choose **W**indow from the control menu, and then choose **M**ove. Your mouse will appear in the middle of the window, and you can immediately move it and place the window wherever you want. When you're done, just click mouse button 1.

You can also move it by putting your mouse pointer inside the thick bar at the top of the window, called the *title bar*. Just click and hold down mouse button 2 while your pointer is in that area, and move the window to any place you like.

Minimize and Maximize

In the upper right corner of all windows are two buttons. The one to the left is called the *Minimize Button*, while the one on the right is the *Maximize Button*. They do just what their names imply. The Minimize Button shrinks the window down to an icon (which can be seen in the Minimized Window Viewer); the Maximize Button expands the window to fill your entire screen.

Maximize and Restore

Click on the Maximize Button for the Information folder. It will immediately grow to take up your entire screen, as in figure 7.10.

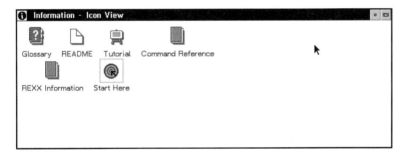

Figure 7.10

The maximized Information folder.

Take a close look at what used to be the Maximize Button; its changed! What you now see is called the *Restore Button*. Its function is to restore the window to its size before you maximized it. Go ahead and click on the Restore Button.

Minimize

Click on the Minimize Button. The Information window will vanish. However, notice that the Information folder on the desktop is still grayed, as in figure 7.11.

Figure 7.11

The grayed Information icon.

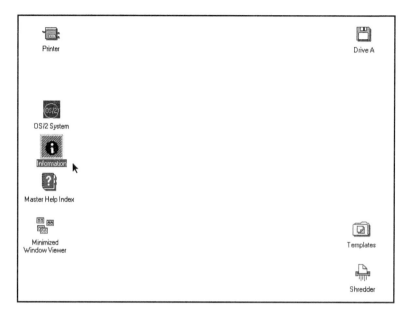

By default, minimized objects are placed in the Minimized Window Viewer. Double-click on the Minimized Window Viewer to view its contents. You'll see that the Information folder is there (see fig. 7.12).

Figure 7.12

The Minimized Window Viewer.

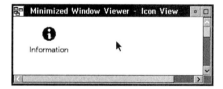

To restore the minimized Information window to the desktop, double-click on it. Now move the Information window up to the top of the screen, so you expose the Minimized Window Viewer (which should be empty now). If you need to, click your mouse once anywhere in the Minimized Window Viewer's window (even if you can only see part of it) to bring it up to the top. Now close it.

I pulled a fast one on you there. You just learned that you can click on any part of a window to bring it to the *foreground*. In other words, you make it the active object or window that will be "on top" of everything else. Just making sure that you're paying attention!

Here's another way to bring back a minimized object. First, minimize the Information folder again. Just like before, it vanishes, and its icon on the desktop remains grayed. To bring it back, double-click on the grayed Information icon.

TRICKS

If the object that you minimize is a program that is doing something, the program will continue running while it's minimized. You can go get coffee, go to the bathroom, or work with something else as it continues. That's multitasking in action!

Scroll Bars

Let's say that you have a window open, and it's not big enough to display everything in it, even if you maximize it. In other words, there are objects inside the window that you can't see. How would you work with such a window?

Give up?

The answer is to use the window's *scroll bars,* which are used very frequently in OS/2.

First, clean up your desktop and close any windows that are still hanging around from all the playing that we've been doing. Now, open up the OS/2 System folder (with a double-click) and find a folder called Productivity. Open it up, too. Your screen should look like figure 7.13.

All of the neat icons you see here are the OS/2 productivity programs that came with your system. You can learn more about them in *OS/2 for Non-Nerds*, available from New Riders Publishing at finer bookstores near you!

Notice the vertical bar that's pointed out for you. That's a *vertical scroll bar.* There are also *horizontal scroll bars,* but they work exactly the same way, only sideways. Following are three ways to scroll through a window using the scroll bar.

Figure 7.13

The Productivity Folder.

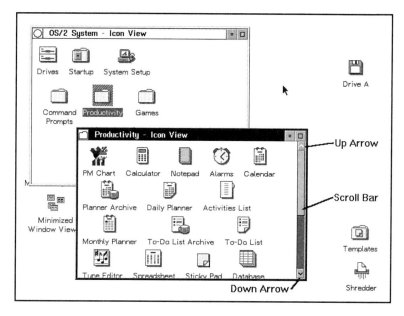

Grab and Drag

Notice the lighter colored part of the scroll bar. This lighter portion is sort of a "handle" that you can move with your mouse.

You can click on that with mouse button 2 (the right one) and drag it up and down. Notice how the window "view" changes as you do that.

Use the Arrows Buttons!

You can also click on the two arrow buttons. Just put the tip of your pointer on either arrow and click once with mouse button 1 (you use mouse button 1 here because you're pressing a button rather than moving something directly). For each click, the window will change view slightly (by a line or so) in the direction of the arrow you're clicking.

Scroll by "Windowfuls"

See the darker area of the scroll bar? Sort of the background to it? If you click on that with mouse button 1, rather than on the lighter colored portion, the window will scroll by an entire "windowful." Try it!

Scroll Bars for Programs

Almost every program that you use will use scroll bars in lots of places, so it's an important tool to get used to. The bad news is that in some programs, when you move a scroll bar by directly dragging the "handle," the screen won't change as you do it. Some programs make you let go of the handle before they redisplay the contents the way that you want them. Just wanted to warn you. The specific behavior all depends on the program that you're using. Most OS/2 programs scroll immediately.

Creating New Folders

First, close all of the windows that are still open on your screen. We want to be off to a clean start here. All done? OK, let's get going.

As you work more and more with your computer, you'll start accumulating more and more junk, and you're going to need places to keep it all. To store all of this stuff, you're going to be creating folders to hold it all in.

Creating a new folder is simplicity itself:

1. Open up the Templates folder.
2. Locate the template called Folder.
3. Drag it onto your desktop.

That's all there is to it! While you're doing this, notice that the original Folder template is still in the Templates folder after you've finished. That's how the templates work—they let you "peel" off copies of whatever it is you're creating. Sort of like an infinite pad of paper that never runs out. In fact, that's why all of the templates look like those little yellow sticky pads you have stuck all over everything.

Renaming Your New Folder

Because your desktop would get pretty boring with a bunch of folders all called "Folder," you'll probably want to assign some deep, meaningful names to them. (I have one that says: "Thanks a lot for letting me buy this computer, honey!")

The easiest way to rename a folder is to hold down the Alt key while you click mouse button 1 on the folder (this actually works with all objects).

When you do this, the little flashing bar at the left end of the name is your cursor. You can use the normal editing keys to change the name of the object. In other words, press Del, Backspace, or the arrow keys; plus the rest of the keys to type in the new name (you probably guessed that part). Also, you can enter in multiline descriptions just by pressing the Enter key to go to a new line. When you're done, press mouse button 1 to save your folder's new name.

Creating Still MORE Folders

One of the nice things about the WPS is that you can embed stuff in many levels, as deep as you want. So you can open up your new folder, and create another folder inside of it. Then you can create still another folder inside that one, and so on. In fact, there's hardly any limit to how many of these things you can create! (It may be infinite.)

Shutting Down

STOP!

Before turning off your computer, always perform a proper shutdown with OS/2. Failing to do this could cause you to lose data, and generally ruin your day.

Now, before turning your computer off, you should always shut OS/2 down properly. Failing to do this is not a good idea (yes, I'm being repetitive, but this is important).

To shut down OS/2, follow these steps:

1. Make sure your mouse pointer is on top of blank desktop space.

2. Click mouse button 2 (normally, the right one). You should see the desktop get surrounded by a dashed line, and the desktop menu appear.

3. Click on Shut **D**own.

If any programs are still running, OS/2 will ask if you want to end them. Go ahead and click on any OK buttons that come up. You will then see OS/2 display a message that says `Please wait, shutdown still in progress`. Wait until this message says `Shutdown has completed`. It is now safe to turn off your computer, or restart the system by pressing Ctrl+Alt+Del.

Go ahead and turn it off!

CHAPTER

8

Mo' Better Software— Get What You Want, Pay What You Must

When people exclaim "That $#&%* PC," they actually mean "That $#&%* DOS, OS/2, or Windows program" that their PCs are running. The software may not be intuitive, it may need more memory than is available, or it can simply *crash* (your computer becomes frozen in time and needs to be restarted). If anything, the computer is only an innocent victim. (Help me, I'm being assaulted by a piece of software!) If you have to choose software for yourself, your office, your wife, your child, or your mother, you can avoid the traps of problem software. The secrets of successful software purchases are uncovered in the following topics:

- Do you know your software?
- How to make smart choices
- What's the best deal?
- Can you really pay less and get more?
- Avoiding the pitfalls of pirated software
- Installing DOS and Windows

Avoiding common installation pitfalls

 HELP!

 Do you need to trade in the old model for a new one?

So Many Software Packages, So Little Time

What you buy to make your computer perform the task you want (for example, to record personal or business financial information) is referred to as a *software program*, *software package*, or *software application*. Software program is the nerdiest of the terms because it refers to what the software is made of—the final program lines written by some nerdy programmer. In many cases, software application refers to a category of software. For example, Lotus 1-2-3 is a spreadsheet application software program. The phrase software package often refers to the physical box, manuals, and disks you purchase.

SAVE
THE DAY!

Avoid the common mistake of buying your computer before determining the software you need. The software program you want to use may require more memory, speed, and disk space than the computer that best fits your budget or is the "best buy" in the store. Some accounting programs, for example, may require a math coprocessor chip, which many computers don't have.

Buying a computer before determining what software you want is similar to buying a house with one-tenth acre of land, and then deciding you want to raise a horse on the property.

Choosing a Software Package

Consider some basic factors when you choose your software tools:

 What tasks do you need to accomplish?

 How accessible are the software's features to perform that task?

What kind of technical support is available?

 What do you really need to do?

Most important, select the software package that can accomplish your specific tasks. Identify and prioritize the tasks you need to perform before you begin researching software. Add to your list as lower priorities those specific items you would like to do or use if you had more time.

> What a package can do is often less important than what it does easily.

NERDY
DETAILS

Table 8.1 lists several categories of software and a few popular software packages. If you are shopping for a PC, the recommended minimum CPU configuration also is included. This helps if you know what software package you plan to use. Whether a math chip is required probably isn't that important unless you want to redesign the Brooklyn Bridge or make a new double hull Valdez—drafting programs and a few other applications benefit from a math chip.

Table 8.1
Popular Software Categories

Category	Product	Recommended Min. CPU	Math Chip
Operating Systems	Microsoft DOS* (MS-DOS)	286	No
	IBM-DOS (PC-DOS)*	286	No
	Digital Research DOS (DR-DOS)	286	No
	NetWare 386	386SX	No
Word Processing	Q & A Write	286	No
	WordPerfect 5.1	286	No
	Microsoft Word for Windows	386SX	Optional

* These CPUs recommended for the best memory management.

continues

Table 8.1
Continued

Category	Product	Recommended Min. CPU	Math Chip
Databases	dBase IV	386	Optional
	Alpha IV	286	No
	Q & A	286	No
	Reflex	286	No
Spreadsheets	Lotus 1-2-3 for DOS	286	Optional
	Microsoft Excel	386SX	Optional
	Quattro Pro	286	Optional
Personal Finance	Quicken	286	No
	Managing Your Money	286	No
Accounting	DacEasy Accounting	286	No
	MYOB for Windows	386SX	No
	Peachtree Complete	286	No
CAD/CAM	DesignCAD 2D	386	No
	AutoCAD Release 12	386DX	Yes
	Intergraph PC Workstation	386DX	Yes
Scientific Software	LabView for Windows	386DX	Yes
	MathCAD	386DX	Optional
Communications	PC Anywhere	386SX	No
	Procomm Plus for Windows	386SX	No
Desktop Publishing	PageMaker for Windows	386DX	No
	QuarkXPress	386DX	No
Graphics	Windows Paintbrush	386SX	No
	CorelDRAW!	386DX	No
	Micrografx Designer	386DX	No
	Adobe Illustrator for Windows	386DX	No
Forms Design	Perform Pro	286	No

Category	Product	Recommended Min. CPU	Math Chip
Integrated Software	Microsoft Works for DOS	286	No
	Microsoft Works for Windows	386SX	Optional
	LotusWorks	286	No
Networking/ Multiuser	LANtastic	386SX	No
	NetWare 386	386DX	No
	Windows for Workgroups	386SX	No
Programming	Visual BASIC for DOS	386DX	No
	Visual BASIC for Windows	386DX	No
Development Tools	Borland C++	386DX	Optional
Project Managers	Microsoft Project	386DX	No
	Timeline	386DX	No
Personal Information Management	CA-UpToDate	386SX	No
	Desktop Set	386SX	No
	Polaris PackRat	386SX	No
Contact Management	ACT!	286	No
	Maximizer	386SX	No
Optimal Character Recognition	OmniPage	386DX	No
Games	Falcon 3.0	386DX	Optional
	Lemmings	286	No
Educational	SpeedReader	386SX	No
	Compton's Multimedia Encyclopedia	386SX	No
Utilities	Norton Utilities	8088	No

Suppose that you are interested in purchasing word processor software for legal writing. You may have different requirements than someone who wants a word processor for simple memos. Legal writing often requires you to strike through unwanted text, place footnotes on the same page that the footnote occurs, and integrate comments and changes from several sources. Similarly, an executive who occasionally uses the computer to write business letters has no need for such fancy features; instead, the executive wants a program that is easy to use, despite its irregular use.

Next, think about the software. Which features are crucial to your work? Which features are helpful but not crucial? By making a prioritized list, you can begin the search for software that fits these needs.

Using Magazine Reviews

Computer magazines are a good place to start selecting software. Magazines such as *PC World*, *PC Magazine*, and *Byte* often review several software programs in head-to-head competition.

Some magazines may give an "Editor's Choice" or "Best Buy" award to one or more of the programs reviewed. Although these reviews are helpful, don't always rush out to buy the top dog. Often, the reviewers fail to develop a working relationship with the software. Also, the reviewers may become entranced with a program's bell or whistle, such as an eye-popping pie chart in 256 colors, and overlook an Achilles' heel, such as sluggishness on slower computers or an awkward menu design. At most, these software reviews point you to the top three or five software packages from which you can choose.

Referrals: Is Anybody Else Using This Stuff?

Another way to choose a software package is to find other sources. Table 8.2 lists several helpful references and contacts:

Table 8.2
Sources for Selecting Software

Source	Pitfalls to Avoid
Magazines	Don't limit yourself to the "Editor's Choice." The reviews may be overly-written with feature-itis.
Current Owners	Consider the source, and ask about other programs they personally examined.

Source	Pitfalls to Avoid
Consultants	Make sure they don't sell the software you are considering buying.
Store Salespeople	Try to gauge how well the salesperson knows the software. Don't accept a salesperson's recommendation just because a product is a best-seller. You don't want to follow the herd.
Computer Clubs	These members often have the same software needs as you. By pooling your experiences and observations, you can make a good buying decision.

Consult with your local computer user group, friends, and peers. If you find that no one else is familiar with the software program you're interested in, beware. If you ever need a helping hand, you'll find yourself alone.

A free and more universal opinion can be gotten from a computer club. If you don't mind speaking in front of an audience, and have no aversions to large groups of nerds, stand up at a meeting and toss your question out to the whole group.

Even though nerds can be irritating, they know software inside out and love to show off their knowledge. Also, computer club members usually neither sell software nor hardware but can provide unbiased information on both. Find out when and where the next PC club meeting takes place, and don't be shy!

Make sure you talk to users of the current version of a software program, not last year's release. Software programs are updated more often than some people's underwear.

TRICKS

Evaluating Your Choices

Once you have a handful of software programs that meet your critical needs, the next step is to evaluate each program.

Software use with accessible features helps you in the short- and long-term. Easy access to features shortens your learning curve which, in turn, cuts training time. On-screen help and easy-to-remember sequences of commands cut production time for everyday tasks. Clunky software can drive you crazy; software with direct and simple commands, even for complicated tasks, is pleasant. The choice you make concerning software used on a day-to-day basis can affect your productivity and morale (as well as that of your employees) more than any other computer-related decision.

Besides ease of use, consider these other software features:

 Error recovery. All software should provide error-recovery capabilities that are easy to use. Does the program enable you to "undo" things? We all make mistakes; if you make a wrong choice, you should be told so in English rather than encounter a cryptic message and be kicked out of the program and sent back to an empty screen.

 On-line help. A good software program has an easier way to find help rather than scrambling for the manual. Many programs provide on-line help—you can press a key and browse through a list of available help topics or access help for the part of the program you are using. When you finish, you simply close the help window and return to your work without ever opening the manual.

 Speed. The software you are evaluating should be speedy on most computers. Some software programs are known for being agonizingly slow on certain systems.

NERDY
DETAILS

You should evaluate the software before you purchase a computer. If you already own a computer, make sure the desired software is fast enough on your machine.

 Easy exit. Your software should exit easily and elegantly. If your work has not been saved before you exit, the program should prompt you to save the information.

 Good documentation. When you need the manual, is it complete? Good documentation includes diagrams and notes. Important information and warnings should be prominently highlighted.

Documentation should describe the features of the software logi-cally, not just spew out every piece of information. Finally, the index should list key words for solving problems and the actual tasks performed by the software ("Setting up the printer," for example).

Another consideration: Is there a quick reference card or keyboard template of the most often used commands? These "cheat sheets" can save you from hunting through the manuals.

 Capacity. As you become familiar with your software, you'll demand more from it. Does the program accommodate your growing needs? Some word processors, for example, use the computer's memory to hold the entire document. This often limits you to about 50 pages of text. If you later plan to work with longer documents, you'd better shop around.

 Company credibility. Does the software manufacturer appear credible? How long has it been in business? Does the company periodically improve its software, or provide "bug fixes" to minor problems that passed through its testing staff? Has anyone else heard about the company? If not, the software company may be here today, gone tomorrow.

Of course, no one except you knows how you will react to a new software program. The best acid test is to sit down at your local computer store and put a software package through its paces. Jot down your reactions to the program. Do you feel extremely confused? Are the instructions clear? Are the commands you want arranged with common sense or is the layout a farce?

Buying the Software You Want

When you finally choose a software package, you then must decide where you want to purchase it. Typically, this means buying *commercial software* (software you pay for up front).

See the "Software for the Taking" section for inexpensive alternatives to commercial software.

NERDY
DETAILS

One option for cheap software is software mail-order companies listed in computer magazines, such as *PC Magazine*, *PC World*, *Computer Shopper*, and *PC Sources*. Another option is local software stores, where help is always available should you have any questions.

If you already own a computer, complete the form in Chapter 5 and have it with you when purchasing your software. Often, software packages list minimum system requirements on the outside of the package, such as "4M disk space required," "VGA monitor required," or "Mouse highly recommended." Make sure your system more than meets these requirements. Microsoft Windows, for example, can run on a lean two megabytes of memory, but consider getting four or more if you want to avoid snail-pace performance.

Returns from Hell

Whichever company you buy from, double-check the company's return policies. Software purchased by mail often cannot be returned if opened. Major retail stores, however, such as Egghead Discount Software and Software Etc., accept returned software. If you want to have this return option, buy from a company that lets you return software, even if opened. This peace of mind may be worth a slightly higher price.

TRICKS

Some stores only accept returned software if the gummed envelope that contains the floppy disks remains unopened.

One way to avoid opening the gummed envelope and to find out whether the software is as promising as your research indicates is to read the manual first, before you install the program. If the capabilities you need are not found in the manual, you can easily return the software because the envelope isn't open.

Software for the Taking

You do not need to spend a lot of money for quality software. Two types of software are available for under $50, or even free of charge:

   Freeware, or public-domain software

   Shareware, or "try-before-you-buy" software

Freeware, also known as public-domain software, is available free to anyone who wants the program. You simply use your modem to *download*, or copy, the software from a local electronic bulletin board system (BBS) or a major on-line service (such as CompuServe).

Shareware is software distributed by the software's creator, or author, without requiring you to pay up front. This type of software is sold on the honor system. If you like the program, shareware authors ask that you send a modest registration fee. Registered users then receive discounts on future releases of the software and often receive printed documentation. If you continue using shareware without registering it, built-in annoying messages or delays may appear.

Like freeware, shareware can be acquired from a BBS. Shareware helps both the author and customer. This concept enables small software companies (usually one or two people) to distribute their software without incurring enormous marketing costs. The consumer can test a shareware program before purchasing it—consider shareware "try-before-you-buy" software.

TRICKS

Do you have a modem? If not, you can obtain shareware from mail-order businesses, such as Public Brand Software or Software Labs, which only charge a modest processing fee ($3-$5 per disk). You can request their catalogs by contacting:

Public Brand Software, P.O. Box 51315, Indianapolis, IN 46251. Call (800) 426-3475.

Software Labs, 100 Corporate Pointe #195, Culver City, CA. Call (800) 569-7900.

Software Piracy: Don't Walk the Plank

Often, it's tempting to give a friend or colleague a copy of a software program that you like. Some electronic BBSs even specialize in providing copies of software, charging callers a fee to access the stolen software. This practice is not only unethical but illegal. As of October 29, 1992, massive software piracy is a felony (no longer a wrist-slapping misdemeanor).

Anyone caught distributing more than 50 illegal copies of a single software title faces a prison term of up to five years and a fine of up to $250,000.

According to the Software Publishers Association, a trade association for over 1,000 software manufacturers, software piracy costs software makers about $1.2 billion yearly (see fig. 8.1).

Figure 8.1

Losses due to software piracy have diminished recently.

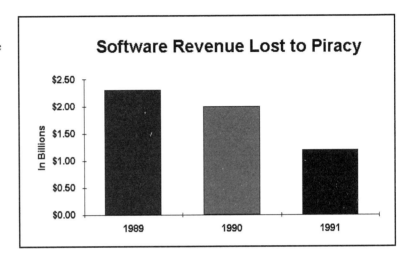

It is now a felony, not a misdemeanor, to copy commercial software! Go directly to jail, do not pass go. How long in jail? Up to five years, and pay up to $250,000.

STOP!

Installing and Running New Software

When you buy software, it usually comes in a big box with not much inside. The more expensive the software program, the larger the box (something about perceived value, eh?). Software packages contain:

 Disks. The actual software program is stored on what are called *floppy disks*. You insert these disks into your disk drive and run an installation software program by typing **A:INSTALL** or **A:SETUP**. These disks often are placed in a sealed envelope that lists the license agreement on the outside. When you break the seal, you agree to abide by the terms of the license agreement.

STOP!

A license agreement says that you do not "own" the software in the traditional sense. Rather, you are licensing it from the manufacturer for a fee. If you break the terms of the license agreement by illegally copying the disks or by some other means, the software can be taken from you.

NERDY DETAILS

Make sure you select software packages that contain the same size disks as your computer's disk drive. Although some programs come with both 3 1/2-inch and 5 1/4-inch disks—called *dual-media*—some packages clearly indicate the type of disk they contain. Select software packages that contain software for the width of your disk drive. If your computer has both 5 1/4-inch and 3 1/2-inch drives, you need not worry about which disks come with the programs.

 Manual. Although few people have the patience to read software manuals, these references are important. In the manual, you'll find the phone numbers to call for technical help and customer service.

NERDY DETAILS

A technical support person once said, "I wish they'd RT*#@$%M!" "What's 'RT*#@$%M?'," I asked. "Read The *#@$%& Manual!"

 Registration card. Complete this card and send it to the software manufacturer. With the information on the card, the company can provide you with improvement notices, lots of junk mail, and technical support.

 Miscellaneous. Other items may also be included, such as a quick installation card, a quick reference card to the program's main features, sales flyers, or an addendum to the manual.

Insert, Insert, Insert...Installed

The process of installing software is the same as spoon-feeding your computer. To load the program onto your computer, several floppy disks are placed, one at a time, into your disk drive. (The original disks can be used to install the program again, if necessary.) During the installation process, you are placing a copy of the software inside your computer. Software loaded from your computer's hard disk drive is much quicker than loading software from individual disks.

Steps for installing software are pretty universal:

1. Open the software package. Be careful not to tear or crumple the box because you may want to return the software. In addition, keep the receipt.

2. Find the installation instructions in the manual or on a separate card. This information typically is placed so that you see it first.

STOP!

Your computer relies on two start-up files, AUTOEXEC.BAT and CONFIG.SYS. When you install new software, these two files are often modified to provide the best working environment for the new software. You should have a backup of these two files to protect your computer from some overbearing new software program. To copy these crucial files, enter each line as follows:

```
COPY C:\AUTOEXEC.BAT C:\AUTOEXEC.BAC
COPY C:\CONFIG.SYS C:\CONFIG.BAC
```

If after installing your software, you find something terribly wrong, you can restore these files to their original condition by typing each of the following lines, and then pressing Enter:

```
COPY C:\AUTOEXEC.BAC C:\AUTOEXEC.BAT
COPY C:\CONFIG.BAC C:\CONFIG.SYS
```

Now that you have a safe backup copy of your system's files, you can proceed with the installation.

3.   Insert the first disk—labeled "Disk 1" or "Installation Disk"—and type either **A:\INSTALL** or **A:\SETUP**. Your software may install differently; consult your manual or separate installation instructions.

The installation program starts.

4.   You may be asked to enter a serial number found on the disk, on the registration card, or on the box. You also may be asked to provide your name and that of your company.

The information you enter is then recorded on the disks. If someone illegally copies your software, this embarrassing information appears when the "bootlegged" copy starts.

5.   You may be asked where to install the software, as well as some other questions. Often, the installation program may make some recommendations, which usually are best for your system. When these recommendations appear, say "Yes" to everything, or keep selecting "OK."

6.   Insert each disk as the installation software requests it. Microsoft Windows, for example, requires the installation of at least six disks. When the disk drive light turns off, insert the next disk, and close the disk drive door or latch. Press Enter to tell the installation software you have placed the next disk in the disk drive.

NERDY
DETAILS

> You must restart your computer after a software installation changes your AUTOEXEC.BAT or CONFIG.SYS start-up files. Most installation programs ask you to restart the system. If the installation for your software does not ask, restart it by turning off your computer for a few seconds or by pressing Ctrl, Alt, and Del at the same time.

7.   When you finish, view the "read-me" file and jot down the command required to invoke the software. This is usually a three- to eight-letter name, such as **WIN** (for Microsoft Windows). As the installation software nears completion, it may recommend that you view a "read-me" file (often called READ.ME). This file is a newsletter-on-disk, with last-minute instructions and warnings. Make sure you read this document.

TRICKS

If you decide to read the "read-me" file at a later time, look for this file in the directory in which the program was installed. It can be called READ.ME, README.TXT, or even WHATSUP.DOC. (What a wascally wabbit.) To read the file, type

> **TYPE READ.ME ¦ MORE**

or

> **MORE < READ.ME**

To conserve the amount of space on your hard disk, you may want to view this file, and either print it or delete it if its information does not pertain to you.

Installing Windows Programs Pane-lessly

Installing a Windows program is often very simple. The same general steps as outlined in the preceding section apply, but with Windows, the process is more like a picture book:

1. Insert the first disk—labeled "Disk 1" or "Installation Disk."

2. Start Microsoft Windows. Typically, you start Windows by typing **WIN**.

3. Open Program Manager.

4. Choose **R**un from the **F**ile pull-down menu (see fig. 8.2).

5. When the **R**un dialog box appears, type either **A:\INSTALL** or **A:\SETUP**. Consult your manual or check the first disk for the right command.

6. Answer the questions, and insert the disks as requested.

7. When the installation finishes, your new software is typically placed in its own window pane, which is called a "program group."

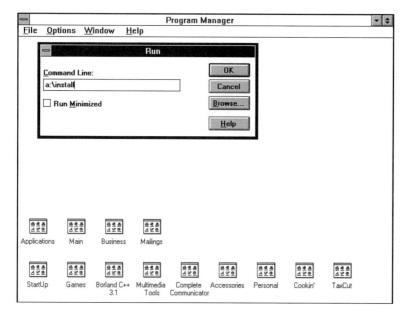

Figure 8.2

Installing Windows
software is pane-less.

TRICKS

Some software cannot be installed if you are using an alternative to the Program Manager, also known as a "Windows shell."
One such shell is Norton Desktop for Windows, which is
designed to replace Program Manager. If you are using a shell
in place of Program Manager, you may have difficulties
installing your software. Consult your manual to see how to
temporarily disable a Windows shell.

Windows software modifies the AUTOEXEC.BAT and CONFIG.SYS files just as
DOS programs modify these files. Three other files related to Windows also
may be modified when you install Windows software:

WIN.INI

SYSTEM.INI

PROGMAN.INI

Most software copies these files to a backup name. Nevertheless, to prevent unwanted changes you should copy these files by typing the following at the DOS prompt:

```
COPY C:\WINDOWS\WIN.INI C:\WINDOWS\WIN.BAC
COPY C:\WINDOWS\SYSTEM\SYSTEM.INI C:\WINDOWS\SYSTEM\SYSTEM.BAC
COPY C:\WINDOWS\PROGMAN.INI C:\WINDOWS\PROGMAN.BAC
```

Common Error Messages

A new software program may display an error message when it starts. One message, for example, is `Not enough file handles`. When your computer starts, a certain amount of memory is set aside to track the number of computer files you are using. A word processor, for example, may require your PC to open five files from the disk. The more files your software requires to be opened, the larger this number should be. You can have up to 255 files open at one time; a value of 20 often is adequate for most people. Some programs, such as Microsoft Windows, require a higher number of files, such as 40.

The installation software often modifies the CONFIG.SYS start-up file, so that the program being installed has the resources it needs to start. One of the lines in the CONFIG.SYS file reads:

```
FILES=xx
```

The *xx* parameter is the number of files your computer currently can open.

NERDY
DETAILS

See Chapter 5 if you need more information on the CONFIG.SYS file and the AUTOEXEC.BAT file.

How do you increase the number of files? DOS 5.0 includes a text editor called EDIT.COM, which enables you to create or edit simple text files, such as CONFIG.SYS and AUTOEXEC.BAT. If you have DOS 5.0, type:

```
EDIT C:\CONFIG.SYS
```

Change the line that contains the FILES= command to a higher value. Then, save your work by pressing Alt,F,S. Press Alt,F,X to exit. To make the changes effective, restart your computer by pressing Ctrl-Alt-Del.

TRICKS

> If you do not have DOS 5.0, use your own word processor to edit CONFIG.SYS. When you use a word processor to edit this file, you must save the file as an ASCII, or text, file.

Another message that may appear is DISK FULL. The installation software does not have enough room to copy all of its files to your computer. This message is seen less as installation programs become more "aware" of computers on which they install software. Most installation programs check the hard disk drive for enough disk space before they begin. If you encounter this message, delete some old letters, unwanted software, or outdated software to make room for new software.

Help!

After buying software, you may need some help. Often, the store from which you purchased the software does not directly support it. Questions usually can be answered by the manufacturer. If you have a question, you usually dial a long-distance phone number and wait to speak to a technical support person.

If you finally reach a technical support person (you may have to endure some Muzak), have all of the information about your computer right in front of you, and have your software open on-screen in the area for which you have a question.

NERDY DETAILS

GEEK

> Be gentle with technical support people; the burnout rate for these professionals is very high. Providing help over a phone wire is very difficult—it's the same as doing brain surgery by fax.

The Lure of Upgrading

If you own software you like, eventually you will want to upgrade to a new, improved version when one becomes available. Software is numbered with version numbers, starting with version 1.0. Minor changes in the software are often noted to the right of the decimal point in the tenths place. For example, version 3.1 is slightly more improved than version 3.0. Version 4.0 is probably a major overhaul of the program.

When you buy a newer version of your software, you do not have to pay the full price that new customers pay. Upgrade prices range from $10 to $90.

When you upgrade your software, you provide proof to the store or the manufacturer that you own the previous version, either by forfeiting the cover of the manual or showing the first disk. You also can order the upgrade directly from the company. If you must order the upgrade by mail, you do not have to prove your ownership because you are in the company's files (if you sent in the registration card).

TRICKS

Run away from software that starts with version 1.0. My experience has always shown that first releases of new software are often very troublesome. Some features may not work, or the program may conflict with your computer.

You also may want to avoid (if possible) versions 2.0, 3.0, 4.0, and so on. The jump to the next whole number implies great improvements but also greater chances for trouble. The new features may not have been fully tested before the software was shipped. Don't be a programmer's guinea pig; wait for versions 2.1, 3.1, 4.1.

After you own a software program for some time, you have three options: stay with your current software, upgrade to a newer version, or buy a different program altogether. Ask these questions before upgrading your software:

 How many extensive upgrades (jumps from 2.0 to 3.0 to 4.0) have been introduced since you purchased the program? (Do not include upgrades to correct bugs in previous versions.)

How often does your software make you feel limited in what you can do? Put your wish list of features aside for the moment. Desired features are the icing—think about the cake.

Does an upgrade involve buying other software? The cost of an upgrade can be deceptive if you also have to invest in other software or a new operating environment, such as Windows or OS/2. These add cost, learning curves, and complexity to the way you work.

How often do you turn to external programs or stray from your computer altogether to make up for your current software's "inadequacies"? When evaluating an upgrade's features, consider those that simplify the way you currently do your work.

How often does your current software prevent you from sharing work files with friends, family, and colleagues? Many upgrades accept a broader range of file formats than earlier versions.

Count the upgrade's most appealing features. How many of them truly are important to you? Count only those features that you will actually use. These days, software manufacturers tack on software bells and whistles you may never need. How many features will really help you work smarter?

How much work and time are you willing to devote to your upgraded software? Estimate the time that it will take you to get up and running the way you actually plan to use the software.

Will your software require new hardware, such as more memory (RAM), a larger disk drive, a laser printer, or a mouse?

Would a whole new software program, not merely an upgrade, better satisfy your heart's desires? You may love your current program and not know you've outgrown it. When the job at hand substantially outstrips your software's capabilities, an upgrade probably won't help. It's time to look for another program.

PART 4

Things You Have To Deal With

"I HATE IT WHEN THEY EAT JUST BEFORE THEY COME IN.
THIS ONE JUST HAD A WHOLE BAG OF CHIPS."

Unlike Nerds,
Your PC Has Guts

D on't worry if you know nothing about what's inside a PC's case; most people don't even know what's inside their own bodies! When you feel it's time for some exploratory surgery (or if you're just bored), and you do open your PC, what you see are the same things you'll find in every PC. The reason: every PC has the same parts; what makes one PC more expensive and more powerful than another is some parts are faster or larger or both. In this chapter, you'll learn about:

- The guts of your PC
- The measurement of your PC's brain
- Adding a math coprocessor, for some serious (nerd-oriented) computing
- Memory chips may look alike (black squares with legs), but they're different
- Expansion ports can make your computer more fun
- Adequate power for your PC, in good times and bad

Your computer is made up of many different physical parts. Together, these parts are called *hardware*. As mentioned in the previous chapter, your hardware runs *software*. Together, hardware and software help you work better and faster.

Hardware includes any part of your computer you can touch. When you purchased your computer, you probably received a keyboard, system unit, monitor, and mouse. Your computer may also have other parts, such as a modem that connects it to other PCs by phone lines, or a printer to get your work on paper. These items are covered, respectively, in chapters 19 and 14.

Inside the System Unit

This chapter is concerned mostly with the system unit—the square box that sounds hollow when you tap it (there are parts in there). When people talk about their computer, they usually mean the system unit (see fig. 9.1). The system unit holds your computer's "guts." In fact, removing five or six screws from the rear outer edge of the system unit usually enables you to remove its cover and examine these things:

 Microprocessor (also called the processor, central processing unit, or CPU)

 Memory

 Expansion cards and slots

 Power supply

The *motherboard* is a thin, rectangular circuit board that forms the foundation of your computer. It contains many computer chips and connections, providing your PC with various capabilities. (Hopefully, your motherboard won't become the "mother of all computer evils.")

NERDY
DETAILS

GEEK

The motherboard is actually an example of a printed circuit board, or PCB. A PCB is a green or brown piece of fiberglass with computer chips attached to it. (Don't confuse a PCB with PCBs, a dangerous toxic substance used in electrical transformers.) These chips communicate with each other through thin copper wires, or "traces," that crisscross the PCB like city streets.

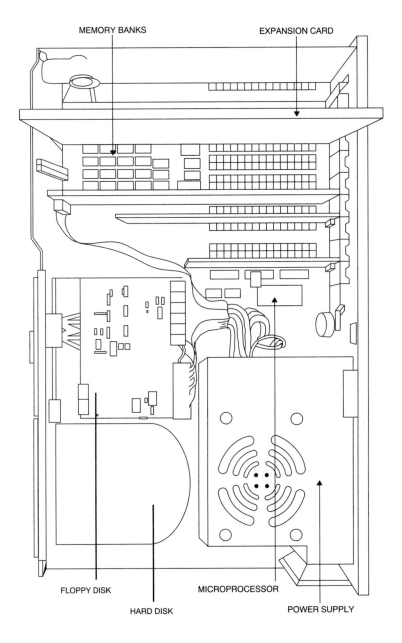

MEMORY BANKS EXPANSION CARD

FLOPPY DISK

HARD DISK

MICROPROCESSOR

POWER SUPPLY

Figure 9.1

The system unit contains the meat of your PC.

The electronic morsels on the motherboard include:

 The processor. Your computer's "brain."

 Math coprocessor. An optional computer chip that gives your processor faster math skills. Your PC can still handle numbers without this chip; the "co" in coprocessor simply means it assists the processor (ever heard of codependency?).

 RAM. Working memory for your software is called *random access memory* (*RAM*). Rows of memory are inserted on your motherboard. Often, you can add these chips yourself.

 ROM. *Read-only memory*, or *ROM*, chips control your computer. The most important ROM chip is the Basic Input/Output System, or BIOS (pronounced "buy-ose" which rhymes with "comatose"). The BIOS is the crucial but little-known computer chip that makes your PC "compatible" with the original IBM PC. In other words, it is the standard upon which all PCs operate.

This PC ROM stuff confuses most non-nerds. Check out the section "Other Memory" in this chapter for an understandable explanation.

NERDY
DETAILS

 Expansion Slots. Electrical connections into which you insert *expansion cards*, such as an internal modem.

The Brains Behind the Operation (After Yours, of Course)

One crucial part of your motherboard is the processor. The *processor* is a single computer chip about the size of a matchbook. Its metallic legs are inserted into the motherboard. A processor is like a transistor radio on steroids; each processor contains thousands of small transistors. These small transistors are the building blocks of computer technology. For example, the 486DX processor contains about 1,200,000 transistors (see fig. 9.2).

Figure 9.2

The reason your PC has a fan—the hot and fast Intel 80486 family.

The processor, which does the bulk of your computer's thinking, is the motor behind your software. The processor can calculate the ongoing checkbook balance in your personal finance software, or it can compare your words in a document against the software's built-in dictionary. Other computer chips and circuitry support the processor, but this jewel is the most important part that makes your computer fast.

NERDY
DETAILS

The processor is also called a central processing unit, or CPU (pronounced "see-pea-you").

Several brands of processors are available. Most likely, yours was designed by Intel Corp., although other companies make processors. All processors are members of the same Intel 80*x*86 family of computer chips, but they come in different strengths: 8088, 8086, 80286 (or just 286), 80386 (386), 80386SX (386SX), 80486SX (486SX), and 80486DX (486DX). You may already be familiar with these names because they often are sprinkled throughout conversations with computer salespeople or friends. Since 1981, five families of processors have been introduced—8088, 8086, 286, 386, and 486—each faster than its predecessor (see table 9.1).

Table 9.1
Processors Past and Present

Brand	Year Introduced	Highlights
8088	June 1979	The brain of the first IBM PC introduced in 1981 and used in early PCs and laptop computers (obsolete)
8086	June 1978	A slightly faster version of the 8088 (obsolete)
286	February 1982	The processor behind the genuine IBM PC/AT and much faster than the 8088/8086 (obsolete)
386	October 1985	Also known as the 386DX to set it apart from the 386SX (in style)
386SX	February 1989	A cut-down but affordable version of the 386DX used in laptops and inexpensive home PCs (in style)

Brand	Year Introduced	Highlights
486/486DX	April 1989	Also called the i486, a souped-up version of the 386DX, which includes a math coprocessor (cutting edge power)
486SX	April 1991	The same as the 486DX but without math coprocessor (in style)

NERDY
DETAILS

Note that the faster (higher-numbered) processors are not always the latest. Due to market pressures, Intel Corp., a big and often exclusive manufacturer of these processors, has introduced more varieties of slower processors.

Don't know which processor you have? Remove your system unit cover and "check under the hood." The processor is often the largest computer chip inside your computer. The processor is usually located in the rear center of your case. Numbers on top of this important black square show the type of processor you own. Look for numbers like this:

 80386DX-*xx*

 80486SX-*xx*

xx is the speed (in megahertz, or MHz) of your processor. The higher the number, the faster your PC. If you don't see a number, you can use diagnostic software to give you a list of your PC's features.

TRICKS

If you use Microsoft Windows 3.1, you already own a free diagnostic utility. The Microsoft Diagnostics utility (MSD.EXE) provides extensive information about your PC and is equivalent to programs that cost up to $100. This utility is found in the directory in which you installed Microsoft Windows (typically C:\WINDOWS). To use it, exit Windows and type

MSD

continues

> *continued*
>
> Many options are then displayed (see fig. 9.3). If you have a
> mouse, simply click on each box for details about your computer.
> In the upper right corner, you'll see the brand of processor.

Figure 9.3

Microsoft's utility
gives you complete
information on
your PC.

Doubly Fast

A processor's power is determined by two factors:

 Its clock speed, measured in megahertz (MHz)

 The manner in which it moves information inside itself and to the
rest of the motherboard

Your processor was designed to run at a certain clock speed, which is the
"heartbeat" of your PC. This heartbeat is measured in millions of cycles per
second, or megahertz (MHz). If one PC has a faster clock speed than another,
that means it gets the same amount of work done in less time. In other
words, the higher the clock speed, the faster your PC.

NERDY
DETAILS

Don't confuse this clock with the built-in clock that stamps
your files with the date and time. When you save your work, the
current date and time are saved with the file. To find the
current time on your computer, type **TIME**.

Often, computer owners mistake clock speed as the only measure of a PC's speed. A processor is measured by the amount of information it can move at one time. This information is measured in *bits*, short for "binary digit." A bit is used to measure how much a computer can store and process all information. Typically, eight bits make up a *byte*, that is, a single character (a letter, number or symbol).

The movement of these bytes inside your computer is similar to a highway. If a highway has only one lane in each direction, only one string of cars can drive at any one time. To handle more traffic, you can add another lane and thereby double the number of cars that can drive on the highway at one time. These highways are called data *buses*. If you look on your PC's motherboard, the data buses are all the little lines (lanes) that go to the processor.

Data buses can be both external and internal. You can only see the external data buses; they are the lines on the circuit board that connect to the processor. The second indicator of a processor's speed is the difference between these external data buses and the internal data buses. Some processors can calculate a lot more information than they receive. Like Los Angeles, which has twelve and fourteen lane highways in town, but only two lane roads outside of town, a processor may be designed to handle more information inside itself than it can send to the other circuitry on the motherboard.

Each category of processor (286, 386, 486, etc.) has a set number of internal highways on which information travels. The 8088 and the 8086, for example, have two highways. Each highway can carry eight bits (a byte) of information; therefore, sixteen bits (two bytes) can be processed internally at one time. The 8088 and 8086 processors are called 16 bit processors because they can only handle 16 bits (two 8 bit bytes equal 16 bits) at a time.

Still confused? This measurement is only for inside the processor itself. There may be a different number of "lanes" for talking to the other circuitry in your PC. The obsolete 8086 was a 16 bit internal and 16 bit external processor. The cheaper 8088 was a 16 bit internal and 8 bit external processor. See Table 9.2 for the amount of lanes of other processors.

Table 9.2
Speed Also Is Determined by Data Bus Width

Processor	Speeds	Internal-External Data Bus (in bits)
8088	5, 8MHz	16-8
8086	5, 8, 10MHz	16-16
286	8, 10, 12, 16, 20, 25MHz	16-16
386DX	16, 20, 25, 33, 40MHz	32-32
386SX	16, 20, 25MHz	32-16
486DX	25, 33, 50MHz	32-32
486SX	16, 20, 25, 33MHz	32-32

Out of Date?

In one way, a new PC is like a new car: drive it off the lot and its value drops immediately. A new processor is introduced each year; the power of these processors doubles about every two years. The 50MHz 486 processor is about 50 times faster than the one in the first IBM PC (see fig. 9.4). This list shows the major processors and their release dates:

Processor	Trade Name	Release Date
286-12	80286	Feb-82
386SX-16	386SX	Jun-88
386SX-20	386SX	Feb-89
386SL-20	386SL	Oct-90
386SL-25	386SL	Sep-91
386DX-16	386DX	Oct-85
386DX-20	386DX	Feb-87

Processor	Trade Name	Release Date
386DX-25	386DX	Apr-88
386DX-33	386DX	Apr-89
486SX-16	486SX	Sep-91
486SX-20	486SX	Apr-91
486SX-25	486SX	Sep-91
486DX-25	486DX	Apr-89
486DX-33	486DX	May-90
486DX-50	486DX	Jun-91

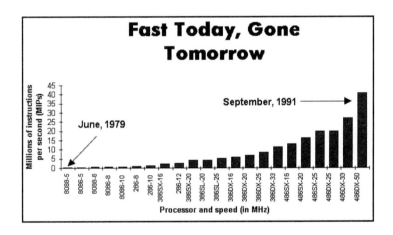

Figure 9.4

PC power has mushroomed since 1981.

NERDY DETAILS

I stumbled across the sales receipt of an 286 PC I bought a few years ago: $2300 and it only had a dinky 44M hard disk! I could buy almost four 286 PCs today for that price, if I could find them.

Upgradable Computers

Some PCs need "brain transplants"—new processors that you add to a large empty socket on the motherboard—to give your PC more power. In 1992, Intel introduced *speed-doubler*, or *clock-doubler*, technology for 486 computers. Chips based on this technology come in two versions: DX2 and OverDrive processors. They run at one speed inside the processor and at half that speed when addressing your PC's memory and other components. The technology works on Intel 486DX and 486SX processors running at 16, 20, 25, and 33MHz. There are no OverDrive or DX2 options for 386 computers.

The DX2 is a processor available on new PCs. You can now buy a new PC with a 486DX2/66 processor, as an example. This processor thinks at 66MHz inside the processor, but talks to the rest of the computer at 33MHz. A 486DX2/50 processor is also available; it operates at 50MHz internally and 25MHz for the rest of the PC.

NERDY
DETAILS

What is the benefit of having a processor that talks at a certain speed inside itself, but at a slower speed with the rest of your PC? Most of your PC work is done within the processor itself. The speed-doubling technology overall increases the speed of your PC, although the results may be slowed by your PC's original design. Still, an increase in speed is better than no increase at all.

The *OverDrive chip processor* replaces the 486SX processor already in your computer. These chips fit in the vacant 169-pin *performance upgrade socket* in your motherboard. (This socket is also called the 80487SX math coprocessor or *OverDrive socket*.) Such OverDrive sockets are available for 16, 20 and 25MHz 486SX computers. Once you plug in the new OverDrive processor, the original processor is shut off.

NERDY
DETAILS

Speed-doubling technology is ideal for computer owners worried about their PC becoming "out of date." By simply inserting a new chip (as easy as plugging in a new fuse), you can almost double the speed of your PC. However, the OverDrive chips themselves cost a few hundred bucks.

If anything, the OverDrive chip creates a good reason to skip the 40-MHz 386 PC and jump to the 25-MHz 486SX. (The two are about the same speed.) Later on, you can upgrade the 486SX. You can't upgrade the 386.

The only disadvantage to Intel's Overdrive technology is by the time you notice your 486 PC can't keep pace (in one or two years), you'll want to own a 586 or 686 PC with a larger hard disk, faster video card, and more memory—all of which will probably cost less than your current PC. This industry changes so quickly that you probably shouldn't plan for the future. It seems like yesterday when the 386 was preferred over the 286. Now, the 386 is considered obsolete. Where does it end?

You can also replace the processor in 25- and 33MHz 486DX computers with a 168-pin OverDrive chip. You simply remove the existing processor from its 168-pin socket and replace it.

Buddy, Can You Spare a Calculator?

To speed up the number-crunching power of your PC, you can add a *math*, or *numeric*, *coprocessor* in an empty socket on the motherboard. Like a calculator, this optional computer chip helps your main processor handle numbers.

Not all math operations use the math coprocessor. Common operations such as addition, subtraction, multiplication, and division still are performed by the main processor. For sophisticated math operations—such as cosines, sines, tangents, and square roots—a math coprocessor can speed up number-crunchin by almost 100 percent, boosting overall performance by 200 to 100 percent. Party!

You can only take advantage of this capability if your software supports a math coprocessor. Usually, spreadsheets (such as Lotus 1-2-3) and drafting and programming software support a math coprocessor. About one in ten software programs support this nerdy chip. If you work with software that accesses a math coprocessor and you use sophisticated mathematical functions, a math coprocessor can be a great addition—no pun intended. Most of these processors are cheap (less than 150 bucks).

How is a math coprocessor added to your computer? Most computers have a socket—an empty hole—for a math coprocessor, usually next to the main processor. You still benefit from a math coprocessor on a 486SX computer (see table 9.3). You have two choices:

 Intel (or Intel-compatible) **math coprocessor.** These are the traditional math coprocessors most people use.

 Weitek math coprocessor. Weitek (pronounced "way-tek") math processors are reserved for the most demanding statistical and design work.

GEEK

Computers that have an 486DX processor do not require a math coprocessor; it's already built into the chip.

NERDY
DETAILS

The type of coprocessor is not the only information you need. You also need to know the speed needed by your computer's design. Like your processor, this speed is measured in megahertz (MHz). The 80387SX coprocessor comes in four speeds: 16MHz, 20MHz, 25MHz, and 33MHz. Each is designed to match the speed of the computer. As a rule, a coprocessor's speed must match the speed of the main processor.

Table 9.3
Processors and Their Companion Calculators

Processor	Coprocessor
8086	8087
8088	8087
286	80287
386SX	80387SX
386SL	80387SX
386SLC	80387SX

Processor	Coprocessor
386DX	80387DX or Weitek 3167
486SX	80487SX or Weitek 4167
486DX	Built-in, no Intel coprocessor needed, or optional Weitek 4167

Installation of a math coprocessor is simple: open the computer case and stick the chip in the empty socket. Then, you tell your software to recognize the math coprocessor, if it doesn't automatically.

Memory: A Place for Your Stuff

Do you have a work area in your house or apartment where you take things that need to be fixed, sanded, or painted? If your chair broke, you wouldn't fix it in the living room—you'd take it to your "work room," which might be the garage, basement, or a corner of your apartment. As silly as this sounds, the motherboard also has a work area called *RAM* or *random access memory* (pronounced "ram"). RAM is memory; software you want to work with is loaded from the hard disk drive into it.

The amount of RAM is measured in kilobytes (K). A kilobyte equals 1,024 bytes, a single character or number. A megabyte (M) equals 1024K. The first IBM PC had 16K of memory; today's computers often have memory amounts of 2M, 4M, 8M, or more.

NERDY
DETAILS

> The phrases "RAM" and "memory" for the most part are interchangeable.

RAM is a type of short-term memory; when the power is turned off, the contents are lost forever. (This is why you must save your work to a floppy or hard disk before you turn off your computer.) Like the top of your desk, this memory is a volatile, temporary workspace. When you want to work on a project, you take your papers and tools out of your desk drawers and put them on your desk within easy reach. With memory, you load a computer program and a file from your disk drive and put them into memory where they are close at hand.

Unfortunately, the disk operating system, or DOS, which coordinates your various computer components, places an upper limit on how much memory your computer can access at one time. (You can have as big a desk as you want, as long as it isn't bigger than your office.) In most cases, your computer can only handle 640K—or 655,360 bytes—of information at one time. Although you may have 8M of memory—that's 8,096K—you may still get messages such as "Program too big to fit into memory" or "Out of memory." Fortunately, memory above this limit can be used for other purposes, as discussed later in this book.

Three Types of Memory

Your PC may divvy up its total memory into three types:

 Conventional memory. The memory into which you load your software and work files. Conventional memory, also known as base or low memory, is any memory below 1M (1024K), although only 640K of it is directly available for your work.

 Extended memory (XMS). Memory above 1M. This memory usually is not directly available to your software. Special software utilities, however, can use it to speed up your computer. If you own Microsoft Windows, this program can directly use the extra memory.

 Expanded memory (EMS). For the most part this is converted extended memory. To use expanded memory, you must use software that expressly says it can use it. Usually a software utility called an *expanded memory manager* (EMM) manages this expanded memory. DOS 5.0, for example, includes such a manager called EMM386.EXE. Older software used this type of memory as a short-term fix to memory shortages. Today's software would rather use extended, not expanded, memory.

GEEK

Extended memory is only available in 286, 386, and higher computers.

NERDY
DETAILS

Adding Memory

The addition of memory (RAM chips) is an inexpensive way to make your computer faster and more capable. The cost of memory at the time of this writing is about $30 per megabyte, and falling. A small dose can be a big boost to your PC's performance. How do you add memory to your PC? Three options, listed in order of convenience and cost, are as follows:

 Adding memory to vacancies on your motherboard

 Replacing your current motherboard's memory with higher-capacity memory

 Purchasing a memory expansion card that occupies one of your expansion slots

Your PC's motherboard may still have room for more memory. Most 286 and higher computers can take additional memory chips directly on the motherboard.

Computer Chip SIPs and DIPs

Memory chips come in different shapes and sizes. All memory chips discussed here are called *DRAM*, or *dynamic random access memory*. DRAM chips are the most common type of computer memory. DRAM chips need to be energized hundreds of times per second to hold information. If you shut off the power, the information is lost. Three types of DRAM chips are shown in figure 9.5 and explained as follows:

 DIP (dual in-line pin). Not to be confused with the kind of "DIP chips" you dunk into jalepeno cream cheese dip, a DIP memory chip is a rectangular chip with 16 metal legs, eight on each side. To install such memory chips, you must plug each one into place. DIP chips are installed in multiples of nine.

 SIMM (single in-line memory module). To install several memory chips in one step, some manufacturers use memory packages in which several memory chips are stored on small circuit boards. The SIMM is the most popular design. In one move, you can install the equivalent of nine DIP chips.

Figure 9.5

Examples of DIP, SIP, and SIMM memory chips.

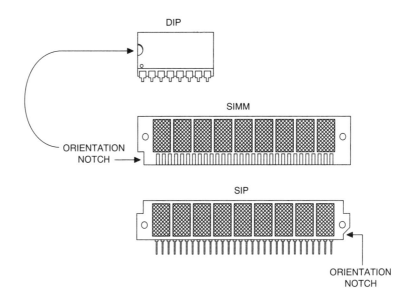

SIP (single in-line pin). The SIP memory package is similar to the SIMM in that it contains several memory chips in one unit. However, the SIP uses DIP-like memory and has thin metal leads that plug into your motherboard. In some ways, a SIP looks like a comb with metal teeth.

NERDY
DETAILS

SIPs and SIMMs eliminates *chip creep*, a process in which memory chips work their way out of place because of the constant heating and cooling that occurs in your computer.

Your PC probably uses just one of these types of DRAM chips, although some use several. All of these types are installed in memory banks. A *memory bank* is a collection of slots on the motherboard that makes up a block of memory. To work, this bank must be completely filled with memory chips, just as your car needs every spark plug to work properly. Table 9.4 typifies the possible memory variations for 386DX and 486 computers that use only SIMMs:

Table 9.4
Filled Memory Banks Give You More Memory

Total Memory	Bank 0	Bank 1
1M	4×256K	
2M	4×256K	4×256K
4M	4×1M	
5M	4×1M	4×256K
8M	4×1M	4×1M
16M	4×4M	
17M	4×4M	4×256K
20M	4×4M	4×1M
32M	4×4M	4×4M

Not All RAMs Are Equal

Besides the size of the memory chips, you must also consider speed. Memory chips are rated by their reaction time, which is measured in nanoseconds, or billionths of a second. How fast is a nanosecond? One nanosecond, abbreviated ns, is the time it takes light to travel 12 inches. The smaller this speed rating, the faster the chip. A 60ns chip is faster than a 100ns chip, for example. Generally, faster chips cost more.

The speed of a memory chip is printed on its surface. On the memory chips, you see an identifying number. The last two digits after the dash (-) are especially important because those digits indicate the speed of your memory. The last two digits indicate the speed in either nanoseconds or tens of nanoseconds. For example, one of my older computers has memory chips with the number "M5K4164ANP 51727F-15." The last two digits indicate these memory chips are 150 nanoseconds fast. Today's faster memory is around 60 nanoseconds.

TRICKS

It doesn't hurt to install memory chips that are faster than required for your motherboard or memory card. Faster memory chips can be a boon if you intend to transplant them to a faster computer in the future. Unfortunately, faster memory won't speed up your computer; your computer's design anticipates working at a certain speed and no faster.

Making the Most of New Memory

Adding memory usually is not an end in itself. Any extra memory you add must be used to load various software utilities that then speed up your computer. Some computer owners simply buy a computer with lots of memory, but never take advantage of that memory. Some possible uses of extra memory include:

 Task switching. With some programs, such as Microsoft Windows and DESQview, you can use extended memory to load several programs at one time and move between them—a process called *task switching.*

 Multitasking. If you have a computer that uses a 386 or higher processor, you can even have your programs perform work in the background—such as printing or downloading a file from an electronic bulletin board system (BBS)—while you are working in another program in the foreground. This capability is called *multitasking.*

 Disk cache. Both extended and expanded memory can be used for a disk cache, which speeds up access to your hard disk. If you work with software that uses your hard disk a lot (you can tell by the frequent blinking of your hard disk's light on the front of your PC), the improvement can be phenomenal. The disk caching utility SMARTDrive comes free with DOS 4.0 and higher and also with Microsoft Windows.

 Print spoolers. Print spooling software enables you to print a long document to extra memory immediately. Then, you can resume your other work while the many pages emerge from your printer one at a time. With this feature, you won't have to wait for your printer to finish before you can get back to work.

Other Memory

Another type of memory called *read-only memory* or ROM is reserved by your computer's operating system to help run your computer. The most important ROM chip(s) you should know about is the Basic Input/Output System, or BIOS. The *BIOS* provides the crude brains that make your PC's components work together. The BIOS chip is usually a 28-pin DIP chip. In other words, it is a rectangular chip that has 14 metal legs on each side. Newer 386 and 486 computers place the BIOS near the processor and math coprocessor socket.

The BIOS is a collection of small computer programs built into a ROM chip. The BIOS collection is the first thing "activated" when you start your computer, even before the operating system is loaded. The BIOS has three main functions:

 Tests your PC's components each time you turn on or restart your PC. This capability is called the *Power-On Self-Test*, or POST. The POST tests your computer's memory, its motherboard, screen, keyboard, and more. You'll often hear a clicking sound as the BIOS tests your memory for any possible defects, for example.

 Finds the operating system and loads, or "*boots*" it. This is called the *bootstrap loader routine*. If an operating system such as DOS is located, it is loaded and put in control of your PC.

 After an operating system loads, the BIOS works with your processor to ensure that software programs have easy access to your computer's specific features. The BIOS tells your computer how to work with your video card and hard disk, when a software program requires it.

With these responsibilities, the BIOS is like a computerized traffic cop, ensuring your computer's safety and providing smooth flow for the demands your software places on it.

NERDY
DETAILS

> Some people call the BIOS the CMOS (pronounced "see-moss"). Chapter 4 refers to the BIOS this way. The two are different, yet related. On most computers, the BIOS lets you change the configuration without having to crack open your computer and set various switches. (Thank goodness!) As your
>
> *continues*

> *continued*
>
> computer warms up, you can start this built-in setup program to tell your computer about added memory, a second floppy drive, or a color video card.

Built-In Expansion

Your PC was built to grow with you. Since their creation in 1981, PCs have been designed with empty slots inside their cases. These slots were set aside so that features could be added by inserting circuit boards.

These empty slots are called *expansion slots* or *expansion ports*. Although the original PC had five slots, your PC may have between three and eight expansion slots. The circuit boards placed into them are called *expansion cards*, *expansion boards*, or *add-on cards*. These "plug-and-play" expansion cards let you add new features to your computer. One popular expansion card is the internal modem, which lets your computer share information with others over a telephone line.

The addition of an expansion card is the most popular way to add new features to your PC. Believe it or not, you can improve your PC yourself with only a screwdriver! The features from these expansion cards are either required for your PC to operate, or provide features above and beyond that of the typical PC. A few types of expansion cards you can add include:

 Video card. The *video card* lets you see your work, such as the words you type in your word processor. The video card, also called a *video* or *display adapter*, controls your computer screen and provides all those nifty colors.

NERDY
DETAILS

A new design in some PCs is to bypass the typically slow expansion bus (into which the expansion card is inserted) and use what is called the *local bus*. Local bus is super fast— as fast as your PC's CPU. In a PC that has a local bus, the expansion card talks to your PC at 32-bit speed, not 16 or 8.

Input/Output (I/O) cards. Another crucial expansion card is the input/output (I/O) card. The I/O card provides various connections to external hardware, such as your PC's printer. Some I/O cards provide only a *parallel printer port* and a *serial port*. Others take up two expansion slots to provide a parallel printer port, two serial ports and a game port for a joystick. Such robust I/O cards are often called *multifunction I/O cards*.

What do each of these ports do? The parallel printer port, or just parallel port, lets you connect a printer. The two serial ports can be used to run a mouse (which enables you to make selections in a software program by pointing and clicking) as well as connect an external modem (which enables you to communicate with other computers). The joystick port enables you to use a joystick for use with computer games, especially ones that simulate flying.

 Disk drive controller card. The *disk drive controller card* also is important. Without a circuit board to run your disk drives, you cannot get information into or out of your computer. You can't copy a file to a floppy disk to share with a friend or peer, nor load new software programs onto your computer. On new PCs, one expansion card may control up to two floppy disk drives and two hard disk drives. Such expansion cards may also provide I/O ports for connecting to other devices. For example, my disk drive controller takes up another expansion slot by providing two serial ports, a parallel printer port, and a joystick port.

NERDY DETAILS

> Some PCs have the equivalent of the disk drive controller card, I/O card, and video card built onto the motherboard. No expansion cards required! One advantage is that the PC is faster because these parts are closer to the central processor. However, if any of these parts die, the whole motherboard must be replaced!

You can add expansion cards for a cornucopia of new capabilities, including:

 Scanning pictures and text for use in your PC's word processor

 Protecting your work by making a duplicate of your hard disk to a small tape, then safely storing it away

Adding a CD-ROM drive so that you can access a wealth of information or simply play an audio CD

 Play high-quality sound in games and other software programs

 Receive and send faxes on your PC without wasting a single tree

NERDY
DETAILS

Expansion slots may vary between PCs. The most popular design is the *PC bus*. Today, it is called the *Industry Standard Architecture* or *ISA* bus.

In 1987, IBM introduced its line of Personal System/2 computers. The PS/2 computers didn't use the ISA bus. Instead, IBM created its controversial *MicroChannel Architecture* or *MCA*, which enabled the computer to process information faster. Sadly, expansion cards designed for the popular ISA bus could not be used with these PS/2 computers. Likewise, you couldn't use an MCA expansion card in your PC.

The inability of the PS/2 to use the ISA bus card prevented people from salvaging expansion cards from another PC and using them in a new PS/2. Because of this non-transferability of cards, many people never considered buying the PS/2 computer. IBM has since produced PS/2 computers that use the ISA bus, however.

To counter IBM's renegade MCA bus, a consortium of PC makers developed an improved bus design that didn't fully abandon the ISA bus. The new bus was called the *Extended Industry Standard Architecture*, or *EISA*. Unlike MCA, this new standard allows you to use your ISA expansion cards from your older computer with the new architecture.

Installing an Expansion Card

When you install an expansion card, you may have to configure it by using *jumpers* or *DIP* (dual-inline pin) *switches*. A jumper is simply a short piece of wire, encased in plastic, that enables you to make an electrical connection between two pins on your card. A DIP switch is simply a little box with a bank of switches you must set either up or down. For example, I installed a Diamond Stealth VRAM video card that required me to change the DIP switch to take full advantage of my NEC 4FG monitor. Fortunately, you often don't need to set DIP switches or jumpers. Most expansion cards have been pre-configured at the factory to work in most situations.

When you remove an expansion card, rock the card back and forth along its length. In other words, do not twist the card from side to side but rather pull up alternately on each end. Be careful where you grab the card; there may be delicate components that you may crush. Carefully grab the card by its metal bracket and edges.

STOP!

Before touching an expansion card, touch a metal object nearby, such as the inside of your computer's case, to drain yourself of static electricity. Do not touch any of the components on the card because any static electricity may damage the sensitive electronic parts on the card. Also, do not touch the gold edges on the card. As you remove each expansion card, set it aside on a clean surface, preferably on the anti-static bag from other cards you have purchased.

SAVE
THE DAY!

After installing a new expansion card, it may not work, or another piece of hardware that used to work, such as a mouse, no longer works. This indicates a *hardware conflict*. The two pieces of hardware—the new expansion card and mouse—are using the same "phone line" to talk to your PC. What causes such a conflict? Four sources of conflict include:

 Direct memory access (DMA) channel

 Read-only memory (ROM) address

 Input/output (I/O) address

 Interrupt request (IRQ) line

Look up these phrases in your manuals and see if both pieces are fighting over the same line. It's possible a just-installed modem may be preset for COM1 (the first serial communications port). This serial port occupies a set I/O address. However, that same COM1 port may be used by your mouse. You will find that neither the mouse nor the modem works. The solution is to change a jumper or DIP switch on one or the other so one continues to use COM1 and the other uses COM2. They will then each have their own phone line. No more party line!

Power, Power, Power

Your computer can't run without electricity. Your computer includes a power supply that turns the 110-volt alternating current (AC) from your electrical outlet into both 5- and 12-volt direct current (DC). The power supply has a tough job. It must start the computer's hard disk from a dead stop to 3600 revolutions per second while providing safe, stable current to the motherboard. The motherboard can be ruined by simple static electricity, not to mention unstable power.

The process of turning high voltages into low voltages generates plenty of heat. This is one reason the power supply has its own cooling fan. The cooling fan also provides cool air to the rest of the computer, which generates heat as the electronic circuits are powered. The cooling fan doesn't draw cool air into the computer. Rather, it blows hot air out the rear of the computer. The result of this decompression is that cooler air is pulled in through the front and then over the components of the motherboard.

Power supplies are rated in watts, or W. Most PCs have 200- or 250-watt power supplies. Because of the demands placed on my computer, I installed a 300-watt power supply. This eases the burden on the power supply, lengthening its life. Also, this power supply has a thermostatic control that increases the speed of the cooling fan as the temperature goes up.

SAVE
THE DAY!

If you ever hear the absence of the cooling fan's slight whir, turn off your PC immediately! Without this fan running, the built-up heat—up to 150 degrees—will destroy your computer. Occasionally check the flow of air being expelled by your PC. Place your hand behind the fan's vent; you should feel a slight but constant breeze. Once, I found my fan working at half normal speed because of a defect.

Leave It On!

The eternal debate among PC users is whether to leave your computer on or off. First of all, a computer is no blender. You can leave it on unattended even if you are gone for an extended period. Nothing will burn out. In fact, your computer may last longer if left on, because it goes through the most stress when turned on. Have you ever seen a light bulb burn out while it was on? No, because they usually burn out when first turned on. Flicker. Dead. Similarly, a PC is most likely to break under the strain of warming up.

As a general rule, turn your computer on and off once a day, but no more. Keeping your computer at a constant temperature is probably one of the best ways to lengthen the life of your computer. This same rule applies to your computer printer.

TRICKS

Plug your monitor into its own outlet, not into the outlet built into the back of the PC. Some people use a special "cheater" cord to plug their monitor into the computer's AC outlet. Unfortunately, this outlet was meant for the original monochrome (single-color) display. Using this outlet is convenient but may overtax the power supply.

SAVE THE DAY!

Do not operate your PC for extended periods with its cover off. Believe it or not, your computer's parts get overheated with the lid off. Why? The cooling fan relies on the cover to suck cooler air from the small vents in the front and out the rear. With the cover off, there is little, if any, air flow. The result: your computer parts generate heat that is not being dissipated fast enough.

Where Lightning Strikes

Your computer's power supply has plenty of built-in power protection. Regardless, it may not be able to handle four electrical foes:

 Voltage spikes. Short-duration surges in the power line. Spikes can be quite short, as brief as a billionth of a second. Although unnoticed by lights and other electrical equipment, your computer may be damaged by these.

 Power surges. A longer version of the spike, these last several milliseconds. Power surges are invisible, but your PC may restart itself or simply shut down.

 An electrical brownout. Also known as a power sag, a brownout is when the line voltage falls below that required by your PC and other electrical devices. During a brownout, you will see lights dim, electrical motors slow down, and the display on your computers monitor may shrink.

SAVE
THE DAY!

Your computer is more sensitive to electrical fluctuations than other office equipment. If your computer restarts on its own or simply blanks out—although the monitor may still be on—turn the power switch off, wait a few seconds, and then turn it on. This resets its internal circuit breaker.

 Blackout. This involves complete interruption of power for more than a fraction of a second. Power failures cost U.S. businesses $12 billion yearly.

According to the National Power Laboratory, a division of Best Power Technologies Inc., a typical office has 443 power errors annually, each of which could gravely affect computerized systems, causing work loss or physical damage. Depending on the importance of your work, you may want to add some power protection. Your options include:

 Surge protectors. These protect you from simple voltage spikes. They're really cheap (from 20 to 200 bucks).

 Line conditioners. More sophisticated than surge protectors, these purify the power and add to it during brownouts.

 Backup power supplies. For highly important work or for areas that have unreliable power, a backup power supply is preferred. Two types exist: *uninterruptible power supplies* (UPSs) and *standby power supplies* (SPSs). The more expensive UPS always runs your PC from a battery that is continually recharged by the electrical outlet. If an outage occurs, you'll have plenty of juice to save your work and turn off the computer until the power is restored. The SPS, on the other hand, works off the outlet but switches in a wink from the outlet to a backup battery when a power outage occurs.

TRICKS

How do you tell the difference between a UPS and SPS backup power supply? If the so-called UPS mentions a "switch time," then it is an SPS, not a UPS. A true UPS always uses its battery, which means it never switches from the AC outlet to the battery.

If you are wondering about lightning... Even though lightning may not strike your building, it can affect your nearby electrical facilities and damage your computer. During a severe storm, save your work and turn off your PC. Leave the computer plugged in. Believe it or not, this gives the lightning the fastest path to the ground. However, you may want to unplug the telephone line to your modem; electrical spikes and surges can find their way to your computer through this line.

TRICKS

A simple way to add extra protection to your equipment in a lightning storm is to tie overhand knots in the power cord. Overhand knots make the lightning surge work against itself and burn out the power cord, not your computer.

Now that you know the guts of your PC, you might start thinking like a nerd. Words like motherboard, power supply, and math coprocessor may pop up in your conversations with others (hopefully, not).

SAM THOUGHT HE COULD GET READY FOR VACATION...
IF HE TURNED UP THE BRIGHTNESS ON HIS MONITOR.

CHAPTER
10

Into the Looking
Glass...with Knobs

D o you watch TV more than your neighbors watch you? If so, you
probably know how to use a TV. PCs also use TVs, but they're called
"monitors" and they don't have as many stations. This chapter introduces
monitors by helping you:

🔧 Know how monitors and video cards work together to let you see
your work

🔧 Decipher terms such as MGA, CGA, EGA, VGA, SVGA, etc

🔧 Select a video card and matching monitor

🔧 Make the most of your monitor

Although early computers didn't have monitors (only printers), yours does.
The *monitor*—also called the *display* or simply *screen*—lets you see your
computer work. The monitor typically sits on top of your computer and
provides the visual link between you and your PC. Without it, you would be
operating blind. You couldn't see the results of your calculations or mis-
typed words on the screen.

The monitor is actually only half of the video equation. The *video card*—also
called the *display adapter*, *video adapter*, or *graphics card*—sends the image
from the PC to your monitor. What's the point? Believe it or not, the video

card is the more important of this video duo. It determines how many colors you can display at one time and which monitor you can use. Terms like CGA, EGA, and VGA indicate the type of video card you own. (More on this later.)

NERDY
DETAILS

The video card is one example of an expansion card. Typically, it sits in one of your computer's several expansion slots to become a working part of your PC. Other computers, including laptop computers, have the video card built into the motherboard. For more information on laptop computers, see Chapter 15.

How Do You Change Stations?

A monitor is very similar to a TV, except you can't change channels. However, you can't use a TV with your PC because the TV was designed to show pictures viewed from across the room, not small text 18 inches away from your face. Like a TV, a monitor has a few knobs or buttons along the side or front:

 Brightness. This dial lets you increase or decrease the overall brightness of the screen.

 Contrast. This dial increases the brightness of images in the foreground compared to the background. If you turn down the contrast, for example, your image will not stand out from the background. The result: a dim-looking and muddied image.

 On/off (power) **switch.** The on/off switch usually is found either on the front or side of the monitor. Some manufacturers are cruel and place it on the back of the monitor. Sometimes, this switch doubles as the brightness control.

TRICKS

The brightness of your screen fades as its internal parts become less efficient over time. To have your monitor last a long time, keep the brightness dimmed to a tolerable level. The less light hitting the screen, the longer your monitor will last.

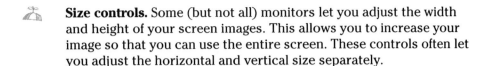

Size controls. Some (but not all) monitors let you adjust the width and height of your screen images. This allows you to increase your image so that you can use the entire screen. These controls often let you adjust the horizontal and vertical size separately.

Horizontal and vertical controls. With these, you can move the screen image up, down, left, or right to center it on your screen. Typically, you won't need to use these controls.

Degauss button. Some color monitors include a "degauss" button to preserve their color clarity. Degaussing eliminates built-up magnetic fields that throw your monitor out of whack. (This is a cleansing ritual for monitors.) After pressing this button, the screen briefly "jumps and wobbles" a bit but then settles down.

TRICKS

If you have a degaussing button, press it at least once a week. Otherwise, turn your monitor off for at least half an hour from time to time. When you start the monitor again, it will degauss itself automatically. You should not press the degauss button more often than every 20 minutes.

Your monitor may include other goodies, such as:

Tilt-swivel stand. This stand attaches to the bottom of your monitor so that you can adjust it to the angle best for your use. For example, tilt it down to avoid the glare of an overhead light. The swivel part allows you to turn the monitor towards friends or colleagues so they can see too. (The tilt-swivel stand also lets you have your monitor nod in agreement with you...uh-huh.)

Anti-glare lens. Some monitors may include an antiglare lens, to cut down the harsh light reflected off the screen and into your eyes. Glare is discussed later.

NERDY
DETAILS

Most computer monitors use a cathode-ray tube (CRT)— the same technology found in TVs. CRTs, as they are called, consist of a vacuum tube enclosed in glass. One end of the tube contains an electron gun that shoots a stream of high-speed electrons to the inside of the TV screen. On the way, a

continues

continued

special coil steers the beam to a specific point. When the inside of the screen, which is coated with phosphorous, is struck by the beam, the screen glows.

This is the light you see when watching TV or using your computer. This glow doesn't last long, so the electron beam must constantly redraw the screen (about 70 times per second). The electron beam moves quickly, sweeping from left to right in lines from top to bottom.

The 1950s Revisited: Black & White vs. Color

How many of you own a black-and-white TV? Not many, huh? Surprisingly, many PCs can work well with a monochrome (black-and-white) monitor. However, many games and other software programs work best with color.

The One-Color Monitor

Monochrome, or *TTL*, monitors produce images of one color. The most popular is amber, followed by white and green. The background color is then black. These monitors can also show flashing, underlined, and bold text. Although most people want a color monitor, monochrome monitors do have their place. A monochrome monitor is ideal for software that requires just viewing letters and few if any graphics, such as bar graphs and pie charts. For example, using a word processor or a spreadsheet or database program does not require color. In fact, your eyes may become less tired using a monochrome monitor. Even Microsoft Windows software can work adequately on a monochrome monitor. Most importantly, monochrome monitors are cheap, usually costing under $80.

NERDY
DETAILS

Early monochrome monitors and video cards couldn't display graphics, such as a pie chart. However, special types of video cards—such as *Hercules* or *monographics*—can handle these tasks. Almost all monochrome video cards can display graphics, although not to the fine detail and colors of color video cards.

The Multicolor Monitor

Just as color TVs are much more popular than black-and-white sets, color monitors are more popular than their monochrome counterparts. By being able to show many colors at one time, these monitors are ideal for displaying charts, painting images, and playing computer games. And programs like Microsoft Windows take advantage of the colors. Color monitors use more sophisticated (i.e., more expensive) technology than monochrome monitors. A monochrome monitor uses one electron gun to paint the screen; the color monitor uses three—red, green, and blue. A color monitor often costs $200 or more.

Whichever monitor you own, it displays *text* or *graphics* or both. Text includes letters, numbers, and symbols you see on the screen. The typical color or monochrome monitor can display up to 25 rows of text by 80 columns (80 characters wide). This is about a half page of single-spaced text.

TRICKS

> Want larger text from your color screen? From the DOS prompt, type: MODE 40. The text on the screen is now twice as large. To change the text back, type: MODE 80. Unfortunately, this doesn't change the size of the text in your software programs. Also, some software programs reset the screen to its normal 80-character-wide format when you are done using them.

Graphics include pictures, images, squares, lines, circles, and possible text thrown in. This distinction is important. Some monochrome monitors cannot display graphics, such as the many multicolored images in a computer game.

Sizing Up Your Monitor

Like a TV, the size of a monitor is measured by the number of inches between opposite corners, from an inexpensive 12" monochrome monitor to a 21" color monitor. And like a TV, the larger the monitor, the more you'll pay. The larger monitors are handy for seeing more under Microsoft Windows or designing a newsletter using desktop publishing software. With a larger monitor, you can see an entire 8.5"×11" page in a 100-percent view. The paper matches the screen. In other words, what you see on the screen virtually matches the page to be printed. This is called *what-you-see-is-what-you-get (WYSIWYG)*. By seeing the whole page at its actual size, you can save yourself from printing several drafts before you get it right.

Picture-tube quality is another consideration. Many monitors are curved because it's easier to send an electron beam across them. Flat-screen monitors, which are a bit more expensive, look better to most people. As a general rule, the less curvature a monitor has, the less glare it will reflect into your eyes.

Monitors also come in two orientations: *portrait* and *landscape*. A portrait monitor is higher than it is wide, enabling you to view an entire page of a document. They differ from standard monitors because they stretch image height to about 66 lines, enabling you to see the equivalent of a full printed page on one screen. A landscape, or dual-page, monitor is the exact opposite of a portrait monitor, suitable for viewing two pages, side by side, at once. Most general-purpose monitors are landscape (wider than they are tall).

TRICKS

To test a monitor you want to buy, try these tips (make sure the monitors have the same video card):

 Draw a circle with the graphics program and ensure the circle is a true circle, not oblong. If things look squashed, check the width and height controls.

 If you are using Windows, type some words in 10- or 12-point type (one point=1/72"). If they are fuzzy or if the black characters are fringed with color, select another monitor.

Turn the brightness up and down while examining the corner of the screen's image. If the image blooms or swells, it's likely to lose focus at high brightness levels.

Load Microsoft Windows to check for uniform focus. Are the corner icons as sharp as the rest of the screen? Are the lines in the title bar curved or wavy?

NERDY
DETAILS

Consider the size of your desk before you think about monitors 16 inches or larger. A 16" monitor is typically at least a foot and a half deep, and a 20" monitor will take up 2 square feet. (Typical 14" monitors are 16 to 18 inches deep.)

It's In the Cards

The video card is the brains behind your monitor. Although tucked neatly inside your PC, this electronic wonder determines the type of monitor you'll have on your desk. Some PCs have the video card built into the motherboard—your computer's main circuit board. Most systems, though, use a video card that fits into an expansion slot.

Most importantly, a video card determines how sharp your images will be. This sharpness, or *resolution*, is measured by the number of horizontal and vertical picture elements, or *pixels*, the video card can display on your monitor. For example, a VGA video card must be able to display 640 by 480 pixels on your screen. The greater the number of pixels, the more detailed your images. High resolutions (such as 640×480 pixels) can provide photographic clarity; low resolutions can make letters look crude. The diagonal lines that form the letters have little stair steps notched into them.

The video card also determines how many colors you can display at one time. Many games, for example, can display 256 colors at one time. As a general rule, the more pixels being displayed on the screen (a sharper image), the fewer colors your video card can display. A video card that can display 256 colors at a resolution of 640×480 pixels can display only 16 colors at a sharper 800×600 pixels.

Which Card Do You Have?

To prevent a mishmash of pixel combinations (659×224, 762×129, etc.), a video card follows one of several industry standards (see table 10.1). The first IBM PC in 1981 had a monochrome (one-color) display that used the *Monochrome Display Adapter (MDA)*. This video card could only display text in a resolution of 720×350 pixels. A company named Hercules released its own video card called the Hercules Graphics Card, or HGC. This card displayed sharper text and could display graphics, such as pie charts. The Hercules standard was a de facto standard for monochrome video cards.

Table 10.1
Video Card Standards at a Glance

Acronym	Meaning	Type	Max resolution (in pixels)	Comments
MDA	Monochrome Display Adapter	Monochrome	720×350	
HGC	Hercules Graphics Cards	Monochrome	720×350	Can display graphics
CGA	Color Graphics Adapter	Color	320×200	Displays four colors of 16 choices
EGA	Enhanced Graphics Adapter	Color	640×350	Displays 16 colors of 64 choices
VGA	Virtual Graphics Array	Color	640×480	Displays 256 colors of 256,000 choices
SVGA	Super-VGA	Color	800×600 1024×768	Displays 256 colors of 256,000 choices
XGA 8514/A	eXtended Graphics Array	Color	1024×768	Displays 256 colors of 256,000 choices

The first color video card was the *Color/Graphics Adapter (CGA)* from IBM. This card had a lower text resolution than the MDA, typically 320×200 pixels, and could display only four colors from a selection, or palette, of 16. One drawback of a CGA video card is that it produces *flicker* and *snow*. Flicker is the annoying tendency of the text to flash as you move the image up or down. Snow is the flurry of bright dots that can appear anywhere on the screen. (Arghhh, a blizzard!) The *Enhanced Graphics Adapter (EGA)*, also from IBM, increased resolution to 640×350 pixels. Also, you could show 16 colors at one time from a palette of 64. Both CGA and EGA are crude by today's standards.

TRICKS

Avoid EGA video cards because they are limited to 16 colors and are only 62 percent as sharp as a VGA card. Also, VGA and SVGA cards let you run CGA and EGA software on your VGA monitor.

The true video revolution came in 1987 when IBM introduced its Personal Systems/2 (PS/2) computers. These computers sported the *Virtual Graphics Array* video card, or *VGA*. (Some people mistakenly call VGA "video graphics adapter.") The most popular standard today, VGA adapters produce a maximum resolution of 640×480 pixels, and are able to display up to 256 colors from a palette of 256,000. (That's a lot of crayons.) An emerging standard is *super-VGA (SVGA)*, which provides a maximum resolution of 800×600 pixels and the same colors as VGA. There are also video cards that display 1024×768 pixels, such as XGA (eXtended Graphics Array), which is also called the 8514/A standard.

Aren't sure which video card you have? A VGA or SVGA card has a 15-pin connector. Otherwise, consult your manual.

Changing Frequencies (or Why Monitors Can Tire Your Eyes)

Because a video card determines which monitor you can use, you must match the monitor to the video card. Like a radio station, a monitor operates at a certain frequency to display the images it gets from your video card. This frequency indicates how often the screen is "repainted" by the electron gun. Most displays have a *refresh rate* (or *vertical scan rate*) of about 70 Hertz (Hz), meaning the screen is refreshed 70 times a second.

TRICKS

Lower refresh rates cause the screen to flicker, and unknowingly tire your eyes. The higher this refresh rate, the better.

Some monitors are *fixed frequency*. They are locked into a single frequency. To use such monitors, you must get a video card that matches the desired frequency. You get a VGA monitor with a VGA video card, for example.

A monitor that supports a range of different frequencies is called a *multiple frequency monitor*. It can work with a range of video cards. One example is the NEC MultiSync 4FG, which supports all popular video standards up to 87Hz. Different vendors call their multiple frequency monitors by different names, including *multisync*, *multi-frequency*, *multiscan*, *auto synchronous*, and *auto tracking*. They're all the same. One convenience of a monitor that covers a wide range of frequencies is that it can be used with video standards that are not yet introduced. In other words, a multisync monitor prepares you for the future.

NERDY
DETAILS

Monitors also appear in two styles: digital and analog. These styles describe how they accept signals from the video card. A digital monitor indicates obsolete technology because this type of monitor can only display a certain number of colors. Some common digital monitors are: MDA, CGA, and EGA. Analog monitors are more popular today and include VGA and SVGA monitors.

Pixel Dust and Other Monitor Magic

When shopping for a monitor, your two biggest concerns are resolution and dot pitch. Your monitor must have a resolution that supports your video card. For example, a VGA monitor must have 640 horizontal by 480 vertical pixels.

NERDY
DETAILS

To handle sharper resolutions, some monitors work in *interlaced* mode. In the conventional *noninterlaced* mode, the electron beam sweeps the screen in lines from top to bottom, one line after the other, completing the screen in one pass. In interlaced mode, the electron beam also sweeps the screen from top to bottom but in two passes. First the odd lines are drawn and then the even ones. This technique redraws the screen faster, reducing any possible flickering of the image. One drawback: The interlacing must be so good that your eye can average the two separately drawn sets of lines. A good interlaced monitor can provide very stable-looking images. Interlacing is reserved for only the highest resolutions, such as 1024x768 pixels.

If you want a color monitor, you'll be concerned about the *dot pitch*. Dot pitch is the distance, measured in millimeters, between the blue, green, and red electron guns used to color your screen. The less distance between these guns, the sharper the picture. Conversely, screens with a larger dot pitch tend to produce less clear images. Most monitors have a dot pitch between .25 and .52 millimeters (mm). To avoid grainy images, look for a dot pitch of .28 mm or smaller for 12" and 14" monitors, or .31mm or smaller for 16" and larger monitors.

TRICKS

If buying a new monitor, avoid monitors with .41 mm or greater dot pitches. On fine text and graphics, the clarity is appalling. One test is to start Microsoft Windows and view the text of the icons on the screen. Are they hard to read? If so, look into another monitor (sorry about the pun). Your eyes are worth the extra bucks.

NERDY DETAILS

It's best not to turn your monitor on and off more than once or twice a day. Two reasons:

 Longer life. The surge of electricity stresses your monitor when turned on. The less your turn it on, the less stress.

 Less eye fatigue. Most monitors require up to an hour to stabilize. During this period, image centering, black level, focus, and screen brightness can vary greatly, affecting the screen's readability and your comfort.

VGA? SVGA? So Many Choices, It Hertz

MDA? CGA? EGA? VGA? SVGA? Which video standard should you select? Start by looking at the software you currently use or would like to run. Many games, for example, require VGA. The new multimedia boom, which combines stereo sound, still photos, full-motion video, and a CD-ROM drive, also requires a VGA video card.

Although VGA is popular, SVGA is becoming more so. (Many video cards support both.) SVGA is very popular for many reasons: besides being a requirement for multimedia, SVGA is also convenient for *Microsoft Windows,* allowing you to get more icons and groups on the screen without having to scroll up or down to make your selections. SVGA is also better for your eyes because it has higher refresh rate than VGA—about 72Hz. Because the screen is refreshed more often, your eyes will not feel as tired.

TRICKS

Short on cash? You can buy a color video card today and a special monochrome monitor that will work together. (Typically, color and monochrome parts don't work together.) By buying a VGA video card and a paper-white VGA monitor (or monochrome VGA monitor), you can display color images in 64 shades of gray. This saves you $100 to $200 dollars, but lets you use the latest video standard. For example, NEC Corp. offers the MultiSync GS2A for less than $100.

Some SVGA cards also support a resolution of 1024×768 pixels, but such a high resolution requires a 16" or larger monitor to read the text comfortably. Also, such high resolution slows down your monitor because the video card must draw all those pixels. On the more common 14" monitors, this resolution crams too much detail into too small an area. So overall, the SVGA standard is a good tradeoff of resolutions and colors. Not too big, not too small. You'll need a monitor that supports SVGA; look for one that supports a frequency of 72Hz or higher.

Because SVGA is not a widely accepted standard, an SVGA video card often acts like the less powerful VGA card. To get SVGA or sharper resolutions, you use special software drivers—small software programs—for each software program that can use SVGA resolution. For example, if you use the desktop publishing program *Ventura Publisher Gold* (GEM version), you will need a software driver for your SVGA video card to display more of the page on the screen.

You won't find software drivers for every possible program; they are provided only for the most popular programs, such as: *AutoCAD, Autoshade,*

CADKEY, Framework, GEM Desktop, Lotus 1-2-3, Microsoft Windows, Microsoft Word, P-CAD, Symphony, Ventura Publisher, VersaCAD, WordPerfect, WordStar, OS/2 Presentation Manager, and *Quattro Pro.* If you own Microsoft Windows, a generic SVGA driver is included so that all of your Windows software can run in SVGA's sharper mode. However, the maker of your SVGA video card includes software designed to run your video card best.

TRICKS

Some video cards include a thinking chip that frees your PC from having to draw the screen. Such video cards are called *video accelerators* or *Windows accelerator cards* because they can speed up all *Microsoft Windows* software. A video accelerator card replaces the video card in your computer. In your DOS programs, it functions as a normal VGA or SVGA card. When you enter *Windows* or another software program the video card supports, you'll truly turn on the speed, possibly 10 to 40 percent faster.

More Memory, More Colors, Same Speed

A video card, like your PC, requires memory chips. Often, you can select how much memory you want on your video card, such as 512K or 1M. Most video cards come with at least 512K. More memory doesn't mean more speed. Rather, additional memory allows your monitor to display more colors or higher resolutions. For 256 colors drawn from a palette of 256,000, you'll need at least 512K of video memory. At 1024×768 pixels, you need at least 1M.

TRICKS

If you currently don't need to display hundreds of colors at once or a resolution of 1024x768 pixels, bypass the extra memory and stick to 512K. The next generation of video cards will probably provide other features you may need. On the flip side, the extra 512K of memory is not expensive—typically less than $50.

Glare, Magnetism, and Other Dangers

You may select the correct monitor, but danger may still be lurking once you turn it on. Three culprits are

- Glare
- Electromagnetic radiation
- Phosphor burn-in

Blinded By the Light

Your eyes may ache after working with your computer. The cause is often glare. Glare is light bounced off your screen directly into your eyes. Because most monitors are slightly curved, they channel the light from the sides at you.

You can easily tell if you have a glare problem. First, turn off your monitor. If parts of your screen display an especially bright spot, such as a window reflection or other light source, you've found your problem. The best solution is to buy a monitor with a flat screen and either an etched or coated glass designed to reduce glare.

If you cannot afford a new monitor, here are some affordable ways to reduce glare. First, change the light that is bounced off your screen. Point your screen away from any bright light sources, such as windows and lamps. Also, avoid facing a window directly. Looking at a monitor with a bright window in front of you is especially straining. It's best to have windows to the left or right of your screen. Also rearrange the other lights in your room. Window blinds can control outside light. Meanwhile, reduce the amount of surrounding light in your room without relying on a single reading lamp. A single lamp causes uneven lighting, which also causes eye fatigue. Your goal is to have indirect, uniform lighting.

You can also change the position of your monitor. Tilt your screen down slightly, about 10 to 15 degrees below eye level. An upward-tilting screen is ideal to look at for bifocal and contact-lens wearers, but it reflects more light than one perpendicular to your desk. Also, you should sit more than 18 inches from your monitor. When setting the monitor's brightness, start out at a low level to avoid headaches and eye fatigue. How low? Load a program that has a light background and set the brightness accordingly. You'll not only avoid eye problems but also lengthen the life of your monitor.

A filter of tinted glass or plastic can improve your monitor's contrast by darkening the screen uniformly. These filters, called *glare filters* or *antiglare screens*, are available for as little as $50. Because of the filter, you may need to increase the monitor's contrast and brightness—in that order—so the screen seems as bright as usual. You can get an inexpensive black mesh (nylon cloth) antiglare screen, but it may cause more trouble than it solves. These screens reduce glare by absorbing any light that isn't traveling perpendicular to the screen. Unfortunately, mesh screens absorb light that comes in at sharp angles from the side, producing glare. Also, the coarser meshes may interfere with the screen's images.

TRICKS

It's best to have dark characters on a light screen, rather than the more common light characters on a dark background. *Microsoft Windows* and other programs enable you to change your colors. To create black text on a white background, add the following line to your CONFIG.SYS startup file:

```
DEVICE=C:\DOS\ANSI.SYS
```

Next, restart your computer. Then type: PROMPT $e[7m$p$g. You should have black text on a white background. To make the change long-term, add that command to your AUTOEXEC.BAT file.

Is Your Computer Killing You?

Your monitor generates electromagnetic emissions. Several medical studies indicate that these electromagnetic emissions may cause health problems, such as miscarriages, birth defects, and cancer. The risk may be low, but if you spend a third of your day (or more) in front of a computer monitor, that risk is multiplied.

The concern is that *VLF (very low frequency)* and *ELF (extremely low frequency)* emissions somehow affect your body. These two emissions come in two forms: electric and magnetic. Some research indicates that ELF magnetic emissions are more threatening than VLF emissions because they interact with the natural electric activity of body cells. Monitors aren't the only culprits; significant ELF emissions come from electric blankets and power lines. ELF and VLF are not considered radiation; they are actually radio frequencies below that of broadcasting.

Some monitors reduce these possibly harmful emissions. A low-emission monitor costs about $20 to $100 more than similar, regular-emission monitors. When shopping for a low-emission monitor, don't just ask for a low-emission monitor. Find out if a monitor limits specific types of emission, particularly ELF magnetic fields, or ask if the monitor complies fully with the new 1991 Swedish standard called SWEDAC.

If you don't buy a low-emission monitor, you can take other steps to protect yourself. The most important is to stay at arm's length (around 28 inches) from the front of your monitor. After a couple of feet, ELF magnetic emission levels are reduced to those of a typical office with fluorescent lights. Also, monitor emissions are weakest from the front of a monitor, so keep at least three feet from the sides and backs of nearby monitors and five feet from any copier—a real strong source of ELF.

Etched in Stone (Actually, Phosphorous)

Leaving your monitor on for long periods can permanently etch what is displayed on the screen into the phosphor surface behind the glass. This is called *phosphor burn-in*.

To avoid phosphor burn-in, dim or turn off your monitor if you will be gone for more than one hour. Some people use a software *screen saver* or *screen blanker* to hide or cover up the screen image temporarily. One popular example is After Dark from Berkeley Systems. These utilities place a moving image or a blank screen over your current work. When you return, you press any key or move your mouse to uncover your work.

As mentioned earlier, your monitor dims with time. Setting the brightness and contrast controls correctly prevents you from having to use your monitor at its highest intensity. To adjust your monitor, first turn the brightness way up. Next, adjust the contrast. Finally, turn down the brightness until you can't see the diagonal scan lines.

TRICKS

Microsoft Windows 3.1 includes built-in screen savers. Select the Desktop icon from the Control Panel. Then select one of the many screen savers. Select "Test" to preview each. If you select "Setup," you can even add a password to the screen saver so that no one but you can use your PC when you are away.

There are other ways to make the most of your monitor. Cleaning the screen is the most basic but overlooked way to maintain your monitor. If you often point your fingers at the screen, a smudge will remind you to do the chore. Even if the screen isn't smudged, regularly clean it. When you clean your monitor, use a soft, lint-free cloth and a non-alcohol glass cleaner. Always spray fluid on the cloth and not on the screen.

Also, keep your monitor cool. Unlike your PC, the monitor does not have a cooling fan. This is why monitors have ventilation holes and slots. Keep these free and clear. Never place paper or anything else on top of the monitor. Your monitor may overheat and suffer an electronic aneurism. If you notice dirt accumulating on the openings, use a toothbrush or vacuum cleaner to clear them.

CHAPTER
11

Keyboards and Other Things You Can't Keep Your Hands Off

This chapter covers the various things you use to "talk" to your computer—how to give it commands, cancel your orders, make a selection, and more. The keyboard is the most popular way to do this, followed by the almost-essential mouse. This chapter covers:

- Keyboards with distinct personalities
- Important keys that could save your PC's life and improve yours
- Stupid keys you wouldn't consider using
- Having your keyboard take care of you—Carpal Tunnel Syndrome
- Safeguarding your keyboard from you... and repairing it when you don't
- Typing French or other "foreign" characters, including fractions
- Above and beyond the keyboard—mice and trackballs

Personal computing is a "hands-on" experience. You can yell at your computer all you want, but to really tell it where to go, you must use a keyboard or a mouse. These parts of the computer are called *input devices* because you are giving your PC information with which to work.

Touring the Keyboard

The keyboard is the most popular way to talk to your computer. A keyboard has four parts:

 The typing area, which includes letters and numbers.

 The numeric keypad, where people with 10-key skills (typically accountants) can nimbly add up numbers.

 The cursor and screen controls for paging up and down in your document, and for moving your PC's cursor one character or line at a time.

 The function keys (F1 through F10) that access special features in a software program. When DOS is on-screen and you press the F3 function key, for example, the last command you typed is repeated. Most programs, such as Microsoft Windows, use F1 to display helpful information about the program. (Many keyboards also have function keys F11 and F12, although their absence is no great loss.)

The touch of a keyboard is crucial. Some people prefer keyboards that "click," telling them with each keystroke that the key was pressed. This is called a *click-tactile* keyboard. Others prefer silent, or *non-tactile*, keyboards. If you are a fast typist or work in an office environment, you may prefer a quiet keyboard rather than the staccato of pressed keys.

TRICKS

Most computers come with an inexpensive, low-quality keyboard. You may want to purchase a high-quality replacement keyboard from companies such as Northgate Computers or Keytronics. For between $70 and $100, you can have a warranted keyboard that has extra features. Some even include a solar calculator! These replacements often let you swap a handful of individual keys to your liking. For example, you can swap the Caps Lock, Alt, and Ctrl keys or the asterisk and backslash (/) keys. More on these keys below.

The keyboard plugs into your computer using a five- or six-pin connector. Newer keyboards can be used in older computers. Often, a switch on the belly or back side of the keyboard lets you switch between XT (old technology) and AT (new technology) modes.

NERDY
DETAILS

The placement of the keys on a keyboard can affect your speed. Most keyboards use a funky layout called QWERTY; the top row starts with "QWERTY." A rarer but intriguing keyboard layout is the Dvorak keyboard.

Designed by August Dvorak in 1936, the Dvorak keyboard increases typing speed, comfort, and accuracy by placing the most often used letters in the center, or home, row. The five vowel keys, AOEUI, are on the left-hand side. The five most frequently used consonants, DHTNS, are on the right-hand side.

According to tests, 90 percent of typing efforts are reduced when the Dvorak keyboard is used. The Dvorak keyboard was approved by the American National Standards Institute (ANSI) in 1982. A Dvorak keyboard requires no changes to your computer. Just plug in the new keyboard and it will work. Unfortunately, you have to learn the new style of typing.

All Those Keys

The first IBM PC had an awkward 83-key keyboard. Today's keyboards are better designed, with keys that are easier to reach and LED (light-emitting diode) lights that tell you when certain keys are on. New keyboards have over 100 keys (some have 140!). Most of the additional keys come from a separate numeric keypad (for entering numbers) and arrow keys (for moving the cursor).

No matter what your specific keyboard design, the keyboard has one specific task: to send unique, numeric codes to the computer that correspond to the keys that were pressed. You press the letter "A" and your PC receives a request for an A. These keys are grouped into what they do.

Action Keys

A keyboard's action keys aren't too exciting, but they are used quite often:

 Enter (Return). The most important key is the Enter key. This key, which is usually L-shaped, tells your computer to "go," to do the command you just typed or selected. The Enter key also places blank lines in a document. For your convenience, a second Enter key is on the numeric keypad.

TRICKS

> Unlike a typewriter, you don't need to press the Enter key when you come to the end of a line. Instead, your cursor automatically "jumps" to the next line. This is called *automatic word wrap* because words automatically wrap around to the next line. You do need to press the Enter key, however, when you finish a paragraph and want to start a new one.

 Spacebar. Like a typewriter spacebar, the Spacebar moves your cursor one space at a time (it also makes a great fire button in certain games).

 Tab and **Shift-Tab.** The Tab key (which may only be marked by two arrows) is similar to the Tab key on a typewriter. In some programs, the Tab key moves to the next item, such as from the City to State line in an address database.

By pressing the Shift key with the Tab key, you can move backwards. This is also called a "back tab."

 Backslash (\). The backslash key is used with DOS commands to separate directory names. Here is an example:

```
COPY C:\WINDOWS\SYSTEM\SETUP.INF SETUP.BAK
```

 Forward slash (/). Although it's used often in literature ("Where the hell is that houseboat/RV store anyway!"), the forward slash character is not used often, except when adding extra information to a DOS command. The command DIR /P, for example, pauses each screenful of information to stop it before zooms by.

 Pause. The Pause key is actually an "inaction" key. Press this key to place your computer in suspended animation; press any other key to bring your PC back to life.

You can use this key to pause the screen as things go zooming by in DOS, such as listing a directory of your work files or the details of your PC's memory with the DOS MEM /C command.

TRICKS

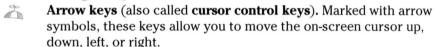

If your keyboard lacks a Pause key, use Ctrl-Num Lock.

Fast-Moving Keys

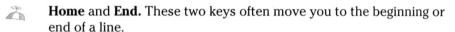 **Arrow keys** (also called **cursor control keys**). Marked with arrow symbols, these keys allow you to move the on-screen cursor up, down, left, or right.

Home and **End.** These two keys often move you to the beginning or end of a line.

PageUp (PgUp) and **PageDown (PgDn).** These two keys typically move your cursor to the next page or screen. In word processing software, these keys move to the next page of your document.

Two-Faced Keys

Some keys turn on or off, changing the behavior of your PC.

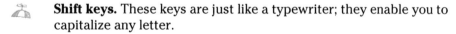 **Shift keys.** These keys are just like a typewriter; they enable you to capitalize any letter.

Caps Lock. The Caps Lock key resembles a typewriter's Shift Lock key. When turned on, it makes all letters you type (but not numbers and punctuation marks) uppercase. Press it again to turn it off.

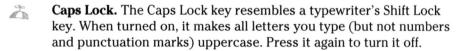 **Num Lock.** The Num Lock key turns on the numeric keypad's numbers. When this key is turned off, the numeric keys double as cursor control keys (the arrows, Home/End, and PageUp/PageDown keys).

NERDY
DETAILS

On most keyboards, the Caps Lock and Num Lock keys have LED lights. When the key is turned on, the light is on.

Timesaving Keys

 Alt and **Ctrl** (Control). These two keys can save you time. Alt and Ctrl often are used with other keys to create unique combinations called shortcut keys. Shortcut keys perform an action (Alt-F3 might save a file in one program; Ctrl-A might highlight and copy information in another) or play back a macro (a collection of prerecorded keystrokes).

The dash means "hold down the first key while pressing the second key."

 Print Screen (or **PrtScr**). This key lets you print instantly whatever's on-screen. In some programs you must press Shift-PrtScr or Alt-PrtScr; the key may not work at all in other programs. In Microsoft Windows, for example, this key prints the screen to a temporary holding space called the Windows Clipboard. The "captured" image can then be saved, printed or copied into another Windows program. Unfortunately, this key only prints letters and not graphics.

If you print to a laser or other single-sheet printer, your page won't emerge until it is entirely filled. If the page isn't full, you must eject it using the form feed button.

Editing Keys

Some keys are used for editing words and lines:

 Insert (Ins). The Insert key typically toggles your computer from insert to overwrite (typeover) mode. In insert mode, the letters you type are inserted at the cursor, moving other letters to the right. In overwrite mode, the letters you type erase the letters to the right of the cursor. It is best to leave your insert key in its natural insert mode. Often when you change between insert and overwrite mode, the cursor typically changes from a thin line to a square block so you can tell which mode you are in.

 Delete (Del). The Delete key deletes the letter at the cursor.

 Backspace (BkSp). The Backspace key moves the cursor backward, mowing over any characters in its way.

Save the Day Keys

Occasionally, you may want to stop your PC and have it do something else. Not as often (but often enough!), your PC may run amuck and need to be calmed down. Try these keys to escape:

 Escape (Esc). The Escape key often lets you escape from your current place. It cancels your changes or returns you to a previous choice. For example, after mistyping a command at the DOS prompt, you can press the Escape key to erase it.

 Ctrl-Break. You sometimes can get your computer's attention by pressing both the Ctrl and Break keys. Your PC typically stops what it is doing at the most opportune moment and gives you control. The Break key may double as the Pause or Scroll Lock keys—look for its name on the face of the key. You also can use Ctrl-C as an alternate to Ctrl-Break.

TRICKS

You can have your PC check more often for the attention-grabbing Ctrl-Break key. Simply add the line BREAK=ON to your CONFIG.SYS startup file.

If you are using DOS 5 (type **VER** at any DOS prompt to find out), type **EDIT C:\CONFIG.SYS**. When the file appears, add the line BREAK=ON near the end.

 Ctrl-Alt-Del. Sometimes, your computer may lose its head and either not speak to you or simply repeat its last command several times. A combination of three keys can stop this nonsense. The Ctrl-Alt-Del (pronounced "Control-Alt-Delete") combination can restart your computer.

This key combination is almost equivalent to turning your PC off and then back on or pressing the reset button on the front of your computer. With a clean slate, you can then get back to work. Unfortunately, the unsaved work you were doing before your computer blew a gasket cannot be regained. For this reason, save your work often.

NERDY
DETAILS

Nerds love the terms "warm boot" and "cold boot." Whenever you press Ctrl-Alt-Del, its referred to as a *warm boot* because your PC is already warmed up. A *cold boot* occurs whenever you turn off the computer (flick the computer switch to off) then turn it on again. You're starting your PC from a cold start.

Stupid Keys

A couple of keys are rarely if ever used, including:

Scroll Lock. Scroll Lock was used to lock a spreadsheet onto your screen so that you could shift the entire screen in different directions.

SysRq. The SysRq key was going to be used by IBM in a future version of DOS. Nothing ever came of it so it remains unused and unloved.

Pipe (¦). The pipe character is used with some DOS commands. Type **DIR ¦ MORE** and press Enter to see an example.

Grave accent (`). This backward apostrophe is rarely used.

Tilde (~). The tilde also is rarely used.

Missing Keys

Some software programs may ask you to press the Help key. No key marked "Help" exists. Instead, most software programs select a key that displays helpful information when pressed. In most cases, the Help key is F1 (function key F1, not the "F" and "1" keys). Sadly, some companies don't follow this style. WordPerfect, for example, uses F3 as its Help key.

Similarly, some programs mention "press any key to continue." Again, no real key is called "any key." Whenever you see this message, press the Enter key or spacebar, just to be safe.

Good Things for Your Keyboard

You can add several things to your keyboard to prevent problems. These include:

- Wrist pads
- Command templates
- Protective covers
- Keyboard accelerators

Repetitive What? Could You Repeat That?

Over the last six years, repetitive strain injuries have increased 1,000 percent. You may know this better as Carpal Tunnel Syndrome (CTS). CTS is caused by the hidden but growing strain of typing at the keyboard. Intense pain develops in the wrist and the typical cure is to wear wrist braces and cease the activity that caused the damage.

CTS not only afflicts typists. A few years ago, a Michigan family sued Nintendo for their daughter developing CTS after hours of playing a Nintendo Entertainment System. (The story called this condition "Nintendo-itis.")

The main cause of CTS, besides too much wrist typing, is curled wrists, which amplifies the strain. For example, I keep my wrists parallel to the floor. Many office desks, however, are too high for this arrangement (if only companies realized that desks are cheap and it's the employees who are valuable). Another way to prevent CTS is to take frequent breaks to reduce stress.

Some products that prevent CTS include:

- **Wrist supports.** This foam rubber pad is placed in front of the keyboard to support your palms when typing. A variation of this is the rolling wrist support, which adjusts to the individual's height.

- **Reminder software.** Some software packages lurk in the background and remind you every so often to take a break from typing.

Keyboard Condoms

Instead of safe sex, you can have a safe keyboard. To avoid feeding your keyboard an unhealthy diet of crumbs, beverages, and dust, you can purchase a cover to place over your keyboard when not in use.

Better yet, you can purchase a second skin for your keyboard. If you work in a rough environment, you can get a molded plastic skin for your keyboard. This see-through, protective cover must match your exact keyboard layout. One such cover is SafeSkin from Merrit Computer Products. You can still use your keyboard, although typing may be slowed somewhat.

Same Typist, Faster Keyboard

You can speed up your keyboard with a software package. Simple programs called keyboard accelerators let you repeat a certain character or move your cursor quickly to where you want it. (Sadly, a keyboard accelerator doesn't speed up your typing.) A keyboard accelerator lets you change the repeat rate and repeat delay (how long you hold down a key before it repeats). Such accelerators are often memory-resident utilities that must be loaded. Unfortunately, these utilities require memory that could be used elsewhere.

TRICKS

Forget the accelerator software and accelerate your keyboard yourself. If you use DOS 4.0 or higher, you can use the MODE command to make your keyboard more responsive. Simply type this command:

MODE CON RATE=32 DELAY=1

Your keyboard should be much faster. You can change the RATE values from 1 to 32; the default is around 20. The higher the number, the faster the keys will repeat. The values for the DELAY range from 1 to 4; the default is 2. The DELAY value is measured in quarter-second increments. To make this improvement permanent, you can add this line to your AUTOEXEC.BAT startup file.

There may be other sources for speeding up your keyboard. Some computer setup programs, which are contained in the BIOS chip (see Chapter 9) let you change the "typematic" rate of your keyboard. And some keyboards, such as the Northgate OmniKey/102, let you accelerate your keyboard.

Cheat Sheets for Your Keyboard

So many programs use a combination of function, Shift, Ctrl, and Alt keys to call up various commands and menus that a map of all these combinations certainly is welcomed. Instead of placing Post-It notes all over your desk and keyboard, you can turn to keyboard templates.

Keyboard templates are plastic or cardboard "cheat sheets" that show the commands for a specific software package. For example, I own templates for Q&A and Lotus 1-2-3. When I use one program or the other, I place the appropriate template over the function keys. Some software programs include a keyboard template; otherwise, you can purchase one in a software store. To prevent these small templates from being lost or accidentally tossed, make a photocopy of the original to set aside as a backup.

NERDY
DETAILS

Because keyboards are designed differently, get the correct template for yours. For example, some keyboards have the function keys on the left side of the keyboard in two columns. Others have these keys along the top in one long row.

Whoops...Splash!
Bad Things for Your Keyboard

If you ever spill a beer (or any other beverage) on your keyboard, the damage can be fixed. As soon as possible, unplug the keyboard from your PC. Next, flush the keyboard with distilled water, not tap water (distilled water won't leave any mineral residue). Next, disassemble part of the keyboard and wash the components with the distilled water. Remove the screws from the base of the keyboard. Once the base bottom is removed, do not remove any internal screws.

If the liquid has dried, let the keyboard soak in some of the water. When the keyboard is clean, pour another gallon of distilled water over it and through the key switches. After the keyboard is totally dry, try it. If the keyboard is not dry, it may short circuit and be ruined.

STOP!

Make sure the keyboard is dry before using it. Keyboards use electrical signals that you can damage permanently if water, which conducts electricity, is inside.

Even if you rescue your keyboard from a spill, you may have shortened its life. Any residue hangs onto dust and other contaminants, making your keyboard dirtier in less time.

Cleaning Your Keyboard

Other items can lodge between your keys, including pencil points, flaking correction fluid, paper clips, and cat hair (yum yum!).

Whether your keyboard is noticeably dirty, it's best to clean it periodically. You can vacuum the keyboard weekly or use a can of compressed air. Before using compressed air, turn the keyboard upside down and tap it gently to make the contaminants fall out.

TRICKS

For more extensive keyboard cleaning, remove each keycap (the individual covers for each key) using a special chip-puller. Some keyboards fall apart when they are opened. For this reason (and for your sanity), photocopy the keytop arrangement (place the keyboard on the copier) for a reference.

After removing each keycap, spray some compressed air into the space under the cap to dislodge any contaminants. Then replace the keycap and check the action of the key. Sometimes, it is best not to remove the spacebar key. On 83- and 84-key keyboards, this key is difficult to reinstall.

If you really don't give a hoot about cleaning your keyboard and would rather use it until it disappears in a cloud of dust and cookie crumbs, go for it. Computer keyboards are so inexpensive and difficult to fix that getting a new one may be the best solution.

Plug-In Problems

The major keyboard difficulty is the cord becoming unplugged. This cord can become disconnected from either the back of your PC or the rear of the keyboard. Another common problem is accidentally bumping the switch on the rear or bottom of the keyboard that switches it between XT and AT mode. If bumped to the wrong mode, your keyboard won't be recognized no matter how firmly plugged in it is. (In most cases, switch your keyboard to "AT.")

Your Shorts Are Showing

Several symptoms indicate the presence of a short in your keyboard. A *short* is simply an unwanted extra electrical connection. Your keyboard may be telling you something if:

- A key appears to be pressed all the time (characters fly across the screen).

- Several keys print whenever you press one key.

- Different characters appear on-screen than what you type, or at least appear to be different because they are being mutated by the Shift, Ctrl, or Alt keys.

- Your PC starts to beep when you turn it on. (Don't confuse this with the one or two beeps you hear when your computer starts.)

The opposite of a short is an *open circuit*—the key is missing an electrical connection. For the most part, open circuits are the most common keyboard failure. The reason: any foreign object that falls into the keyboard has lots of opportunities to block one of the keys from making contact. A few symptoms include:

- The key does not respond to normal typing

- Different keys fail at different times

- More than one key fails

To fix this mess, clean the keyboard (read "Cleaning Your Keyboard" and get brownie recycling points) or shell out another 100 bucks for a new one (after all, you are a "consumer").

Can You Type ½ Fräulein?

Sometimes, you may want to type a non-English word or a fraction. How do you type résumè or Fräulein with an English keyboard? How do you type ½? The answer is to use letters above and beyond the typical 26-letter alphabet. These letters are called *extended ASCII characters*. By pressing the Alt key and one to three numbers, you can type these non-English characters.

In the back of the DOS manual, a table shows the codes for all the special characters. To type an extended character in DOS or in most software packages, simply hold down the Alt key and enter the number assigned to the character you want. Alt-65, for example, produces the capital letter A. The number must be typed from the numeric keypad on the right. Make sure the Num Lock key is on (lit). After typing the numbers, one after the other, release the Alt key. The extended character should appear.

See table 11.1 for the more popular extended characters.

Table 11.1
Popular Extended Characters

Key	Extended Character	Key	Extended Character
Ç	128	ï	139
ü	129	î	140
é	130	ì	141
â	131	Ä	142
ä	132	Å	143
à	133	É	144
å	134	æ	145
ç	135	Æ	146
ê	136	ô	147
ë	137	ö	148
è	138	ò	149

Key	Extended Character	Key	Extended Character
û	150	ñ	164
ù	151	Ñ	165
ÿ	152	´	171
Ö	153	¨	172
Ü	154	£	156
á	160	¥	157
í	161	÷	246
ó	162	±	241
ú	163	"	253

TRICKS

If you will be typing several non-English characters, you can change your keyboard to that of another country's with a few changes. You first need to select the country you want your PC to adopt. You also need to change the personality of your keyboard, printer, and display (KEYBOARD.SYS, PRINTER.SYS, and DISPLAY.SYS, respectively). For full information, check your DOS manual about turning your PC into a world traveler.

Just as you might want a non-English character in your document, you also may want to type a fraction, such as ½ or ¼. Other symbols, such as division (÷), plus/minus (±), and square (²), also are available. Again, you must hold down the Alt key and then type the code for the fraction you want.

TRICKS

If your keyboard has a few keys that don't work, you can use this Alt key technique to type those characters. Suppose, for example, the semicolon key (;) doesn't work. Rather than throw away the keyboard, you can press the Alt key and type 5-9 on the numeric keypad. If only a couple of keys are dead and you don't use them often, you can get by comfortably until you save enough for a new keyboard.

Mousing Around

Most software today, especially Microsoft Windows, works best with a mouse. Mice are small plastic objects about the size of your palm. They usually have two or three buttons used to select items. Typically, a small ball in the exposed belly of the mouse rolls across your desk to register your movements. You move the mouse to move a corresponding pointer on the screen. This pointer on the screen usually is called a *mouse cursor* and is shaped like an arrow or box. There are four basic mouse techniques: pointing, clicking, double-clicking, and dragging.

When you move your mouse, you move it to point the corresponding mouse cursor at parts of the screen. Once the pointer is where you want it, you click the mouse button to select the item. When you click, you press and quickly release the mouse button. Double-clicking means quickly pressing the button twice before you release it. Often, clicking is used to open an item and double-clicking is used to close it.

Sometimes you need to move objects around your screen, and that's where you use dragging. To drag an object, you hold down a mouse button and move the pointer while keeping the button held down. Dragging also lets you select a portion of the screen for resizing. Learning a mouse is all "thumbs" at first, but with time you will master it.

The most popular mouse is the Microsoft Mouse. Because of this, most mice are Microsoft-compatible. Your mouse usually has a "tail," a cord that connects to your PC. There also are cordless mice that transmit your movements to a radio or infrared receiver in your PC.

Mouse on Its Back

A trackball is like a mouse on its back. Instead of moving the ball in the mouse across the desk, a trackball stays in one place. You use your palm to move the ball. Two or three buttons are placed in front of the ball. If you are short on desk space, a trackball is ideal because it doesn't need to be moved around your desk. You also don't have to move your arm or wrist. Otherwise, a trackball works the same as a mouse, requiring a software driver to make it work. A trackball, such as the Logitech TrackMan, costs about as much as mouse (about $75).

Light Mouse

Instead of a mouse, you can use a pen to click on things and to move stuff around. One type of pen pointing tool is the digitizer tablet. A digitizer tablet resembles a sketch pad. You draw on the pad with a pen or a mouse-like cursor (sometimes called a *puck*). This pen is attached to the computer. If the tablet is really nice (Wacom tablets are nice… and expensive), the pen is cordless and pressure sensitive. For artists, the digitizing tablet is ideal because it enables them to trace a drawing and save it to a file.

A light pen is a variation of the digitizing tablet that eliminates the tablet. Instead, you point to the screen. The pen is attached to a cord. When not in use, it attaches to the side of your monitor. The tip of the pen is sensitive to light and reacts to changes in brightness on the screen. The pen tells your computer when it "sees" a portion of the screen light up.

CHAPTER
12

What's So Hard About Disk Drives?

After sweating over a long document or address database, you want to save your work so it won't be scattered to the four winds. Floppy and hard disks are the two most common (and cheapest) media for preserving your work. Once your work makes it onto these media, you can rest easy knowing all your effort is safe. This chapter shows you what it means to be floppy and hard, and throws in a few extras:

- What a floppy drive and disk are, and why you should care
- How to buy disks (get in your car, drive to the store...)
- How to care for your floppies when no one else will
- How to format disks (they won't work until you do this)
- The differences between hard drives and floppy drives
- Alternatives to hard disks (hard squares?)
- How Windows takes over the hard disk (Veni, Vidi, Vici!)
- Finding free space on your hard disk for storing more stuff
- How to care for your hard disk when no one else will
- How to find lost files in the hard disk's filing cabinet

Disk Drives: A Place for My Stuff

When you use your PC, it's like working at your desk. You take papers and other tools out of the drawers and temporarily lay them on the desktop where they'll be handy. At the end of the day, you usually (or should) clear your desktop. Put the scissors back where you found them and the pencils separate from the pens.

Similarly, you sit at your PC and take out your favorite software. You might run your new game or write a letter with your word processor. When finished, you want to save that top score or shining written proposal. If you couldn't save these things, you'd have to start over each time you used your computer. This is why disk drives are used to store your work. The fruits of your labors can be saved permanently to a disk drive so you can resume later.

There are two types of disk drives: floppy disk drives and hard disk drives. With both, you save your work to what are called *files*. A letter to your brother, for example, may be saved as one file. Another letter to your insurance agent is another file. You can save many files to a disk drive. In fact, disk drives act as large file cabinets for your work. (Hence, the name files.)

Why Floppies?

A floppy disk drive, or simply floppy drive, allows you to store your work and take it out of your computer. Your PC has at least one floppy drive and probably two. The floppy drive is the thin, often horizontal opening(s) in the front of your PC. The floppy drive comes in two sizes, based on the size of this opening:

 5.25". This was the size of the original IBM PC disk drive.

 3.5". When IBM introduced its PS/2 line of personal computers, the 3.5" disk drive became very popular for the PC. Why? These disk drives, although smaller, can hold more information.

Your floppy drives are given lettered names. Your first drive is called drive A, or, in DOS lingo, A:. This is the drive your PC attempts to use each time you turn it on. If you have a second floppy drive, it is called drive B, or B:. Often, the topmost drive is drive A, although the order doesn't matter. To prevent confusion, you can label each drive with adhesive stickers.

A floppy disk of the same size (3.5" or 5.25" wide) fits inside the floppy drive. Once you tell your PC to save your work to the floppy disk, a small light turns on until the work is saved. This is called the drive light. When the drive light turns off, you can safely remove the disk for safekeeping, sharing with a friend, or travel elsewhere. The floppy drive is only the tool that records your work to the disk. When you want to retrieve information from the disk, you insert it into the floppy drive. Your PC then places the information into its memory for manipulating or printing.

GEEK

NERDY
DETAILS

Why the name floppy disk? The 5.25" disks are made of a thin material in a flexible plastic jacket. Although not meant to be bent, these disks "flop" around when shook.

Your original information is still safely tucked away on the disk. However, you may decide to save your updated work to the same disk. Your software program typically asks you to provide a name for your work. The software program asks for a *file name*. If you decide to save your work to the same file name, you will overwrite the original disk information, or file, with the new updated information. In most cases, this is what you want. If you want to preserve the first draft of your work, you often can tell your software to save the updated information to a different file by using a different file name. In many software programs, this option is called a "Save as" because you want to save the new work to a different name.

Anatomy of a Disk

The two types of disks—5.25" and 3.5"—are designed differently. Consider the highlights of each (see fig. 12.1 and fig. 12.2):

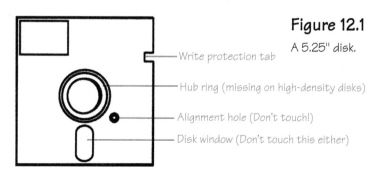

Figure 12.1

A 5.25" disk.

— Write protection tab

— Hub ring (missing on high-density disks)

— Alignment hole (Don't touch!)

— Disk window (Don't touch this either)

Figure 12.2

A 3.5" disk.

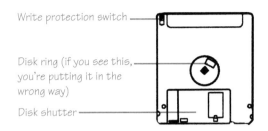

Write protection switch

Disk ring (if you see this, you're putting it in the wrong way)

Disk shutter

When you look at a 5.25" disk, you notice several things. First, it has a hole in the center called the spindle hole that is used to center the disk in the drive. Below this hole is an elliptical cut in the jacket, exposing the actual disk material.

> Do not touch the exposed area of a floppy disk! The oils from your fingerprints can ruin it.

STOP!

On the right side of a 5.25" disk is a write-enable notch. When left uncovered, this notch allows you to save your work to the disk. Adhesive stickers called write-protect tabs are usually included with each new box of disks to cover this notch. If you don't have these, you can use masking tape. When this notch is covered, you cannot erase or change information on the disk. This feature is similar to one on VCR and cassette tapes; when you knock out the plastic tabs, you cannot record over a previously recorded program or song. A disk with a write-protect tab over this notch is called a write-protected disk. You still can copy the files from the disk to another disk. The write-protect tab is handy when you have important work you want to protect.

When you look at a 3.5" disk, the construction is more sophisticated than its larger counterpart. Instead of a gaping hole in the center, this type of disk has a metal hub. Along one side of the disk, a spring-loaded sliding metallic shutter protects the disk from being touched. On the right side, a sliding write-protect switch write-protects the disk. Unlike the 5.25" disks, you don't have to find an adhesive sticker to stick to the disk; simply move the switch. When this sliding switch covers the hole, you can save your work to the disk. When you can see through the hole, you can't.

**SAVE
THE DAY!**

If you try saving your work to a floppy disk and receive a message such as **Write Protect Error**, don't worry. The disk is simply write-protected so that your files cannot be erased. To unprotect the disk, simply remove the adhesive tab for 5.25" disks or flip the write-protect switch for 3.5" disks so that you can't see through the write-protect notch.

**NERDY
DETAILS**

What makes up a disk? A floppy disk consists of a thin circle of somewhat flexible, coated polyester film that must spin freely within a protective plastic jacket. The thin circle of coated film is formed from a material that is coated on both sides with iron oxide and then burnished to a mirror-smooth finish. The iron oxide coating is what allows the disk to hold information. The floppy drive's read/write heads (like a cassette recorder) magnetize the coating so that the iron oxide particles hold information long after the disk is removed from your PC. When retrieving information from the disk, the heads read and amplify the small magnetic field contained in the coating.

The disk's jacket is very important because it contains a liner that keeps the disk clean. The jacket also protects the disk from heat. One 3M executive likens a disk rotating in a disk drive to running through the Sahara desert while trying to remember over 300 pages of information. This heat can cause the jacket to warp, and if the disk inside warps also, information can be lost. Almost all disks can handle disk drive heat up to 125°Fahrenheit before warping. With the thicker jackets, a disk can handle up to 140°F.

Buying Disks

When you buy floppy disks at the store, you may be faced with such choices as "DS/DD," "DS/HD," and "2S/2D." Which disks do you buy? These terms simply describe how much information the disks hold. As technology has progressed, drive and disk makers have been able to cram more information onto the same size of disk. The amount of information that can be stored is measured in kilobytes, or simply K. Disks that hold more than 1000 kilobytes are measured in megabytes, or M (one megabyte=1024K). These different densities are as follows:

5.25" low-density. Other names include 360K, low capacity, DS/DD, or 2S/2D (double-sided/double-density). Few people use such disks anymore because the amount of information that must be stored on them has grown so much. The disk drives that use these 360K disks were on the original PC and are obsolete today.

 5.25" high-density. Other names include 1.2M, high-capacity, DS/HD, or 2S/HD (double-sided/high-density). Although the same size, these disks hold about four times more information than their low-density brothers. Newer computers typically have this size disk drive.

 3.5" low-density. Other names are 720K, low-capacity, and DS/DD (double-sided/double-density). Not many computers have 720K drives, but the disks are more affordable for use with 3.5" high-density drives.

 3.5" high-density. Other names are 1.44M, high-capacity, quad-density, and DS/HD (double-sided/high-density). Newer computers typically include this size disk drive.

 3.5" extra-density. Other names are 2.88M, ultra-density, and DS/ED (double-sided/extended-density). A newer standard, 2.88M disks have yet to gain in popularity.

Use table 12.1 for more information:

Table 12.1
Sizes of Disks

Size	Density	Capacity
5.25"	Single-sided, double-density	160K*
5.25"	Single-sided, double-density	180K*
5.25"	Double-sided, double-density	320K*
5.25"	Double-sided, double-density	360K*
5.25"	Double-sided quad(or high) density	1200K (1.2M)
3.5"	Double-sided, double-density	720K

Size	Density	Capacity
3.5"	Double-sided, quad (or high) density	1440K (1.44M)
3.5"	Double-sided, ultra (or extra) density	2880K (2.88M)

Obsolete

Unfortunately, a 2.88M disk may not work in your drive. Your disk drive must match or exceed the size of the disks you want to use. For example, a 1.44M 3.5" disk drive can read any 1.44M disk or 720K disk. How can you tell a low-density disk from a high-density disk? Use these tips:

- The disk box label or the disk label may indicate double-density (low) or high-density.

- The actual disk used in a low-density (360K) 5.25" disk is a chocolate brown color and has an extra, darker ring around the center hole.

- A high-density (1.2M) 5.25" disk uses a darker charcoal color for its disk material.

- A low-density (720K) 3.5" disk has a square hole on only one side of its plastic case. This disk also has the phrase "DS, DD" or "2S/2D" imprinted on its sliding metal shutter.

- A high-density (1.44M) 3.5" disk has two square holes on both sides and the phrase "DS, HD" or simply "HD" imprinted on the metal shutter or its plastic case or both.

Which size disk drives do you own? Check your computer's manual, sales receipt, or invoice. If you don't have these, follow these steps:

1. Put a usable disk into your disk drive.

This may be a disk you've used in your floppy drive before.

2. Next, type the following command:

```
CHKDSK A:
```

A: is the drive whose size you want to check. For example, you may want to check drive B, your second floppy disk drive, if you have one. (By the way, CHKDSK is a simple DOS utility.)

Your computer will then display various information about your disk drive space and memory (see fig. 12.3, which uses the C: drive as an example).

Figure 12.3

The results of the CHKDSK command.

```
c:\>chkdsk

Volume PROGRAMS     created 11-24-1992 5:21p
Volume Serial Number is 0D37-18DD

 133101568 bytes total disk space
    100544 bytes in 7 hidden files
    350208 bytes in 122 directories
 130754560 bytes in 5484 user files
   1888256 bytes available on disk

      2048 bytes in each allocation unit
     64991 total allocation units on disk
       922 available allocation units on disk

    655360 total bytes memory
    512960 bytes free

c:\>
```

The first line shows the total disk space, in bytes, of this disk.

3. Divide the number in the first line by 1024.

4. Round up the resulting number to the closest value in table 12.1.

If CHKDSK reports 1,457,664 bytes, for example, you have a value of 1423 after dividing by 1024. Rounding this number up to 1440K indicates you own a 3.5" high-density (1.44M) disk drive.

Care and Feeding of Floppies

Disks are cheap (about $1 each) but your work isn't. When you work with floppy disks and disk drives, try to treat them like a fragile egg. Use these tips:

 Keep your disks organized. A new box of disks comes with adhesive labels you can place on each. Clearly label each disk.

 On 5.25" disks, do not use pencils or ballpoint pens to label. Labels should be written with a felt-tip pen to avoid making indentations on the disk.

 Never attach paper clips to a disk. They can cause a crease in your disk.

⚱ Never bend your disks or place anything on top of them.

⚱ When you insert a floppy disk into a disk drive, don't bend its jacket. Don't force it into the drive; instead, align and insert it carefully.

⚱ When not in use, place disks in their protective envelopes (5.25" disks only) and in clean storage containers, such as a disk storage box. 3.5" disks come with plastic wrappers that may be used for extra (unnecessary) protection. Keep disks upright so they don't warp.

⚱ If you are mailing a disk, use a disk mailer. These stiff cardboard envelopes give your disks extra protection. However, you may have good luck mailing 3.5" disks in regular envelopes because of their protective cover.

⚱ Use a disk drive cleaning kit every three to six months. A kit, costing under $20, consists of a paper-like disk made of an absorbent material. Once cleaning solution (typically alcohol) is put on the material, you insert the disk into the drive like a normal disk. As you attempt to use the drive, the read/write heads are cleaned.

⚱ If you're moving your computer a long distance, insert the special cardboard or plastic disk that came with your computer, or acquire one from a local computer store. Insert the disk and close the drive door. Do not use an actual disk; this will do more damage than good because traveling jiggles the drive's parts.

There are other hazards to your disks, including:

⚱ **Magnetism.** Because your work is saved as a magnetic signal, disks should never be stored near anything emitting a magnetic field. Avoid putting your disks within six inches of monitors, magnetic paper clip dispensers, electric typewriters, radios, vacuum cleaners or any electrical device that has a motor or transformer. Even fluorescent lamps with transformers in their bases and magnetic copy holders emit a magnetic field strong enough to erase data.

⚱ **Contaminants (yucky stuff).** Coffee, eraser crumbs, and even smoke can prevent your disk drive from reading your disks. In fact, small particles of dust, food, liquid, and lint can damage your disk drives. Keep the ashtray off your desk—and out of the office, if possible! A smoke particle is more than twice as large as the gap between the read/write head in the drive and the disk. Likewise, the oil of your fingers can ruin a disk, so don't touch its exposed surface. The oil will attract dust and debris.

GADS!

Heat. Most disks can handle temperatures of 50 to 125 degrees Fahrenheit. A disk exposed to direct sunlight, however, is in danger. To avoid losing your work, allow a disk arriving from a different climate (or from a cold car to a heated office) to warm up or cool down. Pretend it has jet lag: wait a few hours for the disk to return to its normal size so its information can be read correctly.

One myth is that airport X-ray machines can damage floppy disks. Not so. X-rays are merely a type of light. What may damage your disks is the handheld and walk-through metal detectors because these use magnetism, not light. Yet, airport metal detectors should be gentle enough for floppy disks. A power of 25 gauss, a measurement unit of magnetism, can affect a 360K disk. For high-density disks, even more magnetism is required. Metal detectors in the U.S. use no more than 1 gauss.

SAVE
THE DAY!

If your 5.25" disks ever get beverages spilled on them, don't panic. You can clean the disk and salvage your work.

First, carefully slit an edge of the floppy's outer cover. Next, remove the circular disk inside without touching its surface. Instead, grab the disk by its edges or inner circle. While holding the disk, rinse it carefully in a sink of warm water.

Once rinsed, set the disk on a clean, soft cloth and wipe it with a damp, soft cloth. As it dries, find a blank 5.25" floppy that you can sacrifice. Slit it open and remove the disk, but keep its plastic cover. Carefully insert the now dry disk into the new jacket and tape the slit. With this patchwork disk, insert it into the disk drive and make a copy of it as soon as possible.

Formatting Your Floppies

Before you can use a floppy disk to save your work, you must prepare it. A new floppy disk is like a record that has not yet had grooves etched into it. This preparation is called formatting; you must *format* each disk before you can save information to it. This formatting is typically done once to each disk. Then you can save many files to it.

You format a disk with the FORMAT command that comes with DOS. In general, you must format a disk at a capacity less than or equal to the capacity of the drive. For example, you can read a 360K disk in a 1220K (1.2M) drive. However, you cannot read a 1.2M disk in a 360K drive. To format a disk, follow these steps:

1. Place the disk into your disk drive.

As you insert the disk, make sure the label is on top. For 5.25" disks, insert the disk with the elliptical exposed area going in first and its indented notch on the left-hand side. For 3.5" disks, insert the disk with the sliding metal shutter first. An arrow imprinted on the plastic shell also shows which side is up.

2. Begin formatting the disk.

From the DOS prompt (C:\), type

  FORMAT A:

A: is the drive letter of the disk you want to format. The drive begins to format the disk. If you have DOS 4.0 and later, you can format a disk to a lower (but not higher) capacity with the /F switch. To do this, just type

  FORMAT A: /F:*SIZE*

Enter the following number for *SIZE*:

Type This Number	To Indicate This Capacity
360	360K
720	720K
1200	1.2M
1440	1.44M
2880	2.88M

NERDY
DETAILS

After a floppy disk is formatted, you can copy and delete files to it. However, sometimes you will want to start with a clean slate. The quick format option in DOS 5.0 lets you delete all the files on a previously formatted disk. To format a disk quickly, type

FORMAT A: /Q

A: is the letter of the drive whose disk you want to format.

3.   When formatting is completed, you will be asked to enter a name for the disk.

You can enter a volume name of up to 11 characters for this disk or simply press the Enter key for no name. Later, you can determine the name of the disk by typing

VOL A:

A: is the drive with the disk you want to check.

4.   Answer Y (yes) or N (no) to format other disks.

If you have other disks to format, enter Y.

TRICKS

You can bypass all this volume and yes and no stuff every time you format a disk by using a secret command. Simply type

FORMAT A: /AUTOTEST

This super-secret, for-nerds-eyes'-only AUTOTEST switch formats a single disk quickly without asking for a single question.

NERDY DETAILS

You can also use the FORMAT command to make a system, or boot, disk. Every computer owner should have a boot disk handy. This floppy disk is an emergency disk if your computer suddenly does not start normally. The computer may go through the motions of warming up, but somehow it simply doesn't come to life. It won't be broken, but it won't let you work on it, either.

To make a bootable disk, place a blank disk in drive A:, your first and possibly only floppy disk drive. (Boot disks usually do not work from drive B:.) From the DOS prompt, type

FORMAT A: /S

The /S switch adds system information to the disk so that it can start your computer when needed. You can test the boot disk by placing it in your drive A: and restarting your computer. If the disk works, you should be asked the date and time and shown an A: prompt (A:\).

A boot disk is a lifesaver if you make a deadly change to the startup file CONFIG.SYS. A boot disk lets you bypass the CONFIG.SYS file and start your computer from the floppy drive. You can then get to your CONFIG.SYS and correct your error.

What Makes a Hard Disk "Hard"?

You can think of a hard disk as a large floppy disk drive that you don't remove. The hard disk is also called a hard drive, Winchester drive, or fixed disk drive. Almost all computers that are five years old or younger have a hard disk. A hard disk is just like a floppy disk drive, except:

 A hard disk is not removed from your PC (although there are special removable drives, described later). All your work and software programs are stored in one convenient place.

 A hard disk can hold much more work than a floppy disk (usually about 150 times more!).

 A hard disk can store and retrieve your work more than 10 times faster than it can from a floppy disk drive.

Instead of one single disk, a hard disk may have several disk platters stacked on top of each other (like a jukebox with a bunch of 45s stacked up). This is one way the hard disk can store so much more than a floppy disk. A hard disk gets its great speed because it is permanently mounted inside your computer and sealed; this allows it to be built to fine mechanical tolerances. For example, the hard disk spins around at 60 times per second, or about 56 MPH. In other words, bumping your computer while its hard disk is working could cause an accident.

SAVE
THE DAY!

Because a hard disk is so intricate, contains so much information, and cannot usually be repaired (in the event it "breaks"), you should copy your important work to floppy disks. Like any mechanical equipment, a hard disk is going to fail someday.

A type of software called backup software copies the entire contents to floppy disks, often compressing the information to require fewer disks. Backup software often works with tape drives, which are a type of hardware that can copy your entire hard disk onto one or two special tape cartridges. In case of a disaster, you should make a second copy and place it somewhere else, such as a safe deposit box, a neighbor's house, or your workplace.

Like a floppy drive, a hard disk typically has an LED light to show when it is being used, such as recalling your work or software program. When you are waiting for a program to load, this light turns on. Like a floppy drive, a hard disk is given a lettered name. The first hard disk is called drive C, or C:, even if you don't have a second floppy drive called drive B. Other hard disks are assigned higher letters, such as D, E, F, etc. You can have disks up to drive Z, but this is very rare.

When a Hard Disk Isn't Right

Your PC's original hard disk is not always the best storage solution. There are a number of ways to give your PC more storage space, including:

 Hard cards. A hard card is an expansion card with a built-in hard disk. A hard card allows you to add another hard disk when there is no room for one inside your PC. For example, most narrow, or slimline, computer cases have room for only three devices. These spaces may be used up by two floppy drives and the first hard drive.

Hard cards may cost more than most regular hard disks, but installation is quick and easy.

 Removable drives. You use a removable drive as you would a normal hard disk. At the end of the day, you can remove a single cartridge and tuck it away for security reasons or send it across the country. These cartridges make perfect backup devices. Unlike tape drives, removable drives let you copy the contents of your hard disk and instantly use the copy elsewhere without wrestling with restoring the information to your hard disk. The most popular removable storage devices are the Bernoulli Box from Iomega Corp., and the Syquest Cartridge from Syquest Technologies.

 Rewritable optical drives. Although these babies are expensive (around $2000), rewritable optical drives offer 128M or 650M of storage per cartridge. The cartridges cost about $200 per disk. For big storage needs, an optical drive is a good investment.

 Floptical drives. A variation of the rewritable optical drive is the super floppy, or Floptical, drive. A super floppy drive provides 20M of storage on an inexpensive ($25) 3.5" removable disk. At the same time, these drives can double as a 1.44M/720K floppy drive. Floptical drives are no faster than floppy drives, but are convenient for copying large files or entire directories.

 Portable drives. If you want a hard disk for on the go, consider a portable drive. These handheld drives attach either to an expansion card inside your PC or directly to your PC's parallel printer port (you still can print). When attached through the parallel port, these drives are not blazingly fast, but they provide enough speed for most work. A portable drive that attaches to your parallel port is ideal for moving large amounts of data between two or more computers.

Getting Up to Speed

Like your floppy drive, a hard disk is measured by its storage capacity. Because they can hold so much information, hard drives are measured in megabytes, or simply M. One megabyte equals roughly one million characters. The size of the hard disk in the original IBM PC/XT was 10M. Today's computers typically have hard disks with capacities beyond 100M. Some hard disks hold gigabytes (G) of information (one gigabyte equals 1024M).

Although size is important, speed should be your main concern. Why? From your hard disk, you will start your major software programs, and save and copy your work files. The slower your hard disk, the more time you'll spend twiddling your thumbs. A hard disk's speed is measured in two ways:

 Search speed. Your hard disk often finds information you want in under one-tenth of a second. Most of this time is spent physically moving the drive's head to the position where the information is stored. The time spent to locate this information is called the drive's *seek time* or *access time*. The information may be found anywhere on the disk; as a result, this search time is usually based on the average seek time. This access time is measured in thousandths of a second, or milliseconds (ms). The lower the number, the faster the drive. A typical hard disk may have an access time of 28ms. A fast hard disk may have an access time of 15ms or better.

 Data transfer rate. The average seek time tells you how fast your hard disk can find information; the data transfer rate tells you how fast it can "shovel" the information to the rest of your computer once it is found. The data transfer rate is measured in kilobits per second (Kbps) or megabits per second (Mbps). This number is often more important than the speed of your hard disk. (The data transfer rate often is limited by the drive's interface, described next.)

> Disk software, such as Norton Utilities or PC Tools, can tell you the access speed and transfer rate of your hard disk.

TRICKS

Your hard disk is connected to an expansion card called a disk drive controller. (Often, this controller also handles your floppy drives.) Your hard disk uses the drive interface to talk to the rest of your computer. Two types of drive interfaces are popular (also see table 12.2):

 SCSI. The Small Computer Systems Interface, or SCSI (pronounced "scuzzy"), is another high-end interface. One SCSI controller lets you connect up to seven peripherals (external PC gadgets) such as hard disks, tape drives, CD-ROM drives, and printers. (For more information on SCSI, see Chapter 13.)

 IDE. The Integrated Drive Electronics, or IDE, interface appeared a few years ago as an inexpensive, effective hard disk interface that competes with the SCSI interface. Most drives today use IDE.

Table 12.2
Types of Hard Drives

Interface	Maximum Data Transfer Rate	Comments
SCSI	10Mbps	Ideal if you are adding a number of storage devices, such as a CD-ROM, optical, or other removable drives
IDE	4Mbps	Affordable, yet fast

Unfortunately, you cannot examine your hard disk and tell if it supports one interface or another; all the cables and connections are identical. To discover which interface your drive uses, check your PC's manual or invoice.

Find Free Disk Space

A hard disk is essential for today's PCs. At first, it seems as if it can hold an unlimited amount of information. Eventually, however, you will probably run out of room. How full is your hard disk? One easy way to find out is to follow these steps:

1. Turn on your computer.

2. From the DOS prompt (C:\ or D:\), type

    ```
    CHKDSK C:
    ```

C: is the drive whose size you want to check.

Your PC will then display various information about your disk drive space (similar to fig. 12.3).

3. Calculate your drive's size. The first line shows the total disk space, in bytes. To find out how many megabytes your hard disk can hold, divide this number by 1,048,576.

4. Calculate your free space.

The last line in the first section shows how many bytes are available on disk. To find out how many megabytes you have remaining, divide this number by 1,048,576.

5. Calculate the percentage of free space.

Divide the number in step 4 by the number in step 3. This is the percentage of disk space you have free on the hard disk.

6. Repeat this step for each drive letter you have, such as drive D:, E:, etc.

Windows and Your Hard Disk

If you own Microsoft Windows, a portion of your hard disk may be reserved as overflow memory. When Windows runs short of actual memory (RAM), it may then use your hard disk as *virtual memory*. In other words, Microsoft Windows can use more memory than your PC actually has. One drawback: your hard disk is much slower than actual memory, but at least you can get your work done without receiving an Out of Memory message.

This memory trick is done through a *swap file*. The term "swap file" refers to a Windows capability, in which Windows temporarily swaps information from your PC's memory to the hard disk.

Pack It Tight

As your hard disk becomes full, you may use a software program to place the same information on less disk space. For example, PKLite from PKWare Inc. increases your disk space by compressing only your program files (files that end with EXE or COM). PKLite reduces the size of these programs by an average of 40 percent.

A more radical alternative is to use a data compression program such as Stacker or SuperStor. These products reduce the space required by your files by 50 percent or more. How? By encoding your files, this compression software keeps the content of your files and trims the waste. When you request information from your hard disk, the encoded information is de-compressed on-the-fly with little or no wait. Once viewed as risky, data compression is now becoming a part of some operating systems. For example, DR-DOS 6.0 from Digital Research Inc. includes a variation of

SuperStor. To speed up decompression, some manufacturers include an optional expansion card that uses a thinking coprocessor.

Handling Your Hard Disk

You can take a few steps to protect your hard disk:

 Keep your work area clear of smoke and dust. Although hard disks are sealed and have a built-in air filter, a clean environment can help prevent catastrophes. When a dust or smoke particle sits on any single disk platter, the read/write head crashes into it at about 56 mph. This crashing is inevitable; a dust particle is about two times taller than the gap between the head and the disk surface.

 Keep your hard disk at a near-constant temperature. In a few minutes, your hard disk may go from room temperature to over 100 degrees. Saving information at one temperature may make it difficult to find when it is retrieved at a different temperature. When you first start your computer, do not use it immediately. Give it about five minutes to warm up. During that time, get ready for your work, grab a cup of coffee, or read the paper.

Some laptop computers often "die" when taken from a hot or frozen car into an office and turned on. Usually, the change in temperature and humidity causes condensation, leading to water droplets on the platters. Always give your computer time to adjust to the humidity and temperature of its surroundings before turning it on.

Turn Your Hard Disk into Parts

You may have one tangible hard disk, but it can often be broken up into separate drives called partitions. For example, I have one 245M hard disk, but I have used the DOS command FDISK to break my drive into three separate drives. My drive C is 100M, drive D is 70M, and drive E is 75M. Before DOS 4.0, you could not create a partition larger than 32M. Now, you can select almost any size. Why do this?

 Organization. Drive C can be used to store all your software programs; drive D can store all your work files (called data); and drive E can store the really important stuff, such as games (separation of work and play). By placing the fruits of your labor on drive D, you can use backup software to back up only that partition. If your hard disk suddenly dies, you can always reinstall your programs and game software, but the work you've sweated over could never be replaced.

 Speed. By breaking your hard disk into several smaller hard disks, your PC has less stuff to search through. This means you'll find your work more quickly.

 Less waste. Like the government, your hard disk has built-in waste. If a saved file doesn't fill up an entire unit on the hard disk (called a *cluster*), the rest is simply left unused. By creating smaller partitions, the size of these clusters can be reduced (as shown in table 12.3). The result is less waste overall. Notice that the most waste is for a partition of 512M or greater; if I save a 2K file to an 8K cluster, 6K (75 percent) will be wasted. This waste is also called *slack*.

Table 12.3
Cluster Size in Different
Versions of DOS

Partition Size(M)	DOS 3.3	Compaq 3.31	DOS 4.01/5.0
0-15.9	4K	4K	4K
16-32	8K	2K	2K
32.1-63.9	n/a	2K	2K
64-127.9	n/a	4K	2K
128-255.9	n/a	8K	4K
256-511.9	n/a	8K	8K
512+	n/a	16K	16K

STOP!

You can create partitions only when you have a new hard disk or have made a backup of your current hard disk. If you use the FDISK command, you lose all information on your hard disk.

Finding Files

A hard disk has so much capacity that you may have trouble finding a certain file. One easy way to find a file is to go to the root directory of your hard disk and use a variation of the DIR command. Follow these steps:

1. Type

    CD

This places you at the top of your hard disk so that you can search every place beneath it.

2. Type

    DIR *filename* /S /P

filename is the name of the missing file, such as PROPOSAL.DOC or TODO.TXT. You can also use wildcard names, such as *.DOC to find all the files that end in the extension "DOC," or BOB.* to find all the files that start with the name "BOB."

Your screen then displays the files that meet your search. If more files than can fit on your screen are displayed, you'll be asked to press any key to display more.

Armed with floppy and hard disks, you can save your work and share it with others. By taking care of your hard disk, your hard disk will take care of you.

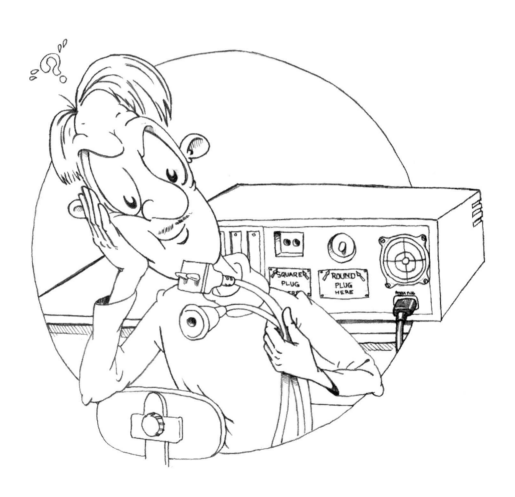

Round Peg, Square Hole—Ports and Cables

E ver wired a stereo before? You probably think PCs are just as ornery, with a jungle of cables through which even King Kong couldn't slash. Believe it or not, you can bushwhack your way through this mess, and connect extra goodies to your PC. It only involves understanding a PC's "ports," which are those covered holes and funny looking connectors on the backside of your PC's case. This chapter will teach you about:

 The number and types of "ports of call" your PC has

 How to be a matchmaker between the cable and connector for each port

 How to love and care for your cables

Several cables are connected to your computer, such as those to the keyboard, printer, and modem. These things are connected to your PC through ports. Confused? Suppose your car was a computer; your gas tank opening would be called a port. The filler hole allows you to connect a gas pump nozzle to the gas tank so that you can "fill 'er up." For your PC, ports are used to send or receive small electrical signals. For example, when you move your mouse, its wire tail sends a signal to the mouse port that you have moved it. A mouse cursor on the screen then moves a proportionate amount of distance.

Your PC may have several ports, including a:

- Parallel port
- Serial port
- Mouse port
- Game port
- Monitor port
- Keyboard port
- SCSI port

These ports may have alternate names, such as those in table 13.1.

Table 13.1
Ports and Their Aliases

Name	Aliases
Parallel port	Printer port, parallel printer port, Centronic port, LPT port
Serial port	I/O Port, RS-232 or RS-232C port, COM (communications) port
Mouse port	None
Game port	Joystick port
Monitor port	Video port
Keyboard port	None
SCSI port	None

Cable Talk

Ports are merely the destinations for cables. Cables are made up of several wires bundled inside a plastic sheath. At the end of a cable or in the port to which the cable attaches, these wires culminate in a collection of pins. Over these thin wires, electrical signals are transmitted. A cable may have as few as five pins or as many as 50.

Every cable must end; the end is called a *connector*. The wires in a cable must attach at both ends to two pieces of hardware, such as your PC and its printer. Most cable connectors are one of three types:

 D-shell. This connector is shaped like the letter "D" and has pins.

 Centronics. This connector, which is used only with parallel printers, doesn't have pins. Instead it has a rectangular mouth lined with copper plates into which you insert the cable.

 DIN. This connector is a tubular plug that is most commonly used to attach a keyboard to your computer.

These connectors use different numbers of pins to make it more difficult to plug the wrong cable into the wrong connector.

Gender, or sex, is also used to reduce error. A male connector has pins that protrude out and are inserted into the female connector. As you can guess, the female connector has small holes that accept the male's pins. For every cable connection, the cables that plug into a connector must be of the opposite sex. Ads sometimes use phrases like male-to-female, male-female, M/F, or F/M to indicate the gender of the two connectors on a cable. The first gender should refer to the end that plugs into the PC.

Communications Ports

The basic ports in any PC are the serial and parallel ports. These are often called *communications* or *I/O* (input/output) ports. The serial ports are used to run mice, scanners, and even printers. The parallel port is used mostly to send your work to your printer. On older PCs, serial and parallel ports were mounted on an expansion card (called a *multifunction I/O card*); modern PCs have two serial ports, a parallel port, and even a game port right on the motherboard.

Parallel (and Printing) Port

The parallel port is often called the parallel printer port, printer port, or Centronics port. Why? In most cases, this port is used to attach your printer to your PC. However, this port also can be used to attach a portable hard disk to your PC.

Your computer may have more than one parallel port—up to three (big fat computers have a lot of parallel ports). Each parallel port has a name: LPT1, LPT2, and LPT3. *LPT* stands for line printer. Your first parallel printer port is LPT1, your second one is LPT2, and so on.

Each parallel port on the back of your PC has two parallel rows of 12 and 13 holes—25 altogether. The matching parallel printer cable with its 25 pins connects to your parallel port on the back of your computer and then to your printer. The connector contains 25 individual protruding pins (called DB-25). The other end of your parallel printer cable has what's called a 36-pin Centronics connector.

NERDY
DETAILS

One disadvantage of printer cables is that the signals that travel through any of the 25 wires may bleed over to the others, corrupting anything that's printing. This is called crosstalk. The longer the cable, the greater the chance of crosstalk. For this reason, most manufacturers recommend parallel cables be no longer than 10 feet.

If you want to put your printer more than 10 feet away from your computer, you should buy a special double-shielded or low-capacitance printer cable. With the proper shielded cable, you can place your printer 50 feet away or more.

Serial Killer?

The serial port is ideal for sending and receiving information to a peripheral, such as a mouse or a modem. Some printers also can use a serial port, although they require special cables. The serial port is also called the RS-232 port. The name *RS-232* comes from the name of the standards developed by the Electrical Industries Association for this port. Like the parallel port, each serial port has a name that only a nerd would love (it's confusing): COM1, COM2, COM3, or COM4. Your PC most likely has at least two COM, or communications, ports although it can support up to four.

Unlike the parallel printer port, two types of serial ports are made; therefore, two types of serial cables also exist:

 25-pin. This traditional RS-232 port has 25 pins in a D-shell connector (DB-25 connector).

 9-pin. The newer serial port design has nine pins (a DB-9 connector).

The two serial ports work the same. In fact, you can buy a serial cable adapter to convert a 25-pin cable to the 9-pin connector, or vice versa. Because the serial port has pins, it requires a serial cable with a female connector. In other words, the end of the serial cable has holes instead of pins.

For example, imagine you are ordering a serial cable to connect your new external modem to your PC's serial port. When you order the cable, you must know whether you'll be using it with a 9- or 25-pin port. The port connector is male, requiring a female DB-9 or DB-25 connector.

NERDY
DETAILS

> Many people have old laser printers (such as the original Hewlett-Packard LaserJet) that only work through a serial port. To make a serial printer act the same as a typical parallel printer, type these commands from the C:\> prompt:
>
> ```
> MODE COM1:96,n,8,1,p
> MODE LPT1=COM1
> ```
>
> When you print to LPT1 (the first parallel port), the printing will be sent, or redirected, to the COM1 port (the first serial port).

Mouse Port

A mouse often is connected to your PC's 9-pin serial port; hence, the name *serial mouse*. A mouse attached to its own expansion card is called a *bus mouse*. Some mice, however, use the special mouse port found in PS/2 computers; they are called *PS/2 mice*. (Some video cards also include a PS/2-style mouse port, such as the ATI VGA Wonder XL.)

Game Port

A *game port*, or joystick port, is used to connect a joystick to your PC. Joysticks are used to play computer games, especially those that simulate flight. Sometimes, the multifunction I/O card (discussed earlier) or a sound card (if you have one) may include a game port. Otherwise, you can get a game card: an expansion card that lets you connect up to two joysticks.

NERDY
DETAILS

If one reason for buying a PC is to have the ultimate game machine, you might want to buy a game card. Often, a separate game card is best for today's speedier computers. A typical game port on a multifunction card sometimes gets confused by all the other work it must do while you are playing. Occasionally, I've found my plane upside down!

A game card that is strictly for a joystick gives more enhanced performance in your games and makes them more fun. If you plan to purchase a game card, make sure the game card can handle the speed of your computer, which is measured in megahertz (MHz).

Monitor Port

Your monitor must get a video signal for you to see your work. The monitor can only get this information from one source: the video card. Your video card must match your monitor. For example, monochrome, CGA, and EGA video cards have female 9-pin ports (DB-9) that connect to 9-pin monitor cables. VGA, super-VGA and XGA video cards connect to a female 15-pin port (DB-15) that connect to your monitor's cable. Check out Chapter 10 if you want to know about monitors and video cards.

Keyboard Port

Your keyboard uses a connector called a DIN connector. This tubular plug attaches your keyboard to your PC. It typically is a 5-pin connector, although IBM PS/2 computers use six pins. Pretty simple, huh?

SCSI Port—Clearcut the Cable Jungle

The Small Computer System Interface (SCSI) usually is an expansion card (it's part of the motherboard on fancy PCs) that you can use to connect up to seven external hard disks, CD-ROM drives, printers, and more to one port. When several SCSI (pronounced "scuzzy") devices like these are connected to one port, they are said to be *daisychained*. The SCSI port contains the most pins of all ports: 50. A SCSI port often is not included with a PC. It is typically a card you add later.

NERDY
DETAILS

Corel Systems Corp., maker of CorelDRAW!, introduced a new SCSI (Small Computer Systems Interface) card, the CorelSCSI LS3000, which Corel says is the first to offer a feature called "intelligent termination."

Before the LS3000, SCSI cards would lose information if one of the daisychained devices connected to the card was disconnected while the others were still connected. This could happen if, for example, the computer was moved from one location to another. Fixing this problem required you to open your computer to adjust switches to compensate for the missing device. With intelligent termination, no case-cracking is required. This SCSI card is smart enough to recognize one end has been terminated (disconnected) and terminate the other end. When the missing device is reconnected, the card knows that as well. Corel provides a software kit called CorelSCSI to add this intelligent termination feature to other SCSI cards besides its own.

SCSI Benefits—Imagine a Line of Elephants

SCSI does have its advantages; it's 20 percent faster than the IDE interface and, through daisychaining, can handle up to seven peripherals using just one port. A small desktop PC can have up to 21 SCSI devices hooked up to it through only three expansion slots. In other words, you don't need to buy an expansion card for every hard disk, tape drive, CD-ROM drive, and scanner you have in your PC. One card fits all.

Another benefit is that the SCSI bus is self-contained; it has its own intelligence and operates independently from your PC. SCSI devices connected together can transfer data among themselves without your PC breaking a sweat. For example, a SCSI tape drive could back up your SCSI hard disk while you're playing a game.

SCSI Disadvantages— There Aren't Many Elephants Around

The SCSI port has been popular on the Apple Macintosh computer but has not been popular on the PC because of a lack of standards. One reason: the standards for SCSI are fuzzy. For example, a SCSI host adapter may not be able to talk to a SCSI disk drive. Even if the two did make a connection, you may not be able to add an additional SCSI device that shared the same vocabulary.

If you successfully add a SCSI device, you probably will earn a PC purple heart. The Achilles' heel of SCSI is compatibility problems when you try to get several (up to seven) SCSI devices to share one SCSI adapter. You may find yourself resolving conflicts between port addresses, interrupt lines, and ROM space (Yuck!). Fortunately, a new set of standards called SCSI-2 will help solve some of these limitations.

If you plan to buy a new PC, you may be tempted to equip it with a SCSI hard disk. Unfortunately, a SCSI hard disk is not that fast on a single PC; an IDE drive is faster. However, SCSI is best for a network or multiuser PC that is shared between several people. In addition, SCSI cards save you big bucks even though they cost about $100 more than other interface cards. How can this be? You only need one interface card for seven gadgets!

Most likely, the SCSI interface will continue to be the Holy Grail of the PC world; it will be sought after but never found. SCSI probably will be adopted by the corporate world but not by home computer users.

Cable Cleanup

Cables are so small and inexpensive compared to the purchase of a PC, they are easy to overlook. Often, PC users rely on the cables that either came with their computer or were chosen by the salesperson. Thanks to the industry standards discussed earlier, you can get your cables from almost anywhere. For example, you can buy your parallel printer cable from any-where and it will work with your IBM-compatible computer and printer. In most cases, your hardest decision may be whether you want a 6- or a 10-foot long cable.

Cables also can be the source of many troubles. A loose keyboard cable, for example, may cause the message No keyboard present to display and prevent you from using it any further. A loose printer cable may make your laser printer print entire pages of black. Here are some tips for caring for your cables:

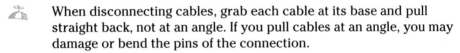 When disconnecting cables, grab each cable at its base and pull straight back, not at an angle. If you pull cables at an angle, you may damage or bend the pins of the connection.

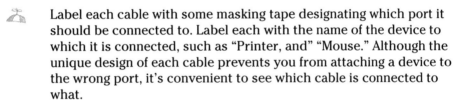 Label each cable with some masking tape designating which port it should be connected to. Label each with the name of the device to which it is connected, such as "Printer, and" "Mouse." Although the unique design of each cable prevents you from attaching a device to the wrong port, it's convenient to see which cable is connected to what.

To prevent the rear of your PC from looking like a plate of spaghetti, tie your cables together using garbage bag ties. You can also buy flexible plastic tubing about 1" in diameter. Slit the tub lengthwise and place your cables inside.

Never wedge your PC, printer, or monitor against the wall (it's tempting though because these PCs are so big). The cables need to have room to extend from these devices and bend out of the way. Try to leave 6" between the back of the computer and the wall.

Avoid connecting and disconnecting each cable as much as possible. Over time, the friction that holds the cable in place may be diminished.

Some ports have parts that hold each cable in place. Otherwise, a cable may have screws or screw knobs that hold it in place. Use these parts to keep the cables well-connected.

With the right cables connected to the right ports, your PC's peripherals can stay in touch with each other. A cable connection is the next best thing to being there.

CHAPTER
14

A Press on Every Desk

One of the author's favorite quotes is: "Freedom of the press only applies to those who own one." Today's falling printer prices allow you to have your own printing press on your desk. Like Gutenberg, you can crank out multiple copies of your great American novel, print mailing labels, send letters to loved ones, and threats to telemarketers.

This chapter clues you in to printer pluses and minuses. After reading this chapter, hopefully you will know once and for all whether the printer you have is all you'll need or if the new crop of laser printers and dot matrix printers is your only option. This chapter describes:

- The printer lineup—the good, the bad, the acceptable
- Buttons you see on every printer but never use
- Fonts that are persuasive even if you're not
- Shopping for a printer ("I will not be duped!")
- Getting more life from your printer, even after you have used it to death
- Testing and fixing the old paper-regurgitator

Whatever you put into your computer you eventually need to print. Another term for stuff you print is *hard copy*. If you hear someone say, "Can I have a hard copy of that," he or she needs the printed pages.

PC printers come in many designs and work differently. One may be fast; another might offer high-quality type; one may do envelopes; and another excels at mailing labels.

As with everything else in the computer industry, the prices of printers have fallen drastically. Laser printers, which once cost more than $5,000, now can be purchased for under $600.

Families of Printers

Technically, two families of printers exist: impact and non-impact. But most of you are more interested in the cost and quality of printers. (If you want more details on impact versus non-impact printers, read the following note.) For convenience, this chapter compares printers that cost less than $500 with those that cost $500 and up.

NERDY
DETAILS

What's the primary differences between impact and non-impact printers? Impact printers strike the page and leave an impression. These printers are ideal for inexpensive printing or printing that requires duplicate copies from carbon or carbon-less forms. Without the impact, duplicates can't be made.

Non-impact printers silently produce superior print quality without relying on striking. These printers are typically faster than impact printers: they measure speed in pages per minute (ppm) rather than characters per second. The most popular non-impact printer is the laser printer.

Cheap Ways To Print Your Work

Many choices are available for printing on the cheap. The least expensive printers are dot matrix printers. A dot matrix printer forms images on the page out of dots. Several wire pins in the printer are struck by small hammers to leave an impression through the ink ribbon (just like a typewriter). The more pins used, the better the image.

Dot matrix printers give you a choice of quality: 9-pin and 24-pin. The more pins, the better the print quality. Nine-pin printers are used for inexpensive, fast printing. At best, these printers provide near letter-quality (NLQ) print quality.

Don't be duped by a salesperson; near-letter quality is just that—near letter quality. It is adequate, but not good for your important letters or résumés. The 24-pin dot matrix printers provide letter-quality (LQ) print quality. Although typically slower than a 9-pin printer, these printers can be used for correspondence. They can also be scaled back to draft mode so that you can print quickly using a handful of the 24 pins.

With a dot matrix printer, you can print reports on continuous fanfold paper (described later), mailing labels, forms that require duplicate copies, and more. The speed of dot matrix printers usually is measured in characters per second, or cps. The speed may be given for both draft and near-letter-quality and letter-quality modes. For example, a Citizen GSX-140 Plus dot matrix printer has a draft speed of 220 cps and a letter-quality speed of 72 cps. The higher this number, the faster the printer. If you'll be printing hundreds of mailing labels or long reports, you'll want a printer with a higher cps rating.

NERDY
DETAILS

One of the first impact printers for the PC that you now want to avoid is the daisy wheel printer. This printer used a rotating wheel with "petals" for each character. Once the wheel rotated to the correct character, a small hammer struck the character against the inked printer ribbon, forming an image on the page.

Daisy wheel printers are slow, noisy, and fortunately are rare. Some of these loudmouths still are available—avoid them if possible.

For under $500, you can get gorgeous print quality without investing money in a laser printer. An ink jet printer, such as the Hewlett-Packard DeskJet 500, can provide sharp-looking letters and reports. Such printers spray a fine quick-drying ink onto the page from several small nozzles. Despite earlier problems with ink smudging and fading, the latest printers are inexpensive, quiet, but not fast. If you consider the falling prices of laser printers, the ink jet printer does not provide as good a value.

One niche ink jet printers serve is portable printers for laptop computers. An ink jet printer such as the Canon BJ-10e is the size of a notebook computer and sells for under $300. Thermal printers are also used by laptop computers. These printers use heat to print on wax-like paper.

Expensive Printing (More Than $500)

For about $500 or more, you can get a lot of printer power. Most printers in this price range are typically laser printers. These printers use laser beams (high-tech, huh?) to create a burning impression. The pages from these printers are perfect for résumés, important letters, and proposals.

NERDY
DETAILS

How does a laser printer work? It uses a rotating drum that is charged with a high voltage. A negative copy of the image is painted onto the drum by a light source. Where the light falls onto the drum, the drum is discharged. A toner (powdered "ink") sticks to the charged portion of the drum. Next, the drum melts, or fuses, the image onto the paper by pressure and heat.

The most popular laser printers are the Hewlett-Packard LaserJets, which include the LaserJet III and LaserJet 4. Several laser printers imitate the LaserJet, so they can be used in lieu of this popular printer. One inexpensive HP-compatible printer is the OkiLaser 400 from Okidata. These printers use *toner cartridges*, a plastic body that contains enough toner to print about 3,000 pages before being replaced. Dot matrix printers use ink ribbons (cheap, cheap, cheap); a laser printer requires toner cartridges (expensive because they differ for each printer).

Common Printer Hardware

A printer is not difficult to hook up. You simply take the printer out of the box, attach a printer cable to it and tell your software which printer you bought. After you set up your new printer, you can explore the many built-in wonders and gizmos it has. Although laser printers and dot matrix printers look different, they all share a few common hardware features:

 On line/off line button

 Form feed (FF) button

 Line feed (LF) button

 Top of form (TOF) button

On Line/Off Line

A printer is connected to your PC by a cable. Although the printer may be physically connected, it must be made ready to accept information from your PC. This is called "being on line." Most printers have an on-line button. When it is on, the printer is ready to print your work. When this button is pushed off, your printer is said to be off-line.

On some printers, the on-line button is also called the Select button. If you're still unsure about the terms on-line and off-line, think of when you take the phone off the hook. Although your phone is connected to your friends, they cannot get through to you because your phone is off-line (off the hook). The only way your friends or the IRS can call you is if the phone is ready to accept calls (on-line).

TRICKS

The on-line button on a dot matrix printer is handy when printing long lists, such as mailing lists. You can press this button to pause the printer, insert a new ribbon, press the button again, and printing continues as if you'd never stopped.

Eject a Page with the Form Feed Button

The form feed button is used to kick out a page—or the rest of a page—from your printer. You can then see what you've printed. To save you time, most software programs send a form feed after printing your document. Occasionally, you must eject the page manually by pressing this button. If you press the Print Screen (PrtScr) button on your keyboard, for example, the text is printed on part of the page. To see the page, you must press the form feed button, which usually involves these steps:

1. Press the printer's On Line or Select button until the light goes out.

2. Press the Form Feed or Eject button on the printer.

3. When finished, press the On Line or Select button until the light is lit.

A dot matrix printer ejects an entire sheet of paper whenever you do these steps; a laser printer warms up, loads a piece of paper, then spits it out. If you don't return your printer to On Line, your PC won't be able to print.

TRICKS

You can also use the form feed button whenever you need a blank piece of paper.

Use Line Feed To Move One Line at a Time

Like form feed, a line feed also advances your paper in your printer, but line feed moves the paper one line at a time. Line feed is handy when you need to adjust paper inside your printer. (For finer adjustments, some printers even include a micro line feed feature to move the page by hundredths of an inch.) Dot matrix printers usually are the only ones with a line feed button.

STOP!

Avoid using the separate paper advance knob whenever you need to line up paper in a dot matrix printer; this knob can cause uneven friction in your printer, which can mess up the paper path. Use the line feed button instead.

The line feed button typically is the best way to move paper through your printer. To do a line feed, follow these steps:

1. Press the On Line or Select button until the light goes out.

2. Press the Line Feed button on the printer. To advance the paper several lines, hold down the button.

3. When finished, press the On Line or Select button until the light is lit.

If you forget to press the On Line button again, your PC won't be able to print.

Use the Top of Form Button To Move Paper

How does your printer know when it is at the top of a page? Some printers include a top of form (TOF) button. At any time, you can tell your printer the page is at the top by pressing this button. The position you indicate with this switch is considered the starting position even when the printer is off. When you turn on your printer, it knows where the next sheet of paper must be loaded. Like the line feed button, the top of form button is included only on dot matrix printers.

Your printer probably comes with preset top of forms settings for the various papers you may use (described later); you probably will not have to set the TOF unless you use special-sized paper.

STOP!

> Avoid using the paper advance knob (also called the platen knob) on your dot matrix printer to advance your paper. You can confuse the top of form setting by using it. If you use the knob, the printer cannot count the number of lines. Instead, use your printer's form feed and line feed buttons.

Common Printer Software

Whenever you shop for or borrow a printer, you need to make sure the printer will print your work (why else would you need the printer?). You will receive printed output from the mouth of the printer if the printer's software is compatible with your favorite programs. Two types of software are part of every printer's environment: fonts and drivers. These two types of software are unrelated but they both are necessary for printing your lovely work.

Take Advantage of Fancy Fonts

All printers can imitate a typewriter. Both dot matrix and laser printers can print the Courier-type characters you see on paper. The growth of desktop publishing and Windows software demands that your pages look better than ever. Who wants to send a memo with a typewriter look to it? All computer printers now offer fonts to add flavor to your printed page.

To understand fonts, you must know two simple terms:

 Typeface. A *typeface* is a family of type of a certain design. Courier (used by many typewriters) is an example of a typeface. Helvetica, Swiss, Dutch, and Times are a handful of thousands of popular typefaces.

Font. A *font* is a typeface subset. It is a set of characters of a particular style (bold, italic, or regular) and size generated from a typeface. A 10-point Courier bold, for example, is one font.

> *A point is a typographic method of measurement. 72 points equal one inch.*

NERDY
DETAILS

Fonts are often confused with typefaces. Printers always come with at least one font, such as Courier; the total number varies with each printer. A printer that includes 26 fonts sounds like a versatile printer, no? Those 26 fonts, however, may come from a meager four typefaces. As always, caveat emptor (let the buyer beware).

Bitmapped Fonts

Font software can be divided into two types: *bitmapped fonts* and *scalable fonts*. Some fonts are bitmapped fonts, which are fonts of a certain size and style.

The characters in a bitmapped font are made up of thousands of individual dots, or bits—like a painting. Because each character is "painted," a bitmapped font must be made for each size you want. The larger the size, the larger the painting. The result is that bitmapped fonts require lots of disk space. Hard drives can quickly fill with many megabytes of bitmapped fonts.

To view a bitmapped font on-screen, you need matching screen fonts. These also must be painted from individual dots. Many of the fonts in printers are bitmapped fonts—they are of a certain typeface at a certain size in a certain style.

Scalable Fonts: Any Size, Any Way

Scalable fonts use mathematical formulas to describe to the printer how the font should be printed. The style and size of scalable fonts can be changed and printed any way you want. Scalable fonts are similar to a photographic negative. If you want a bigger photograph, you blow it up. You want a wallet-size photo? Shrink it down. Scalable fonts can be drawn to virtually any size.

Older PC software was not compatible with scalable typefaces. Today, scalable typefaces are very popular. For example, the HP LaserJet III and LaserJet 4 laser printers include several scalable typefaces. They also include some bitmapped fonts.

NERDY
DETAILS

In the early days of PC computing, what you saw on-screen wasn't always what appeared on paper. Computer users quickly realized how much easier it would be if they could see on-screen the exact same thing they wanted to print. The computer industry recognized this need and developed software that is WYSIWYG (what-you-see-is-what-you-get) capable.

WYSIWYG-capable programs display on-screen the same layout and format of text and images that appears on paper when the file is printed. The desktop publishing revolution is a product of WYSIWYG programs; PostScript font technology gave users the ability to manipulate and view characters exactly as they appear on the printed page.

The two biggest contenders in the scalable fonts business are PostScript and TrueType fonts.

 PostScript. PostScript fonts (and the printers that use them) are very popular, especially with people who use desktop publishing. PostScript scalable fonts are called PostScript Type 1 fonts. Often, at least 35 PostScript fonts are included with a PostScript laser printer.

PostScript fonts can be rotated in any orientation, stretched, skewed, reflected, shadowed, filled with any pattern, outlined, reversed out, or printed in any shade of gray (whew!).

PostScript fonts work on many kinds of printers. For example, you can design a document on your PostScript laser printer and then take it to a service bureau typesetting machine to print it at magazine-quality resolution. You simply print your document to a PostScript disk file instead of to paper. This disk is then brought to a service bureau where the PostScript file is printed at the higher resolution. You typically pay $6 per page for this service.

TrueType. TrueType is a font technology introduced with Windows 3.1 that lets you use scalable typefaces to produce WYSIWYG results. With TrueType, you can select any typeface outline you have on your computer and use it at practically any size. It doesn't matter if the font isn't supported by your printer; TrueType sends the page as a picture, requiring no fonts from your printer. Adding more TrueType fonts is easy—you can get 20 TrueType typefaces for as little as $25.

Add Extra Fonts for More Printing Pleasure

Scalable and bitmapped fonts are either already included with your printer or available through software. Built-in fonts are called *resident fonts* because they already reside inside your printer. A printer may come with as few as two resident fonts or as many as 45.

The number of resident fonts can be increased by inserting a font cartridge into your printer. A *font cartridge* is a small plastic box that contains small computer chips with permanently recorded fonts. Many dot matrix and laser printers accept font cartridges so that you can upgrade the amount of typefaces the printer can print.

Another way to add fonts is through software. *Soft fonts* are loaded from a disk into your computer. They are then downloaded to your printer when you're ready to use them.

Some soft fonts are available from on-line services and your local bulletin board services (BBSs). This is a cheap way to add more variety to your printer.

TRICKS

Driving Your Printer with Drivers

Each software program you own must have a printer driver to work with your printer. A *printer driver* is simply a small piece of software included as part of your software package to run your printer. Often, your software program has you pick from a list which printer you have. This tells the software program to load the appropriate printer driver.

If your exact printer isn't listed, pick one that is similar to yours. If a Panasonic 1124i printer isn't listed, for example, pick either 1124, 1123, or 1624. The printer will work trouble-free because the drivers for these printers are pretty much the same. If your HP-compatible laser printer isn't listed, simply select the Hewlett-Packard LaserJet that most closely imitates it. An Okidata 400 printer, for example, can print the same way the LaserJet prints. If your software program doesn't list the Okidata 400 as a possible printer, just select the HP LaserJet. It works anyway.

NERDY DETAILS

Your software programs and even DOS are designed to work with certain brand-name printers, such as Hewlett-Packard, Epson, and IBM. Other printer manufacturers may imitate the operation of these printers, saying they are "Epson-compatible" or "HP-compatible." Some printers may imitate a couple of printers.

Each type of compatibility is called an *emulation*. A Panasonic dot matrix printer, for example, emulates an Epson or IBM printer (it prints your work as if it were an Epson printer or IBM printer). Printer manufacturers emulate printers from other companies so that their printers are compatible with as many software programs as possible. Why reinvent the wheel?

Hundreds of brands of printers are available. Your number one concern when choosing or working with a printer is that it is compatible with your software, not your PC. WordPerfect, for example, works with over 800 printers.

Microsoft Windows is a little different from other software. You don't need to select a printer driver for each Windows software program you own because Windows manages the printer driver for other Windows programs. You simply select and set up your printer once using the Windows Control Panel. Then, your printer can be used with any of hundreds of Windows programs. How convenient!

TRICKS

Often, printer manufacturers and software manufacturers provide newer printer drivers for various software programs. Newer drivers may speed up printing, provide new features, or solve past printing problems. Call these companies for the new drivers.

Picking a Printer

The best way to select a printer is to answer four questions:

   What quality does your printing require?

   How fast do you need your printing?

   How much printing do you intend to do?

   Does your software support the printer?

Never select a printer on price alone. Think also about printing speed and the amount of memory. Graphics (pictures and charts), for example, take more time to print and demand more memory than text.

NERDY
DETAILS

> Like your PC, your printer requires memory (RAM). Sometimes, your printer may require a certain amount of memory before it will print a page, such as when you want to print a picture or a heavily-designed page. Desktop publishing programs such as PageMaker and QuarkXpress may produce complex pages that require your printer to have oodles of memory.
>
> One page from a WYSIWYG program can take up to 6M of RAM. The extra memory you may need is purchased and installed inside your printer, not your PC.

Watch out for stripped-down printers. For some laser printers, you must pay extra for the 250-sheet paper tray. What good is fast printing if you have to spoon feed sheets one at a time? Why have crisp-looking text if only a couple of fonts are available? Why bother to get a printer for desktop publishing if it doesn't have enough memory to print a page full of graphics?

Connect the Dots

Selecting a dot matrix printer is relatively easy. Compatibility with your software is rarely a problem because most printers can imitate either an Epson printer or IBM ProPrinter. The hardware for these printers also is similar; all dot matrix printers include a tractor feeder, a device that lets your printer use continuous, pin-fed paper. Unfortunately, a tractor feeder may require you to waste an occasional page when you want to tear off a printed document. You have to advance the paper to get past the sprockets of the tractor feed.

Continuous-fed paper has a row of evenly spaced holes on both sides. These holes mesh with the pins on the tractor feeder. The tractor then moves the paper through the printer. Some dot matrix printers also include friction feed, in which a *platen* (the cylinder against which the printing is done) holds the paper in place and rotates to advance it.

The best dot matrix printers are sturdy capable beasts that can take a lot of abuse and have a ton of options. The more options a dot matrix printer has, the better. You probably will need one of the following capabilities inherent in the best dot matrix printers:

 24-pin versus 9-pin. A 24-pin printer provides letter quality text. If you want to save money and can tolerate lower print quality, select a 9-pin printer. This printer still can print at near-letter quality. If you demand letter quality, stay with the 24-pin printer.

Often, the price difference between a 9-pin and 24-pin dot matrix printer is negligible. Live a little; get a 24-pin model.

 Wide or narrow carriage. Dot matrix printers come in two sizes: wide carriage and narrow carriage. These sizes are also called 132-column and 80-column, in case you're worried about exact width. The wide carriage can handle 11×17-inch ledger paper and wide invoices. If you can live with printing on 8.5×11-inch paper, save about $100 and select a narrow-carriage printer.

 Print buffer. Some dot matrix printers include a small amount of memory, up to 64K. This memory is used to store your document in the printer until it is ready to print. (About 3K holds one page of text.) The bigger the buffer, the sooner you and your PC can work on something else. If you print shorter documents (fewer than 10-20 pages), this memory can be a boon. For longer documents, this buffer doesn't help much. However, you can get back to work sooner by using a print spooler, such as Windows' Print Manager. The print spooler can gobble many more pages than the typical built-in printer buffer.

 Paper paths. Besides the pin-fed tractor feed, you should have other paper options. For example, you may want to feed your printer individual letterhead. If you want to use single sheets and continuous paper, look for a *paper-parking* feature, which pulls the continuous paper out of the way. If you work with labels, envelopes and other heavy paper, you need a printer with a "straight-paper path"; in other words, the way the paper travels through the printer needs to be as straight as possible.

Look for printers with front-, rear-, or bottom-feed paths. For multipart forms, make sure your printer can print on the last page of four- or six-part forms. If you intend to feed several individual sheets through your printer, consider buying a single-sheet or cut-sheet feeder. This device feeds the sheets through without your assistance.

 Noise reduction. Some printers provide a "quiet" mode that slightly reduces the noise of the printer. Other printers, such as the Panasonic 2624, are specifically designed to print as quietly as a laser printer. If your roommate won't tolerate noise after 10 p.m., either buy a dot matrix printer with a quiet mode, get an inkjet printer, or get your own place.

 Fonts. Most dot matrix printers include six or seven bitmapped fonts. Some printers, such as the Epson ActionPrinter 3250, even include scalable fonts. For additional fonts, you may need to use soft fonts. An alternative is to use font cartridges, for which some printers have slots.

Laser Sharp

Even though cheapo laser printers are available for $800, plan on spending $1000 or more—the same as a brand new computer—for a decent printer. These are big numbers for a printer considering a comparable 24-pin dot matrix printer is a fourth the price. The best advice is to do your homework before you step foot in a store or dial your favorite mail-order house. Here are some of the more important considerations of choosing laser printers:

Resolution. Most laser printers print at 300 dots per inch (dpi). This is fine for most work. New printers, such as the HP LaserJet 4, print at 600 dpi. High resolution printers are best for creating in-house ads and other documents that need crisp resolution.

 Speed. Laser printers typically come in two speeds: four and eight pages per minute (ppm). If your printing needs are modest (under 10-20 pages per day), you can save a bunch of bills by buying a 4-ppm printer. 8-ppm printers are designed for the busy home or small office.

 Size. As a rule, 4- to 6-ppm printers tend to be smaller, requiring little desk space. Their paper trays often can be flipped up and out of the way. Faster models are fatter and usually demand their own printer stand or a wing of your desk.

 Processor. The rated speed of a laser printer, such as 4 ppm, is the top speed at which the printer can print. The more complex your page (several typefaces, several font sizes, and graphics), the slower your printer. The speed of the printer's processor is often more important. For example, the HP LaserJet IIP Plus features a 16MHz processor, rather than the 10MHz processor given the original IIP. The actual number of pages that can be printed is increased by the faster processor despite the same engine speed of four pages per minute.

 Emulation. Almost every laser printer imitates the Hewlett-Packard LaserJet. Other printers may use the PostScript (see the following nerdy detail). The important point is that your software must be capable of working with whichever emulation your printer uses. Not all software programs can work with a PostScript printer. Some more expensive printers provide both emulations.

NERDY
DETAILS

A *page description language,* or *PDL,* is the computer language that describes how text and graphics should be placed on a page for printing. Because of their purpose, PDLs determine which fonts work with your printer. PDLs also affect the price of your printer, often by several hundred dollars. When researching printers, make sure you include only printers with a PDL that does not limit the fonts you can use.

continues

continued

Most laser printers understand one of two page description languages that have become standard in the printer industry. The most prevalent page description language is the Printer Control Language (PCL), developed by Hewlett-Packard for its LaserJet printers.

The newer HP LaserJet III and LaserJet 4 use a version called PCL5. The other PDL standard, PostScript, was developed by Adobe Systems.

 Memory. Most laser printers include at least 512K or 1M of memory. This memory is used to prepare a page for printing and is adequate for printing simple text. If you intend to use software-based fonts with your printer or want to print a full page of graphics, you may need more than 1M of memory. Check how much memory your printer can accommodate if more is needed.

 Fonts. Most laser printers include 14 to 45 fonts. Some printers, such as the HP LaserJet 4, even include scalable fonts. Make sure your printer includes some business typefaces, such as Helvetica and Times. For additional fonts, you may need to use soft fonts or font cartridges.

GEEK

NERDY
DETAILS

A laser printer is not picture perfect. For example, a laser printer cannot print to the edge of the page. At least one-quarter of an inch around the entire page is unprintable. Another inconvenience is you can only print 60 lines of text per sheet of paper, rather than the usual 66 (assuming you are using standard typewriter spacing—six lines to the inch). These are minor drawbacks, however.

 Paper capacity. Some laser printers only hold 50 sheets of paper, requiring frequent reloading for large amounts of printing. An optional paper tray may cost $100 to $200 more. Others include trays that handle 200-250 letter-size sheets. Regardless of paper capacity, check to see whether your laser printer can handle envelopes and transparencies.

Selecting Paper

Both dot matrix and laser printers require certain types of paper. A dot matrix printer can use several types of paper, including:

 Fan-fold blank paper. Fan-fold (also called continuous-feed or pin-feed) paper is the most popular paper used on dot matrix printers. A tractor feed grabs the paper by its edges and moves it through the printer as one long continuous sheet. The paper is perforated so that the individual pages can be separated. In addition, the pin-feed edges are perforated so that they can be torn off.

TRICKS

> The perforations on fan-fold paper may be either normal or fine. By using paper with fine perforations, your pages look more professional because they won't have a rough edge left over after tearing off the perforated sides.

You won't find 8.5"×11" (letter-sized) fan-fold paper. The size is often 9"×11" because of the edges required to feed the paper (1/4-inch is required per edge). For wide-carriage printers, you can use 14 7/8"×11" inch paper. The final size of 14"×11" gives you plenty of room for rows of numbers.

 Green-bar/blue-bar. A type of fan-fold paper, this paper has faint horizontal colored bars that make reading columns of numbers easier.

TRICKS

> Continuous-feed paper sometimes is tricky to align. It's often hard to see where the perforation runs, making fast, straight alignment nearly impossible.
>
> Next time you load a stack of paper, use a wide-tipped felt pen to mark the narrow tractor-feed strips on each side of the stack. (You don't want to draw on the paper you'll be printing on, just the discarded edges.) Draw a solid line down the sides of the stack where the paper is folded—not the outside edges. Turn the paper around and mark the other side. Check that the markings are clearly visible. When you load this marked paper into your printer, your alignment problems are over because the tear lines are visible with a passing glance.

Multipart paper. Also a fan-fold paper, you can make multiple copies at one printing. You can order two-, three-, or four-part paper with each sheet separated from the others by a carbon sheet. You can also get carbonless paper, which makes copies without a paper carbon.

For laser printing, the right paper can greatly improve print quality. Your laser printer can use several types of paper, including copier paper. Use relatively smooth, uncoated paper; textured papers (such as 25-percent cotton bond) may be pulled into the printer and print unevenly.

A paper's weight is measured by the weight of a ream (500 sheets) of 17×22-inch sheets. A good laser paper should be just a little heavier than 20-pound copier paper: 24-pound Finch Laser Opaque, Hammermill Laser Plus, Weyerhauser First Choice, and Nekoosa Ardor are good choices. The same paper can be used in inkjet printers.

TRICKS

To save paper, use the other side of discarded paper for drafts of new documents. To prevent this "recycled" paper from curling until needed, place an encyclopedia or other book on top of the stack.

Never use transparencies or sheets of labels unless they are specifically made for use with a laser printer. These things bake under the printer's extreme heat and melt. The result may be serious damage to either your laser printer or its $90 toner cartridge. When possible, consider using recycled paper designed for laser printers.

TRICKS

Want to know how many pages your Hewlett-Packard laser printer has printed to see if you need to get a new toner cartridge (every 3,000 pages)? For a printed report of the current page count of a Hewlett-Packard Laserjet printer, press the On Line button to make it off line. When the On Line light goes out, press the Test button. In the LCD display you'll see the message 05 Self Test. When the printer spits out the first page, check out the left side of the page to see the printer's page count.

TRICKS

Ink jet printers usually print well on standard office stationery, but text on cotton bond stationery often comes out fuzzy. The ink sticks to all the fibers it hits: on bond paper, the fibers aren't as flat as they are on photocopier-style stationery.

To fix this fuzziness after printing, loosen excess fibers by lightly rubbing a well-laundered handkerchief over the bond paper. You'll be amazed by the increased sharpness.

Getting More Life from Your Printer

If someone gave you a purple 1973 AMC Matador, you'd probably treat it like crap, drive it into the ground, and walk off proud you never put a cent into it. Dot matrix printers can be just as ugly, loud, and solid, but don't neglect them. These printers will last for years with a little rough-love and compressed air. To prolong the life of the infinitely ugly dot matrix printer:

 Clean and lubricate the track upon which the printhead (the part that prints the letters) moves. Wipe it periodically with a soft cloth and use a light oil such as sewing machine oil. Avoid WD-40; it doesn't contain enough lubricant. Certainly do not use heavy oil (such as 10W-30)—that's for the Matador.

 Use manufacturer-recommended ribbons. A ribbon not only provides ink for printed characters but also preserves the life of your printer. Ribbons are soaked in ink and in lubricant to help keep the individual pins moving freely. Cheap or re-inked ribbons may not contain enough lubricant.

 Clean the printhead occasionally. A buildup of ink may cause one or more of your printer's pins to stick. If this happens, you will see a continuous white horizontal line through your type or graphics. Clean the printhead with isopropyl alcohol on a foam (not cotton) swab.

 Set the printhead gap according to your paper. The best way to extend the printhead's life is to adjust the gap between the printhead and the platen (the surface behind your paper) according to the paper you are using. Use a bigger gap when you are using thick paper, such as mailing labels or thick multipart forms.

Use the correct paper path. Your printer may be able to accept paper from the front, rear, bottom, and top. Select the best path for the paper being used. Mailing labels, for example, are best used through the front or bottom paper path—not the rear.

Laser printers are definitely worth keeping and caring for (you wouldn't treat a Porsche poorly). If you own a laser printer, follow these tips:

 Clean your printer. Most printer manuals tell you how to clean the printer. Most want you to clean the corona wire and fuser. (The corona wire creates the electric charge that attracts the toner to the paper.) If the corona wire gets dirty, it won't be able to apply the proper charge to the paper. If this happens, you'll get light or even blank streaks on your page.

The fuser is the part that melts the toner onto the page. If you don't keep this clean, the toner may not stick. Streaking may result. Clean these parts with a soft cloth and cotton swabs or the built-in cleaning brush. Avoid solvents and cleaners; they can damage the printer.

STOP!

Never break any wires inside your printer. When I purchased my first laser printer, I broke the corona wire while cleaning it. The printer was useless. The result: a $100 service bill to replace the wire. These wires are very thin and hard to see. Make sure you have good light and a steady hand whenever you approach this thin wire.

 Protect the printer drum. Your laser printer has a photosensitive drum (one of your friends probably has bongo drums). The laser's drum may be built into the toner cartridge (such as in an HP LaserJet). Never expose the drum to light for long periods. Although this drum is covered by a shield, keep the room dimly lit when removing it.

TRICKS

Save the box your toner cartridge and drum ordinarily came in. You can use it to store the drum (it's dark and safe) while you are cleaning your printer. Later, you can use the box to ship the cartridge back to be refilled.

Keep toner cartridges level. Never tilt or store your toner cartridges on one side. This shifts the toner to one side, causing a spill or uneven printing when used.

TRICKS

Does your printer say your toner cartridge is empty? That toner cartridge may have some life left. Remove the cartridge and shake it back and forth to loosen and evenly distribute any remaining toner (this also works if your motorcycle's low on gas). Reinsert the cartridge into your printer and check if the toner empty message is still displayed. If not, continue using the cartridge until it is actually empty.

 Keep print density down. You can extend the life of your toner by turning down the darkness—or print density—until you need to print the final version of your document. You might want to keep your LaserJet's toner dimmed to about 7 rather than the normal setting of 5. (Earth to Hewlett-Packard: why does a higher number print lighter?)

 Replace your printer's ozone filter. Your printer has an ozone filter to trap dangerous ozone gas before it exits your laser printer. (Ozone is good in the atmosphere but not at ground level.) Ozone filters are made of activated charcoal and must be replaced regularly because toner, paper dust, and ozone accumulate in them.

A typical laser printer should have its ozone filter replaced every 50,000 pages or two years. Replace the filter more often if you work in a dry or dusty environment or work alongside your printer. These filters cost between $10 and $45. Sometimes, an ozone filter can only be replaced by the dealer. Consult your printer's owner's manual to see specifics.

TRICKS

Using recycled toner cartridges is a good idea. Most recycled toner cartridges cost 30 to 50 percent less than a brand-new cartridge. The parts in a toner cartridge often last longer than the 3,000 copies and simply require new toner. Consider taking your used toner cartridge to a company that recycles them.

continues

continued

Some recycled cartridges are not as good as others. Look at a test print of the recycled toner cartridge before you choose to recycle. If a sample isn't provided, ask for one before purchasing. In addition, make sure the toner cartridge arrives in a box to avoid exposure to light.

Make It Print! Now!

In Chapter 3, you set up your printer. You can now test it. Before printing with your software, you can test your printer from DOS.

1. Turn on your printer.

2. Make sure the on-line light is lit.

3. Type the following:

    `ECHO THIS IS A TEST AND ONLY A TEST > PRN`

The > PRN redirection at the end of this line sends your command to the printer (PRN). If you have a dot matrix printer, you'll see and hear the results. If you have a laser printer, send a form feed to your printer (discussed earlier in the section "Eject a Page with the Form Feed Button").

TRICKS

You can press the Print Screen (PrtScr) key to send what's on the screen to your printer. Occasionally, you must press the Shift or Alt key with the PrtScr key.

The Print Screen key doesn't always work; in Microsoft Windows, this key prints the screen to a temporary holding space called the Windows Clipboard. The "captured" image can then be saved or printed. Unfortunately, this key only prints the letters on the screen and not the graphics. In addition, you may have to press the Form Feed button to eject the partially filled page.

Setting Up Serial Printers

Most printers are connected to your PC using the parallel port. A few printers use the rarer serial port. Serial printers work just like parallel printers, but require some monkeying around. To use your serial printer with DOS, you must type two DOS commands:

```
MODE COM1:9600,N,8,1
MODE LPT1=COM1
```

If your printer is connected to your PC's second serial port, replace COM1 with COM2.

To use a serial printer with your software program, simply inform the program you are using a serial printer. Most programs can recognize the serial printer.

Printing IBM Graphics

IBM graphics are rare characters, such as shaded boxes and box corners, that don't appear on your keyboard. As discussed in Chapter 11, these are called *extended characters* because they are above and beyond the typical alphabet. To print such characters, your printer must be compatible with an Epson or IBM printer.

Don't confuse graphics characters with actual graphics, such as pictures and pie charts. Virtually all printers can print these, although a laser printer requires a certain amount of memory to print an entire page of graphics.

Common Printer Goofs

Sometimes, your printer refuses to work. Use this list to find the problem:

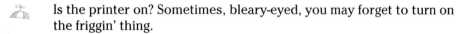 Is the printer on? Sometimes, bleary-eyed, you may forget to turn on the friggin' thing.

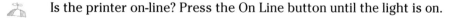 Is the printer on-line? Press the On Line button until the light is on.

Have you run out of paper? Some printers beep at you when they run out of paper. Some dot matrix printers even have a paper-out sensor. If your paper is placed out of reach of this sensor (too far to the left or right), the printer still may think no paper is present.

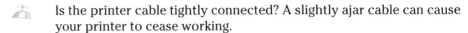

    Is the printer cable tightly connected? A slightly ajar cable can cause your printer to cease working.

    Is a printer ribbon or toner cartridge installed? Some offices on a shoestring budget may be sharing one toner cartridge among multiple laser printers (talk about cheap!).

    Is the print density dial set too light or the printhead gap lever set too far away from the paper?

Paper Jams

Sometimes your printer may choke on the paper it is trying to use. On a laser printer, the paper may be pulled in at an angle or more than one sheet may be pulled through. Your printer may then display a message such as PAPER JAM. No problem—open the "hood" of your printer and gently remove the jammed page(s). In addition, look for any small pieces of paper that might have been torn off.

STOP!

> Avoid the hot parts of your printer, such as the fuser that melts the toner onto the page. Ouch!

Next, remove the paper tray to check for any possible jams there. After closing the printer, you then must turn it on-line again. Often, the jammed page is still remembered by the printer, so no pages have to be reprinted.

TRICKS

> To prevent a paper jam in a laser printer, fan the paper before placing it in the paper tray. Pick up a ream of paper, hold it in one hand, and thumb through it with the other hand. "Fanning" loosens up the individual sheets of paper.

In a dot matrix printer, paper jams most often occur when the paper is not aligned with the printer or the paper is held too taut between the two sprockets of the tractor feed. Try to keep the paper aligned with the printer; it shouldn't be angled going into the printer.

PART 5

Chapters That Didn't Fit Anywhere Else

LAPTOPS ARE RELATIVE!

CHAPTER
15

Living with Laptops

The laptop computer has gone from an oddity to an object of desire. With it, you'll be able to get as much work done outside the office as in it. No longer must you be shackled to the legs of the corporate desk. (If only the boss's attitude was as liberal and liberating.)

In the 90s, the portable PC will be as commonplace as the briefcase and infinitely more useful. For many, the laptop computer provides the freedom to compute outside and on the go. Whether you write a letter in the park or at 20,000 feet, you can choose to work where and when you want. This type of freedom is not found with the stodgy desktop computer. This chapter discusses several points about laptops, including:

- Types of laptop computers
- Different laptop screens and how they affect your work
- Working with your laptop's keyboard
- How to conserve battery energy when you're on the road
- Caring for your laptop
- What to bring when you're traveling
- Where to get laptop insurance

A laptop computer is ideal for the PC owner on the go. From the motel room or roadside stop, you can work at your computer. You don't even need an electrical outlet. Simply turn on your laptop and you can begin working.

Laptop computers have not always been this portable. In the mid-80s, the portable computer resembled a calculator with a thyroid condition. The original "luggables" required a strong arm and an electrical outlet. Today, laptop computers are huggable.

NERDY
DETAILS

> By 1993, one-half of all PCs sold will be laptops.

Typically, people buy a laptop computer as an extension of their desktop PC. More and more people purchase a laptop to serve both needs. For people who can't live without color or full-size keyboards, many laptops plug into a desktop color monitor or have color screens, and most hook up to external, full-size keyboards.

NERDY
DETAILS

> One feature some laptops have that you will learn to love is called the "bookmark," "resume," or "snooze" feature. If your laptop has resume, you can turn off the computer right in the middle of running a program and not lose your place. When you turn the laptop on again, your work appears exactly where you left off.

Portability costs money, however. A typical laptop PC still costs 30 to 40 percent more than a similar desktop model. Sophisticated electronic circuitry is used to reduce space and conserve power; the components, such as the hard disk, must be rugged to handle the bumps and bruises of travel. Big-name manufacturers include AST, Bondwell, Compaq, Dell, IBM, NEC, Tandy, Toshiba, and Zenith.

Different Sizes, Different Needs

The work you plan to do with your portable computer helps you determine the type of laptop you should buy. Here are a few suggestions:

 If you travel a lot and plan to bring your computer along, you want the slimmest, lightest unit you can find.

 If you plan to use your laptop often in an airplane, a customer's office, on the beach, or anywhere away from an electrical outlet, choose a computer with a long-lasting battery charge.

 If you plan to cart your computer occasionally from home to office, bulk doesn't matter. Don't rule out portable computers, which require an electrical outlet. A large laptop gives you a clearer screen, a complete keyboard and even a slot for an add-on board. These larger computers often can be quite affordable.

 If you want to run graphical programs, such as Microsoft Windows, you'll need a fast processor, a high-resolution screen, and lots of memory and hard disk space.

To select from over 100 portable computers is increasingly difficult. How do you recognize the cutting edge in terms of price, processor technology, display technology, battery life, weight, and connectivity? Most importantly, how do you select the portable that's right for you?

Laptop computers are separated by size and features into four categories:

 Portable

 Laptop

 Notebook

 Palmtop

NERDY
DETAILS

This chapter uses the phrase *laptop* to refer to all these types of portables.

Portables: Desktop PCs with Handles

A *portable* computer is simply a desktop computer with a handle. Like a desktop PC, a portable requires an AC outlet for power. Portables usually are more powerful than other laptop computers but less expensive, because they do not require the tightly packed components other laptop computers require for their small size. Portables often weigh about 20 pounds (or more) and sport full-sized keyboards. A portable is ideal if you operate at more than one location and need a machine to run demanding computer chores, such as desktop publishing or drafting.

Laptops: Full-Size Portability

Laptop computers run off batteries and offer large displays and spacious hard disk drives. Unlike "portables," a laptop computer really is portable because it relies on its own built-in power, often nickel-cadmium (NiCad) batteries. A laptop provides the same computing power as that of your desktop computer—the keyboards for laptops also are large and pleasant to use.

Although laptop computers started the laptop revolution, they're considered too big to be truly portable. Like cellular phones and stereo speakers, smaller is better. The revolution continues with notebooks and subnotebooks.

Notebooks: Small but Strong

Notebook computers are designed to be slipped into a briefcase where they are barely noticed. Notebook computers promise to deliver the power of a desktop PC in as little space as possible. Notebooks today mostly offer the 80386SX, 80386SL, and 80486SX microprocessors to run big programs at high speed. Recent ultra-light notebooks (or subnotebooks) weigh under four pounds.

Battery life is a critical design factor for these computers because notebook PCs are likely to be used away from an electrical outlet. Notebook makers have successfully stretched the usual two to three hours of battery life in several ways:

 A version of the 80386 chip, the 80386SL, requires fewer components and less power than the full 80386 processor.

Good notebook computers have a "standby" or "deep sleep" mode. Built-in software turns off the hard drive and screen whenever the computer sits idle for a specific amount of time.

 The processors of some notebooks can be run at slower-than-normal speeds, reducing battery drain. If you're typing a letter, for example, you can reduce processor speed because word processing software doesn't need turbo power CPU speed.

One way to reduce the weight of a notebook computer is to eliminate its built-in floppy drive (subnotebooks lack built-in floppy drives). Floppy drives add weight and thickness to the notebook and also require power. For the mobile worker, floppy drives are not needed if most work is transmitted to the office by modem. Although super-slim, these notebooks require you to haul around an external drive or a cable to transfer files from one computer to another.

The notebook is ideal for those who don't require the ultimate in portable power. By trading a little power for a lightweight design, you can have the equivalent of your desktop computer without the heavy burden. The notebook can be used for word processing, smaller databases, and number-crunching.

Palmtops: PC in a Pocket

Palmtop PCs are designed to be the most portable and efficient. Laptops and notebooks run for a few hours on special battery packs; palmtops live for weeks on ordinary AA batteries.

A good palmtop is an extension of the office PC. A sales representative can download onto the palmtop price lists and sales forecasts at the office, for example, then use the palmtop to record orders and jot down notes about customers' preferences and quirks. Back at the office, the data can be dumped into the PC.

One popular palmtop model is the Hewlett-Packard 95LX. The handheld 95LX stuffs the power of a mid-80s desktop PC into a case not even one-tenth the size. The 95LX even includes built-in software: Lotus 1-2-3. Other software can be purchased on plug-in cards about the size of a credit card. In addition, files can be swapped between HP palmtops without wires; simply place the two gizmos within 8 inches of each other and they communicate with an infrared beam.

Regardless of their efficiency, palmtops are no serious substitute for a larger laptop computer. The 95LX, for example, can display only 16 lines of 40 characters across, enough to view only four or five columns of a spreadsheet. To see more, you have to scroll with tiny arrow keys on a keyboard meant for two-finger typists.

Looking at Portable Displays

A laptop computer has no room for a TV-sized computer monitor, so most use flat screens called liquid crystal displays (LCDs). The latest LCD screens let you see the screen clearly from several angles with better contrast and lighting. Other laptops use screens made of neon-like plasma gas. To improve readability, some laptops include backlighting or edgelighting (also called sidelighting). Backlit screens provide light from a panel behind the LCD. Edgelit screens are lit from small fluorescent tubes mounted along the sides of the screen.

Most laptop screens are VGA-compatible. Instead of colors, shades of gray are used. A 32 gray-scale screen can show 32 shades of gray, for example. If you want color, you likely can connect your laptop to a full-size monitor. Often, a port on the back of your laptop supports an external monitor.

NERDY
DETAILS

How do LCD screens work? Liquid crystal displays (LCDs) use a layer of gooey material—the liquid crystals—sandwiched between two sheets of plastic. A thin layer of transparent electrodes is placed between these two panes. Only light waves parallel to a certain pane pass through the crystals—the same way cheap polarized sunglasses work.

The liquid crystals are twisted to pivot light received through the first sheet and align it with the second. Light makes it through the second sheet to light the screen. When electricity is passed through the electrodes, the liquid crystal molecules are untwisted. Light no longer passes through the second sheet and a black dot appears.

Most LCDs use passive matrix displays. Each dot, or pixel, on the screen shares electrodes with other dots. By sharing electrical contacts, the screens can be slow. Active matrix screens, however, have a separate transistor for each pixel, which provides sharper and richer characters and graphics. For these benefits, laptops with active matrix screens are more expensive.

Most laptops still use the passive matrix design. If you want to take out a second mortgage on your house, you can purchase an active-matrix color LCD. Although these screens have more vivid colors than most color monitors, they are expensive, commanding prices 30 or 40 percent more than conventional LCD laptops.

You may see or hear the phrases "supertwist" and "triple-supertwist" mentioned with laptop screens (chemists call this liquid crystal structure "nematic"). Supertwist LCDs have a more pronounced twist that improves the contrast (the differences between light and dark images).

Gas Plasma Screens

Gas plasma screens are another type of display used with laptop computers. These types of screens are fast and are easy to recognize; their display is orange-colored. Their color comes from tightly-spaced neon-like lamps, one for each pixel.

If you decide to purchase a laptop with this screen, first make sure you can stomach it. Some people find the color irritating. Plasma screens are expensive and power-hungry, and are used mostly in larger laptop and portable computers.

Keyboards

To save space, a laptop keyboard differs from the one on your desktop. The biggest difference is the lack of a few keys common to PC keyboards. Each laptop manufacturer designs its own keyboards; nevertheless, a few shortcuts and compromises are common to all and affect a laptop's usability:

 To save space, the distance between keys or the keys themselves sometimes are reduced. This slight difference may be awkward as you switch between your laptop and desktop keyboards.

 Some laptop keyboards are designed to have a shorter "travel"; the keys do not have to be pressed as deeply to record keystrokes. Keys on "full travel" keyboards must be pushed as far as those on desktop keyboards. A shortened travel distance can be a pain when you accidentally bump a key.

Avoid keyboards that don't have distinct Home, End, PgUp, and PgDn keys. Some laptops require you to press a special function key every time you use these popular keys. This approach stinks!

 Cursor keys in most computers often are placed in a diamond or inverted T configuration so that the Up Arrow key is on top, the Left arrow key is on the left, and so on. Some laptop vendors defy this logical arrangement by using I- and L-shaped variations. These "special" arrangements are especially irritating.

 The Ctrl and Alt keys occasionally are placed in a drive-you-crazy position far from reach. Make sure you can reach these important keys.

Saving Your Juice

The portable PC owner's biggest concern is battery life. If you're not careful, you might lose all your work when the low-power light glares at you halfway through an airline flight. If you saved your work to the hard disk before the dreaded low-power light appeared, it will be safe—but you won't be able to work on it anymore without risking running out of juice.

TRICKS

> The best way to protect your work is to carry a spare battery pack with you for a long flight or emergency situation. If you've put off charging batteries until the day you leave, most laptop AC adapters now can charge up to five battery packs in a row.

Almost all portables today use a rechargeable nickel cadmium (NiCad) battery pack. The battery life of most rechargeable batteries is about two to three hours. One problem with NiCad batteries is the memory effect. The *memory effect* is a condition in which the battery begins to recognize earlier charge points as its limit. If you forget to discharge the battery fully and repeatedly charge it after using only half its power, the battery lasts only half as long. Eventually it becomes unusable.

Your batteries can be recharged at two different rates: fast charge or trickle charge. *Fast charge* recharges your batteries in about one hour while the battery sits in the charger base. *Trickle charge* takes several hours, but lets the battery recharge while you are using the laptop from an AC outlet.

Trickle-charging can contribute to the memory effect. Try to use trickle-charging only after your battery has lost power. If you begin to notice the battery is not working as long between charges as it used to, fully discharge and recharge the battery three consecutive times. This should clear the memory effect.

Nickel hydride (NiMH) batteries—a new type of battery—are slowly replacing NiCad batteries. These batteries give 80 percent more battery life than NiCad batteries and don't suffer from the memory effect. If you already own a laptop, your manufacturer may offer NiMH replacements for your current NiCad batteries.

Built-In Power Savers

Your laptop may have several features that can extend its battery life. Many have utilities that enable you to cut off power to various parts, for example. You can make the hard drive stop spinning whenever it's not used for a preset amount of time. Some programs, such as word processors, do not access the hard disk that often. With these programs, you can set this "spin-down time" to the shortest amount possible.

The shorter the spin-down time, the sooner the hard disk stops after a short period of inactivity. A database or other program, however, frequently accesses the hard drive and requires a higher spin-down time. A spin-down time not adjusted to your software's needs actually can waste power, because the hard disk requires more power to resume normal operating speed than it does to run at a constant speed.

Auto power saving can be customized using power-management options accessed from the computer's setup menu or from a special utility program. Power-management features also enable you to block power to specific ports and peripherals. A disabled internal modem saves precious current, as does reduced backlighting. Small amounts of power flow to all peripherals (internal modem, hard disk drive, screen, floppy disk drive) even when they are not in use; taken together, these can produce a significant drain.

TRICKS

If your laptop has a backlit or edgelit screen, you can save precious battery juice by turning down the brightness.

Another boon to your battery power is a disk cache, such as SMARTdrive from Microsoft. A disk cache puts the most commonly requested information from your hard disk into memory. The retrieval of information from the cache enables you to keep the disk in a spin-down state more often.

TRICKS

Traveling Software Inc. offers a juice-saving software utility called Battery Watch Pro. Battery Watch Pro checks your battery and displays a pop-up fuel gauge on-screen. Based on your current laptop use, it estimates how much time you can continue to work.

Expanding Your Laptop

Your laptop computer has little room for growth. The video card, parallel port, and serial port are built right into the laptop's motherboard (the laptop's main circuit board). An internal modem might also be installed.

Laptops cost so much because most of the equipment within them is specially made to fit in the smallest space possible. Little room is available *inside* your laptop for adding other features. Recognizing this, laptop designers provide ports for you to connect things *outside* the computer.

External Keyboard and Monitor

Most laptops can be turned into a replacement for your desktop PC because they provide ports for a keyboard and monitor. With a monitor and a full-size keyboard at the office, you can use your laptop as a full-fledged PC every day at work. At night, you can use the same unit at home. With this arrangement, you have three computers in one—an office machine, a home machine, and a portable for the road.

Most laptops display up to 32 colors—typically in shades of gray—at VGA resolution. When you connect an external monitor, your laptop's screen is disabled and you use the larger screen instead. When you connect an external keyboard, all the keys on that keyboard work, even though your laptop may not have the same keys.

External Mouse and Docking Station

One thing laptop computers lacked in the past was a mouse. The reason: there wasn't anywhere to put it because traditional mice have been so big. Today, a popular alternative to the big, fat mouse is a small attachment that rests on the side of the case. Microsoft's Ballpoint Mouse and Logitech's TrackMan Portable Mouse are two effective substitutes for a regular mouse and have become very popular with mobile computer users.

Microsoft's Ballpoint Mouse, which has four buttons, can be tilted in relation to the keyboard; Logitech's mouse has three buttons and sits at a 45-degree angle to the keyboard. The Trackman Portable also works as a stand-alone device.

NERDY
DETAILS

Besides Microsoft and Logitech port-a-mice, you have other choices for mousing around. Some are even designed into the case of newer laptop computers. One of the first was the "Isobar," which is a thin bar just below the space bar you control with your thumb. The isobar has had mixed reviews, but it does work. Another more recent addition to some notebooks is the mini-trackball.

If you remember Missile Command, you know that the track ball on that game was larger than a grapefruit and about 10 times as big as these itsy-bitsy additions, which work just as well. If your laptop has one, it may take a week or two before you get used to it. The latest addition is IBM's little red joystick on their Thinkpad notebooks.

Laptop computers typically cannot accept expansion cards such as a scanner card or voice mail card. Some models offer optional docking stations that accommodate add-in slots or large hard drives. Toshiba, for example, offers the Deskstation IV, which provides two expansion slots and ports for external monitor and external keyboard.

These docking stations act as home bases for your laptop. Docking stations are best for laptop owners who work in a variety of locations, travel frequently, and require network access at the office. A docking station can help you eliminate transferring work to a desktop PC.

Docking stations merely extend the external connectors on the rear of the laptop, such as those for your monitor and keyboard. You also have serial and parallel ports, and a power supply that charges your laptop while you are using it at the station. Most docking stations offer one or more drive bays to house additional storage, such as a CD-ROM drive. The beauty of a docking system is that all connections are made to the station bay. You simply slide the laptop in and out—without having to attach and remove cables.

A docking station is not for everyone. Typically, only two expansion slots are provided. (Most PCs have six.) If you require several special expansion cards, the docking station will be inadequate. For most laptop owners, the expansion is not needed, however. The standalone PC is adequate, except for the addition of an external keyboard and color monitor.

Is There Such a Thing as Lapware?

"Laptop software" is a misnomer with today's speedier portable computers. If today's laptops truly are equivalent to the desktop PC, no special software is needed. The same programs you run at the office or at home should also run on your laptop.

The following tips help you take advantage of your current software on a laptop:

 When installing and using software, select the monochrome or Hercules graphics option. (Some software even offers a laptop choice.) These selections may be easier to read than colors that must be converted to shades of gray.

 Microsoft Windows 3.1 includes color schemes for LCD screens. These color schemes use colors best suited for slower, monochromatic LCD screens. To select a scheme, choose Colors from the Control Panel and select one of the three LCD color schemes.

 Cursors on LCD displays often experience something called *submarining;* the cursor disappears whenever you move it because the screen cannot keep pace with the CPU. To fix this problem, select Mouse from Windows' Control Panel and choose Mouse **T**rails. This option displays a ghost image of the mouse cursor whenever you move it. Another way to make the cursor more visible is to increase the speed of the blinking cursor.

Several laptop-only software programs give laptops more capabilities and make them easier on the eyes:

 Cursor enhancers. This type of software enlarges and speeds up the cursor so that you can find it on-screen. One popular product is No-Squint II from SkiSoft Publishing Corp.

 File transfer. Through a cable, you can quickly transfer files between a laptop and a desktop PC. LapLink from Traveling Software is one product. WinConnect, also from Traveling Software, enables you to access the disks of a laptop and desktop PC as if they were one.

TRICKS

> If both your laptop and desktop PCs have 3.5" disk drives, a floppy disk may be faster and more convenient than file transfer software.

 Disk compression. Utilities such as Stacker and SuperStor almost double the size of your hard disk by compressing the information on your hard drive. On faster computers, such as the 386DX, the time spent to decompress this information should be unnoticeable. The delay is often reduced by the small distances your hard disk must search for the information.

 Screen enhancers. You can enlarge the letters on your laptop screen by using a utility such as Laptop UltraVision from Personics. This utility uses larger characters that utilize the entire viewing area, making the characters easier to read. Laptop UltraVision also enlarges the cursor and adjusts the grayscale colors.

Caring For Your Laptop

Laptop computers were designed to handle the hustle and bustle of life. A fall from an airplane overhead bin or a gulp of coffee may overwhelm its built-in hardiness.

The hard disk is the most fragile part of your laptop; it requires precise alignment and is most at risk when it is on and spinning. A simple whack on the case can destroy your valuable work. Whenever you use a laptop, avoid bumping it while it saves or reads information. As a general rule, protect your laptop computer as if it were a '36 Auburn Speedster: don't let anyone or anything touch it! A few other laptop concerns you may want to think about include the following:

- Handle your laptop gently and attentively. Set it down on the table—don't drop it.

- Don't rush to use your laptop. Open and close its clamshell-like screen slowly and with both hands.

- Hook up cables and connectors gently, without bending the pins.

- Avoid beverages and foods like the plague when working anywhere near the keyboard. Any spills on the keyboard can cause disastrous short circuits—and sick stomachs when the repair bill arrives.

- Store your laptop where it can't fall or have anything fall on it.

- Use a padded laptop bag to cushion your PC from life's bumps and bruises.

- Don't spray glass cleaner directly onto the LCD screen. Dampen a cloth with the spray and then wipe the screen.

Laptops are a hot property for PC thieves, so consider these tips:

- Don't let the laptop out of your sight.

- Carry your laptop under your arm or firmly grasp the handle.

- Engrave your name and address on the laptop in an inconspicuous spot, such as on the inside of the battery cover.

- Keep a copy of your laptop's serial number in a safe place.

- Place a backup copy of your work in a bag other than your laptop bag. If someone steals your laptop, you'll still have your work files.

SAVE
THE DAY!

If you lose your laptop, someone will hopefully return it to you when they see your engraved name and address. You can also add lines to your AUTOEXEC.BAT startup file so your ownership is displayed each time your laptop starts. Simply enter these lines anywhere in the AUTOEXEC.BAT file:

```
CLS
ECHO This laptop belongs to ....
ECHO If found, please call XXX-XXX-XXXX collect
ECHO or write to us at .....
PAUSE
```

Include the PAUSE statement so this statement is not overlooked when your laptop starts.

Laptops and Airports

Some people fear that laptop computers can be damaged by airport X-ray machines. This is doubtful. X-rays are merely a type of light. If concerned, simply hand your laptop to the guard when you arrive at the inspection gate. Be prepared to turn on the computer to prove it doesn't contain plastic explosives (almost all security personnel will ask you to do this). Make sure your laptop is fully charged so that you can demonstrate its purpose.

A Laptop Survival Kit

A laptop may end up weighing more than you thought it would after you include its carrying case, battery packs, and AC adapter. You can't help it; you need the following items or the silly thing won't work:

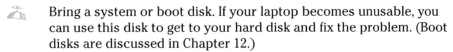

- Bring a system or boot disk. If your laptop becomes unusable, you can use this disk to get to your hard disk and fix the problem. (Boot disks are discussed in Chapter 12.)

- Bring enough floppy disks so that you can copy your important work. Place the backup copy of your work in a bag other than your laptop bag. If someone steals your laptop, you'll still have your work files.

- For extended work, bring at least one extra battery pack.

- Bring your AC adapter. If traveling abroad, ensure your adapter works on 240-volt current. Some adapters can switch automatically, while others require you to flip a switch.

Avoid carrying the manuals for the laptop and the software you'll be using. Instead, bring only the bare essentials, such as the quick reference guide.

 If you'll be using your modem, bring your modem cables.

SAVE
THE DAY!

Even if you purchase an internal modem, you may not be able to use it on the road. Some phone systems are designed only for voice, not data communication. (Some hotel phone systems are digital, which is incompatible with your analog modem.) Connecting a modem to a modular plug in a hotel room also can be a royal pain. The reason: wall jacks and handset jacks come in different sizes.

A digital telephone system may prove tricky to recognize. A general guideline for finding out whether the phone is digital is this: The more features a telephone offers, the more likely that it is digital. Because modems use tones, a hotel phone that uses pulses presents a problem. Users can remedy this, however, by adjusting communications software to dial with pulses instead of tones.

Laptop Insurance

Laptops often don't come with warranties to cover an accidental drop or fatal jostle. The small size of these computers also makes them a great target for theft and an easy item to drop or leave behind.

Computer insurance is your best safeguard against the unexpected. An all-risk policy from a company that specializes in insuring computers, such as Data Security Insurance (800-822-0901), should adequately cover your portable. The Data Security Insurance policy covers fire, theft, accidents, natural causes, and vandalism. Surprisingly, the company also covers accidental drops and erasure of data. With a $100 deductible, the policy costs $75 per year for at least $5,000 worth of coverage.

"HEY, IS THIS THING CABLE READY?"

CHAPTER
16

Networks: Make Your PC Extroverted

T he personal computer is just that: personal. You don't need anyone to assist you in typing at the keyboard or inserting a floppy disk. Armed with a self-contained PC, employees can work independently.

Many PC users formerly used *mainframe computers* and *minicomputers*. Such computers often required entire floors with special air conditioning and electrical generators. Raised floors hid hundreds of cables that snaked from one end of the building to the other. Today's PC requires only an electrical outlet. (If you own a laptop, not even that!)

It didn't take long for the computer industry to bring together maverick PC users. *Computer networks* or *local area networks* (*LANs*) tie several PCs together. (LANs rhymes with tans.)

Networks may seem like the domain of nerds because of all those hacker stories you've seen on the news, but they are for everyone. This chapter introduces networks and shows you:

 Why networks are such big news in the PC world

 How to log onto a network (environmentally correct—nothing to do with deforestation)

The importance of the file server (the what?)

 How cables link together networks, bridges, and televisions

 What to do when your network crashes (coffee break!)

 Network topologies aren't as exciting as they sound

Why a Network?

Basically, a network allows employees to share printers, modems, other hardware goodies (also called peripherals by nerds), software programs, and—your most important business asset—information. The word "local" in local area networks means just that. A LAN often connects the PCs in an office or building, and sometimes a complex of buildings. A handful of LANs that connect PCs between cities and states are called *wide area networks*, or *WANs*.

All LANs primarily resemble a string of Christmas lights. Your office or building is wired only once and employees then join the network through a central pipeline. The addition or movement of PCs and printers in a building is reduced to tapping into the network's cables, which eliminates extensive rewiring.

So, what's so great about networks?

 Networks enable you, your boss, or whomever is paying for your hardware equipment to save money. (If you have anything to do with setting up or running a network, remind your boss how much money you're saving the company!) After investing in PCs, fax machines, and printers, businesses want to maximize their investment by connecting them. For example, one expensive laser printer can be shared by all the PCs on the network. By sharing these network resources, they are used more often near full capacity. More importantly, networks allow you to share information easily, reliably, and quickly.

 You can expand PC networks more easily than mainframe or mini-computer systems, where growth and change can result in expensive rewiring of a network whose cabling may already resemble spaghetti. LANs allow you to add a new PC by simply plugging it into the existing network.

If you're asked to explain to someone, like your boss, what else besides saving money and flexibility makes networks important, tell them that networks give organizations:

 One-stop information. Anyone on the LAN can access centralized information, such as a customer address database or a jointly used software program.

 Electronic messaging. Anyone on the LAN can send messages to and work jointly with others on the LAN. This is called *electronic mail* or *email*.

Before LANs, people used *sneakernet*, which is a kind of nerdy but funny term for saving information on a floppy disk and taking it to another employee on foot. If the information required several disks, delivering it was more troublesome, but at least this network was very personal.

NERDY
DETAILS

You can have a crude network with just two PCs. These can be connected together with a null-modem adapter and serial cable. The null-modem adapter allows you to connect two PCs in the same room. I often use this to transfer files between my laptop and desktop PC (my laptop doesn't have a disk drive). The serial, or modem, cable is the one you normally would use when connecting your PC to another over the phone by modem. The null-modem ("no modem") adapter fools one PC into thinking it is talking to another via modem. To connect the two, you use communications software.

Typically, this method only lets you send ASCII files (plain text) from one computer to another. As a writer, this is typically all I want to do. To move several files between two computers, you can get a file transfer kit to do it, such as Traveling Software's Laplink.

An important advantage of PC networks over larger mainframe and minicomputer systems is PCs on networks remain personal. Employees can use their own software from their hard disk, or they can use the software available through the central computer. For example, they can use the Microsoft Word word processor found on their hard disks or they can use the network version of WordPerfect that most other employees use.

Network versions of popular software programs, such as WordPerfect, are available. Several people can use the network version of a software program at the same time. These network versions are less expensive than buying one copy of WordPerfect for each employee.

STOP!

It is illegal to buy a single-user version of a software package and let several people use it on a network, even if one person uses it at a time. Many software license agreements—the small legalese text that came with your software—state that the software program can be used on "one PC by one person."

Also, the PC's built-in computer chip provides uninterrupted computing power to the single employee. Several employees on mainframe and mini-computer systems must share the processing power of a central computer. As more people use the network, the speed, or response time, is reduced to a snail's pace.

What Parts Do You Need To Install a Network?

What do you say when someone asks, "What kind of equipment do I need to set up a network?" You brilliantly reply, "You need eight parts."

 File (or network) **server.** The main PC that oversees and administers the network.

 Workstations. The individual PCs that use the network (also called *client PCs* because they are customers of the file server).

TRICKS

You can use diskless workstations with your network to save money and provide security. These PCs have neither floppy nor hard disk drives yet have the processing capabilities of a PC. Without disk drives, these workstations rely on the network server's hard disk for software programs and storing one's work. These workstations prevent employees from physically copying information from the network.

 Nodes. Nodes are the individual workstations and other equipment, such as printers and modems, available on your network.

Cabling. Nodes (the PCs and other gizmos hooked up to the network) usually are connected using wire cable. Another type of cabling is wireless: you can now connect PCs by radio signals.

 Network interface card (NIC). The hardware device placed in or near your PC to connect it to the cabling. This is also called a *network adapter* or *LAN adapter* card.

NERDY
DETAILS

Some networks require no network adapter to be put inside your PC. These are called zero-slot LANs because they don't require an expansion slot for this card. Instead, they connect to your PC's serial port. Zero-slot LANs are an inexpensive solution and are useful for transferring files and sharing printers. However, communications may be slow.

 Network operating software (NOS). The software that links the PC, LAN adapter, and the network. In other words, this software runs the entire network show. NetWare from Novell Corp. is one brand of network operating software.

 Hubs and concentrators. A type of wiring clearinghouse that serves as the meeting point for a subset of nodes on the network. What?

 Bridges and routers. Devices that connect one LAN to one or more other LANs. If your little network is not connected to any other networks, these strange items aren't necessary.

What Else Do You Need To Know?

The components described in the previous section affect how your network performs, especially as the network workload increases. With so many parts, the major cost of a network may be more from troubleshooting than from the price of specific products. (One way to trim this cost is to purchase your networking products from a single source.)

For a network to operate best, you need to choose LAN components that work well with the applications you want to use on the network, and then balance the tradeoffs between the costs and performance of those parts.

The most common component of a network is the workstation, the individual PC. How can the workstation better the operation of the network?

Each PC must run a small piece of software called a network driver to tap into the network. The faster the computer, the faster this software operates.

The heart of a LAN is the file server, which is a PC that serves as the "master" computer (all the other PCs are attached to it). A dedicated file server is a PC that is not used by anyone else for daily work but simply focuses on being the brains of the network. (Dedicated file servers provide the most reliable network service.)

Sometimes a PC is set aside to handle some network tasks, such as managing several documents sent to a network printer. These printing jobs are then stored and managed by this print server. Likewise, a PC that handles information received by a network modem is called a communications server. Often, older PCs no one else wants can be relegated to these tasks.

Becoming a Network Guru

If your boss or your co-workers declare you the "Official Network Guru," they will obviously want you to set up the network and make sure everything operates perfectly. You need to make sure the correct equipment is installed. You also need to be prepared for helping users with tasks as simple as logging on to the network or as complex as what to do when the network crashes.

Logging In

When you start a PC that is part of a network, you don't have to use the network. Often, your computer may ask if you want to "log in" to the network. If you decide to log in, the network driver software is loaded and you are connected to the network. Sometimes you must connect yourself manually, such as by typing LOGIN or NET LOGIN.

NERDY
DETAILS

If your business has several file servers, you may have to include a specific name for the file server you want to use. Some companies are so big they have a number of LANs, each of which is managed by a file server. If you work for a big company with many LANs, you might have to specify the LAN you want to log into when you type LOGIN.

As you log in, or connect your PC to the network, you typically have to enter a password. This lets the network administrator, the person who oversees the network, see who is logged in and who has proper access to parts of the network. (Not everyone should be able to see the payroll records!)

After you're connected to a network, the drives on the file server become an extension of your own PC. Rather than just having two drives (C and D), you may be able to use network drives E, F, G, H, and more. I've even seen networks that use drive Z. Sometimes, you have to "attach" the drive with simple commands, but this depends on the network you are using and the software used to operate it.

Some networks do not have a file server. Instead, the connected PCs become the network. This is called a *peer-to-peer* network. With this arrangement, you can use the files on another person's hard disk or they can use the files on yours.

Moving files back and forth over a network is called *zapping* or *beaming*. (Beaming is probably a term inherited by Star Trekkies, who double as nerds. "Beam me your files, McCoy, there's no intelligent life down here.") For example, you can "beam" your sales figures to your boss over the network.

The File Server

The file server is the brains of your network. The faster it is, the less likely the network will slow to a crawl as more people (and their PCs) use it. For this reason, some file servers use a non-DOS operating system to get the most speed. For example, the popular Novell NetWare networking software uses such a proprietary scheme. If you plan to invest in a server, keep these things in mind:

- Buy the fastest and biggest SCSI hard disk system you can afford

- Buy the fastest computer you can get, such as one with an 80486 processor

- Make sure the PC has at least a 300-watt power supply

- Get as much memory as you can for your file server, especially if it uses a non-DOS network operating system

- Hook up your file server to an uninterruptible power supply (UPS) for safety

Place your file server in a smoke- and dust-free environment, and keep it cool

 If you want to save a few bucks, you can use a monochrome monitor

NERDY
DETAILS

Multiuser systems are often confused with LANs. Like a LAN, a multiuser system uses one central PC as the file server. However, the individual workstations are simply dumb terminals. *Dumb terminals* have no computer chips that process information. Instead, these inexpensive terminals rely on the multiuser file server for all their computer power. A multiuser system often has up to 32 people sharing one PC.

Cables: Network Glue

The glue of a network is the communications cable that connects the various PCs. Without wiring there would be no LAN. This cable may be twisted-pair, optical fiber, or coaxial cable installed anywhere on the premises. More exotic cabling methods include microwaves, broadcast radio, spread-spectrum radio, and existing electrical wiring.

Surprisingly, cabling is one of the most important and costly parts of a network. Cabling is important for three reasons:

 Cabling is the most difficult network element to install

 Cabling must be designed to accommodate network changes (such as growth)

 Cabling must be compatible with the upgraded equipment connected to it

Cabling still remains at the top of the list as the cause for a network's failure. Many cables must endure heat, electrical charges, and physical abuse, which eventually destroys them. The more area your LAN covers, the more the cabling becomes a critical design factor.

Twisted-Pair Wire—Nothing Kinky About It

Twisted-pair wire is very popular for networks. Like telephone wires, twisted-pair is made up of two insulated copper wires within a covering. It can carry both voice and computer information.

Coaxial cable, also called Ethernet trunk cable, is a single wire surrounded by an insulator and another solid or woven copper conductor. Coaxial cable comes in two sizes: thick and thin. The thick version is expensive and used only with Ethernet, a type of network design. The thin version—often referred to as cheapernet—is cheaper and easier to work with but may lose data over long lengths.

Fiber Optic—The Future of Communication

Fiber-optic cable consists of hair-thin strands of glass that transmit light pulses rather than electromagnetic pulses from one location to another. Fiber-optic cabling is very expensive, but it does have its advantages:

- **Safety.** The glass cable uses light, which cannot be short-circuited, shocked, or sparked.

- **Capacity.** A single glass fiber can handle more than 240,000 telephone calls.

- **Immunity to electrical disturbances.** Optical fibers do not cause electromagnetic interference (EMI) nor are they subject to it. This makes optical fibers free of electrical "noise" and cross-talk (such as when you can hear other phone conversations).

- **Security.** Fiber-optic cables are almost impossible to tap. If the glass fiber is tapped, the light signal is broken.

The FCC now is allowing phone companies to transmit video signals, which are ideally carried by fiber-optic cables. With precedents like this, the U.S. telephone system is slowly changing from a mechanical (klunky) network into one that carries digital information. When finished, the change will be like going from a scratchy record player to digital audio tape.

Crash! The Network's Down

Networks are not for the faint of heart. Although the benefits are many, they often cause an occasional headache. Sometimes, the network will simply not work. You find yourself unable to log in or stuck in the middle of a software program. This is called a network crash. These crashes can last from ten minutes to an entire day, depending on the cause and your distance from a nerd or someone who knows how to fix the problem. When a crash happens, consider the following:

- Once the network crashes, you can still use your PC. You simply can't use the files or printers that are available exclusively on the network.

- Leave any network problems to the network administrator to resolve. A network is a complex combination of software, computers, and cables—trust the network professional to fix the problem.

- If you are not involved in running the network, use the crash to do other tasks, such as an early coffee break or a reason to run an errand out of the office. If the delay is going to be lengthy, you'd better find something productive before you blow a fuse (your own fuse, that is). Go home early; blame the network administrator.

- If you were printing a document when the network crashed, your document may still be printed. Simply have the network person check the print queue (pronounced "cue"). The print queue should still hold your document. If not, send it again after the network comes out of its coma.

Picking a Protocol

Often, when asked what type of network they're using, people mention words like Ethernet or Token-Ring. These are specific network protocols, or rules for running the network. The protocols used by your network adapter cards and the software that come with them require a certain network topology, or design.

Several topologies exist, including ring, star, and bus. Each describes the arrangement of the PCs and other equipment on the network. For example, ring topologies require all computers to be connected in a closed, circular formation. A certain topology is often dictated by specific network protocols, or rules. Ethernet, for example, requires a linear, or bus topology. A Token-Ring protocol requires a ring topology.

The network choices may appear dizzying, but yours will work out just fine once you get the node (pun intended) from management.

PART 6

Finding Help

CHAPTER
17

Computer Heimlich Maneuvers (Or, Help! My Computer Is Choking!)

C omputers aren't perfect. (Sometimes, neither is the operator.) Some days, your PC may choke. When your PC refuses to run or acts irrationally, its condition can be called a number of things. You can say your PC has "crashed," is "frozen," or has "locked up." What can you do about these conditions?

This chapter illustrates techniques you can use to clear your PC's throat and bring it back from death's door, such as:

- Uncovering changes that may be affecting your PC
- Restarting (rebooting) your PC
- Erasing corrupted files
- Checking loose or unconnected cables outside and inside your PC
- Discovering if your hard disk is about to die
- Tracking down memory-resident or buggy software

- Recovering from internal battery problems
- Determining if competing expansion cards are causing conflicts
- Common printer and mouse problems
- Creating a boot disk
- Restoring accidentally formatted disks
- Restoring accidentally erased files
- Catching Windows errors

Causes of Computer Problems

You can't avoid the occasional computer glitch. (I call them PC "hiccups.") For sometimes obvious but often mysterious reasons, your PC may freeze and lose your unsaved work. The cause may be an imperceptible drop in power from your electrical company, stray cosmic rays, or another user.

When your computer ceases to work or other damage is done, don't panic. The following sections may help you revive it. If not, Chapter 18 points you to technical assistance options.

The Eight Symptoms of Choking

When a person is choking, several signals usually include a reddened face, frantic hand gestures, and bulging eyes. Your choking PC may also offer a variety of signs:

- Your computer doesn't start at all.
- Your PC tries to start, but displays an error code or phrase and stops there.
- The software you are using stops working and displays the same screen, as if it is trapped in time. Sometimes the mouse cursor still works; you can move the arrow all over the screen but you can't make any choices.
- Your PC works, but you can't print anything.

Your keyboard suddenly becomes unusable, and after you press several keys, the computer starts to beep at you.

The screen becomes a multicolored, blinking display of esoteric characters and boxes.

Your PC suddenly restarts itself, even though you were in the middle of using a software program.

Your PC acts slow and sluggish.

The best way to get your PC operating again is to work by the numbers. You can take several steps when your PC is choking.

What Am I Doing Differently?

Sometimes the key to finding the cure to a problem is to analyze what happened before the problem. The key lies in comparing the current condition of the PC to when the PC was working. Ask yourself two related questions: "When was the PC last able to perform the task?" and "What has changed since then?" The correct answers to these questions begin to lead to a solution.

You next need to isolate the problem. Under what circumstances does the problem occur? Does it happen only when you print, or only when you run a particular software program? Does the problem only occur when using a certain software program? One aid in pinpointing problems is to check the error messages that may appear during the self-diagnosis your PC performs during its warm-up. The numbers by themselves aren't very helpful, except to experienced technicians. The message `1790 - Disk 0 Error` means a defective hard disk, for example. A technician may have a manual that lists the solution for that error code.

Start Over

The best way to fix a problem is to start over from scratch. (No, don't buy another PC.) Ninety percent of the time, restarting your PC brings it back to life. Don't rush to this solution, however; if you are in the middle of some work, you will lose the unsaved portion if you restart your PC. Try to do everything possible to regain control of your PC, such as:

Chapter 17: Computer Heimlich Maneuvers (Or, Help! My Computer Is Choking!)

340

 Press the Esc key. The Esc key often regains your computer's undivided attention.

 Press Ctrl-Break or Ctrl-C. Like the Esc key, these key combinations also wake up a snoozing PC.

If these two steps fail, you have three choices to restart it, in this order:

1. **Press Ctrl-Alt-Del.** These three keys perform a *warm boot* to your computer; in other words, you are restarting your PC even though it is already warmed up. These three keys restart, or *reboot*, your computer without requiring you to turn it off.

2. Press your PC's Reset button. Sometimes your keyboard may refuse the Ctrl-Alt-Del command. Press the Reset button on the front of your PC to perform the same thing.

3. Turn your PC off, then on again. As a last resort, turn off your PC. Leave it off for about five seconds so that all those fancy computer chips are cleared of any stored electricity.

Once your PC is rebooted, it often behaves normally. You've cleared its throat and it can now resume eating. If none of these funky key combinations work, read on or call in a PC nerd. Later sections in this chapter discuss other problems that you can fix yourself.

Erase Leftover Files

If you were stuck in the middle of a software program when you had to reboot your PC, you may have some partial files on your hard disk that must be removed. These are called *corrupted files* or *lost chains*. Use the DOS CHKDSK command to clear these. CHKDSK (pronounced "check disk") crudely diagnoses and "fixes" these damaged files. To use CHKDSK, follow these easy steps:

1. From your DOS prompt, type

   ```
   CHKDSK /F
   ```

CHKDSK can recover files only if you have used the /F switch. The report on your screen shows information about your hard disk. If any files are damaged, you will see a message similar to this one:

```
10 lost allocation units found in 3 chains.
Convert lost chains to files?
```

2. Answer "Y" to convert the lost chains.

DOS saves the damaged files to your root, or top, directory, such as C:\ or A:\. These files are saved with the name FILE*nnnn*.CHK, (*nnnn* is the number of the file). The first file is FILE0000.CHK, the second FILE0001.CHK, and so on.

3. You can see if the recovered files might have some value. (They rarely do.) From the DOS prompt, type

    `TYPE FILE0000.CHK`

The file displays on-screen. From this, you should be able to determine if you want to keep these files or can them.

4. If these files are just taking up space and you see no need to keep them, kick 'em out! To do so, type

    `DEL FILE*.CHK`

The recovered files vaporize into the ether of useless information.

Don't Trust Yourself

A computer isn't perfect and neither is its operator. Sometimes we are the cause of computer problems (after all, we're not nerds). For example, I use a switch box to switch between my dot matrix and laser printers. From time to time I'll forget to switch to the printer I want to use. I'll then scratch my head wondering where my document is and why the printer isn't working. Other times, I'll forget that I didn't reconnect all the cables, or that I changed my CONFIG.SYS startup file. But hey, nobody's perfect, right?

NERDY
DETAILS

GEEK

In other cases the problem may be even simpler. I heard of a dBase III teacher who was wondering why a student was staring at the keyboard. "I'm looking for the 'any' key," the student said. The teacher looked at the screen and saw that the program wanted the student to "Press any key to continue." (There is no "any" key, so just press the Enter key or Spacebar.)

Chapter 17: Computer Heimlich Maneuvers (Or, Help! My Computer Is Choking!)

342

Some of these snafus may not be your fault. It's possible that others using your PC have made changes without telling you. They may innocently make changes that are perfectly natural to them but throw you for a loop. They may habitually turn down the brightness of your monitor to prevent phosphor burn-in (see Chapter 10) for example. When you return to your PC, you may wonder why your screen is blank even though the monitor's power is on.

Before you run to the phone to call a computer repair person or the software manufacturer, check to see if you accidentally misinterpreted any instructions or made any recent changes. So remember, before you dial 911 for computers, or send a bomb threat to the software company, ask yourself: "Did I miss an instruction? Is anything different? Could someone else have used my stuff?"

Power, Power, Power

When your PC simply doesn't start, you may have a power problem. Suppose, for example, you turn on your PC and cannot hear the hum of its cooling fan or the familiar starting grind of its disk drives; even the front panel lights are blank. At worst, the power supply inside the PC is broken and needs to be replaced. At best, you may simply have to plug your PC into the wall. Check these items:

- Check that your PC's power cable is firmly plugged into the back of the PC and the wall outlet. Janitorial staff may accidentally pull the plug from the wall, or your outstretched legs may coax the cord from its socket.

- Plug another electrical device—such as a lamp—into the power strip (if you use one) or the outlet. If the lamp doesn't come on, press the reset button on the power strip and try again. If the power strip still doesn't work, plug the lamp directly into the wall outlet. If the wall outlet works, get a new power strip. If the power strip and wall outlet are okay, get a new power supply.

- Check that the wall outlet is on. Some outlets may be turned on by a wall switch.

- Check the circuit breaker. A power surge may cause the circuit breaker to trip, turning off the power. Reset the circuit breaker. If it trips again, you may have a serious power problem. Something in your home or building is causing the circuit breaker to be overwhelmed.

NERDY
DETAILS

The Johnson Space Center in Houston had a confusing power problem. Employees at the NASA center experienced mysterious computer crashes when several LaserJet Series II printers and PCs were on the same power line. Such laser printers often have to draw a substantial amount of energy to keep their heating elements ready for work.

When several printers are periodically "revving their engines" on the same electrical circuit, the power drop can cause nearby computers to restart themselves. This problem occurs only if your electrical system is already marginal and has several laser printers connected to it. What's the cure? Your only choices are to upgrade the line or try filtering the power using a line conditioner.

Hard Disk Hassles

Your hard disk is the most likely computer component to fail, for three reasons:

 The hardware goes bad. The disk controller card, the electronics on the drive, or the cable that connects them may become worn or broken.

 The disk medium may go bad. The thin coating of magnetic particles that cover the drive's platters may be too thin or worn away by a literal crash of the heads onto the platter.

 Software run amok. Some software programs you are running may go berserk and write to areas that are supposed to be off-limits, such as portions of the disk that allow it to start, or boot.

You occasionally see early warning signs of an impending hard disk failure. Some warning signs include:

 You can't retrieve a certain file, or you find unintelligible characters in your work files.

 The drive takes longer than usual to find and load a file.

 The drive occasionally fails to start your computer.

Chapter 17: Computer Heimlich Maneuvers (Or, Help! My Computer Is Choking!)

344

If you see any of these signs, back up your work before doing anything else. Then run a program that will carefully analyze your disk and fix the problem. Often, such software utilities as Norton Utilities, PC Tools, and Spinrite Gold can rescue your hard disk. Sometimes these are only short-term solutions to an eventual outright disk failure. Your hard disk is hemorrhaging and you're only giving it a Band-Aid. If your hard disk requires these utilities, make sure that you back up your work often. The Band-Aid eventually may require a tourniquet—a whole new hard disk.

Make Sure You're Well Connected

Cables are often overlooked when a problem appears. These thin pieces of wire connect the vital parts of your PC, including the printer, modem, CD-ROM drive, monitor, and more. Often, a problem can be fixed by checking the connections:

 Check that all external cables are firmly attached. It's best to use the special connectors on each side of the cable to screw in or clamp to the connected device. For example, printers often have two wire levers that firmly clamp onto the printer cable. Also, check that the ends of each cable are not cracked or frayed. Although the cable may be connected, it may be worn from abuse. You can check the quality of a cable by borrowing a new cable from a friend or using a spare.

 Check that all external cables are attached to the correct ports. Although a cable may fit a certain port, or connector, it may be connected to the wrong one. For example, I have an internal modem that doubles as a voice mail system. The outgoing phone line can be connected to only one of the two telephone jacks. If I plug the phone line into the wrong one, I can still use my phone, but my modem cannot dial out when I call an on-line service, such as CompuServe or PRODIGY.

Check the Internal Cables

Your PC also has internal parts that may jiggle free of their connections. Those parts may include:

 Ribbon cables

 Power cables

Expansion cards

 Memory chips

If you are comfortable with a screwdriver, you can check the inside connections of your PC. Use the steps in Chapter 20 to open your computer.

STOP!

> Before working on the inside of your computer, make sure the PC is not plugged into the electrical outlet. With the risk of electrical shock at hand, not only will your PC need to be rescued... you will too.

The first culprits of your PC troubles may be ribbon cables used to control parts of your PC. *Ribbon cables* look like flattened packs of gray licorice. These are often attached to your disk drives and may come loose when your PC is moved or bumped. Press each end of the ribbon cable to its connection to ensure that they are snugly attached.

Like ribbon cables, power cables inside your PC may also come loose—although this is rare. These power cables are also connected to disk drives and other parts of your PC that require power, such as a tape drive. The power cables are often made of two to four wires. Press each power cable firmly onto each connector.

The expansion cards your PC uses may also cause problems. The constant heating and cooling inside your PC may loosen the card in its slot. The copper teeth inserted into the motherboard also may become tarnished. You can fix both of these problems by removing and then reinstalling each card (often referred to as *reseating*).

STOP!

> Before you touch an expansion card, touch a metal object nearby, such as the inside of your computer's case, to drain yourself of static electricity. Do not touch any of the components on the card because static electricity may damage the sensitive electronic parts on the card. In addition, do not touch the gold edges on the card.

Simply loosen and remove the screw that holds each card in place. When
you remove an expansion card, rock the card back and forth along its length.
Do not twist the card from side to side, but pull up alternately on each end.
Be careful where you grab the card; there may be delicate components that
you could crush. Carefully grab the card by its metal bracket and edges.
After you remove each card, insert it back into its slot and tighten the screw.
By reinserting the expansion card, any corrosion is rubbed off.

TRICKS

You can also clean the copper connectors of each expansion
card. Use a cleaning swab—such as a Q-Tip—and isopropyl
alcohol to clean them. Dip the swab in the alcohol and wipe
each contact. Do not use a rubber eraser to clean these
contacts. Not only can eraser crumbs be left behind, but the
eraser may wear away the contact's copper coat.

Some computer problems are caused by *chip creep*: computer chips work
their way out of place because of constant heating and cooling. Look for
chips on your motherboard and expansion cards that aren't soldered into
place. Give each a gentle push to seat them firmly into their sockets. When
you press a chip on an expansion card, use one hand to support the other
side of the card.

NERDY
DETAILS

It may sound silly to press on a computer chip that already
looks firmly attached. I had an enlightening experience,
however, with a PC I sold to a real estate agent. Soon after
buying the PC, the agent complained that the computer was
acting strangely. The computer was operating at about half
speed and often choked. This was a six-month-old PC, so I was
sure it was not defective. After a visual inspection, I saw
nothing wrong, so I opened it up. After pushing down on a few
computer chips, the PC acted fine. The owner has had no
complaints since.

Conflicting Cards

Some expansion cards that may work fine individually can conflict with
other cards in your PC (these conflicts are discussed in Chapter 9). One way

to pinpoint the problem is to remove all nonessential expansion cards, leaving only the monitor and drive controller. Some PCs have these built into the motherboard—your PC's electronic foundation. If your problem disappears, replace the cards one at a time until the problem shows up again. In addition, disconnect your printer, modem, or other peripherals one at a time to see if the problem persists. Many of these peripherals have built-in selftests. Try them to make sure they're working right.

Clean Up Your Act

Accumulated dust can also cause your PC to choke. A typical house accumulates about 40 pounds of dust each year. What's in dust? Usually soil particles, although 300 million tons of sea salt are placed in the air every year as well. This salt and dirt can corrode and overheat your PC by encasing the individual computer chips with a dust overcoat.

To prolong the life of your computer, occasionally dust off the system unit, keyboard, monitor, and any other related equipment. When your PC is open, use a can of compressed air to blow dust off the expansion cards and chips. Make sure you get computer-grade air, not just air used for camera lenses. This canned air must be free of moisture and contaminants. A popular ingredient to look for is *chlorodifluoromethane*. Avoid canned air that uses Freon TF as a propellant; it generates static electricity as it leaves the nozzle, which could ruin electronic components (not to mention the ozone layer). Blow the dust away from your computer (you want to remove, not just move, the dust).

Blame the Software

Often, a computer problem may be linked to its software. A software problem can masquerade as a hardware failure. Some possible pitfalls include:

 Memory-resident software that conflicts with your other software

 Buggy software

A memory-resident program (also called terminate-and-stay-resident, TSR, and pop-up software) is a second program available to you at the touch of a key. The TSR program lurks in the background until you request it. For example, you can be in the middle of a WordPerfect document and press a key to use SideKick (an electronic calendar TSR program). When you finish entering an appointment, you can return to your document. These TSR programs sometimes fight with other software programs, such as Microsoft Windows. The solution may be to prevent the TSR program from loading to see if it may be the cause of your problem.

Similarly, some software programs are merely the victims of poor design that result in problems. I've owned software programs that have caused my PC to flash in multiple colors and characters because not enough testing was done on the software. If you're having trouble printing, for example, try to print using a different program. If you can isolate your problems to a specific software package, return it and get your money back.

One Little Battery

Your PC requires a little battery to remember crucial information about itself. This internal battery provides the necessary juice to a type of computer chip called a CMOS (pronounced "see-moss"). This CMOS remembers the following information:

 Number of sectors and cylinders contained on the hard disk

 Amount of memory

 Number of floppy disk drives

You're already familiar with this battery; it provides the date and time so that you don't have to enter it each time you turn on your PC. These batteries do not die suddenly; they just fade away, giving intermittent results until they finally expire. One symptom of a dead battery is something you can see: if the date reads Tue. Jan 1, 1980, it's time for a new battery.

A typical battery lasts about five years. If yours dies, your PC won't recognize your hard disk, and therefore, it won't start. You should have a technician replace the battery for you.

GEEK

Some computers use common household AA batteries that you can replace yourself for the clock.

NERDY
DETAILS

The information retained by the CMOS may not be anywhere else. How many cylinders does your hard disk have? What is its landing zone? If you don't know these answers and cannot find them in your computer's manual, you should print this information before it's too late. If you fail to write down this information and disconnect the battery, you may have to waste a few hours getting your PC running again.

All modern PCs have a special Setup program that accesses this information. (Older 8088/8086 PCs do not have a Setup program.) How you get to this information depends on your computer brand. On some brands, you must press the Escape key, Del key, or F1 key as your PC warms up. Watch your screen as your PC starts. Often, a message explains which key you should press. Start this Setup program and look for the number of cylinders and sectors on your hard disk.

When you see this information, turn on your printer, wait while it warms up, then press the Print Screen key to print the information on the screen to your printer. (In some cases you may have to press Shift-Print Screen or Alt-Print Screen to send the information to the printer.) Save this information for future reference. If your little battery dies, you won't get run down getting your PC up and running.

Common Printer Problems

The most common problems occur when printing. Use this laundry list to figure out and fix your printer problem:

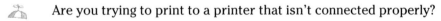

- Are you trying to print to a printer that isn't connected properly?

- Are you trying to print to one kind of printer, such as an Epson, when you actually own a different brand, such as an HP LaserJet? Check which printer you selected from within your software program.

- Are you out of paper or is your printer experiencing a paper jam?

- Is your printer Off Line? Press the On Line button so that your printer can accept your document.

The Trouble with Mice

Although mice are usually very reliable, getting them to work can be a challenge. The first thing to be aware of is that mice need to have some way of communicating with your computer. Most mice do this through one of the serial ports (typically COM1 or COM2).

After the mouse is connected, you need to turn it on by loading the mouse driver software. (If you use Microsoft Windows, don't worry about this.) The mouse driver brings your mouse to life. When you install your mouse, its installation program may alter the CONFIG.SYS or AUTOEXEC.BAT startup file so that the mouse driver software loads every time you turn on your PC. You can activate your mouse yourself: typically, you just type **MOUSE** from the C:\ prompt. The mouse software may tell you that the mouse is indeed connected, plus list some unimportant copyright information.

The most common mouse mistake is when rodent owners don't tell the software which serial port they are using for the mouse—although often, the mouse software automatically finds the mouse on its own. If you install your mouse software and find that the mouse does not work at all, try changing the port into which the mouse is plugged. Here are some other tips:

 Keep in mind that not all software can use your mouse. Only programs that say they support a mouse can be used. Plain old DOS cannot use a mouse, for example.

 Occasionally the mouse cursor (the little arrow) may disappear. Simply move your mouse; this should cause the mouse cursor to reappear.

 Software programs that don't support a mouse may do so with some coaxing. Many mice come with software utilities that enable you to add pull-down menus to your existing software. If you feel like playing around with this, consult your mouse manual.

Tools for a Troublefree PC— The Boot Disk

If you've read anything else in this book, you've probably read about changing the CONFIG.SYS file. Making changes to this file is not difficult, but if you misspell a word or include a space where a space shouldn't be, your computer will freak out every time you turn it on, and you won't even be able to see what's wrong. Your computer isn't broken, it just can't start. For example, you may see a message, such as BAD OR MISSING COMMAND INTERPRETER.

One essential tool every non-nerd should own is a *boot*, or *system*, disk. This floppy disk is an emergency disk that you use if your computer won't start on its own. By having your PC start from this special floppy disk, you can regain control of your PC and fix the mistakes to CONFIG.SYS or fix other problems.

To make a bootable floppy disk, place a blank disk in drive A, your first and possibly only floppy disk drive. (Boot disks usually do not work from drive B.) From the DOS prompt, type

FORMAT A: /S

This command formats the floppy disk. The /S switch at the end adds enough of the operating system to the boot disk to start a computer. After the boot disk formats, you can then copy some DOS files you may need when a crisis looms.

NERDY
DETAILS

When I was called to a high school in southern Minnesota, I used a boot disk to revive a dead library computer. I drove 20 miles and fixed the problem in five minutes. It seemed one of the students accidentally deleted the COMMAND.COM file.

This crucial DOS file allows your PC to start from its hard disk. Without it, you must start your PC from the floppy disk drive. To fix the library's computer, I first placed a boot disk (described in this section) in the PC and started the PC. I then copied the COMMAND.COM file from the boot disk to the PC's root, or top, directory. When I restarted the PC, everything was back to normal.

The following files are highly recommended additions to a boot disk:

- **CHKDSK.EXE.** Provides disk and memory information
- **EDIT.COM.** Provides a simple text editor you can use to edit the startup files and other files (DOS 5.0 only)
- **QBASIC.EXE.** Required to get EDIT.COM to work (DOS 5.0 only)
- **FDISK.EXE.** Changes the size of your hard disk before formatting it
- **FORMAT.COM.** Formats a disk drive

352

Chapter 17: Computer Heimlich Maneuvers (Or, Help! My Computer Is Choking!)

 UNDELETE.EXE. Restores a file that you accidentally deleted (DOS 5.0 only)

 UNFORMAT.COM. Restores a disk erased by the FORMAT command (DOS 5.0 only)

To copy these files to the boot disk, type

```
COPY C:\DOS\filename A:
```

Add any of the files in the list to the *filename* slot.

You should test your boot disk before you throw it in some drawer. Leave the boot disk in drive A and turn off your computer. If the boot disk works, your PC should read it, ask you for the date and time, and then display a plain DOS prompt of A:>. Remove the boot disk and restart your computer again to get back to your normal work.

Unformatting a Disk

Typically, when you format a disk, you are wiping it clean and preparing it to save new information. Still, you may be able to rescue your hard disk or floppy disk after an accidental format. DOS 5.0 includes an UNFORMAT utility, UNFORMAT.COM, that can recover data from an accidentally formatted disk. If you used the DOS 5.0 Safe Format or Quick Format, the files still are on the formatted disk. (The Safe Format is the default method DOS uses to format previously formatted disks.) To unformat a hard disk or floppy disk:

1. Ensure that you have UNFORMAT.COM available.

If you formatted your hard disk, you need to insert either your original DOS disk or your book disk with the UNFORMAT utility on it. If you want to unformat a floppy disk in drive A, the UNFORMAT.COM file is already in your DOS directory.

GEEK

Do not save information to a disk you've accidentally formatted. If you do, you lessen your chances of unformatting it.

NERDY
DETAILS

2. Start the UNFORMAT process. From the DOS prompt, type

`C:\DOS\`**UNFORMAT** `D:`

C:\DOS is the drive and path where your UNFORMAT.COM file is located, and *D:* is the letter of the drive you want to unformat. In some cases, you do not need to type `C:\DOS` because your PC may know where this file is located.

3. Answer "Y" (yes) that you want to update the system area on the formatted drive.

UNFORMAT restores your file information and recovers your disk. If you are unformatting a hard disk, you may have to restart your computer. The unformatting process may take several minutes.

Saving Deleted Files

Like formatting, deleting files from a disk can be undone. Since your PC doesn't erase the actual files (it simply doesn't reserve the spaces occupied by them), you can easily bring these files back to life after accidentally erasing them. Several unerase programs are available. However, DOS 5.0 includes UNDELETE.COM free of charge.

STOP!

UNDELETE is not the godsend it seems to be. It's great to have a command that reverses a stupid mistake, but only if it works all the time. UNDELETE is not 100% successful at recovering files. If you delete everything in a directory by mistake (Oh no, I wanted to delete everything on the floppy disk, but forgot to add the A: to the line!), only about half your files will be recovered successfully.

To avoid having to rely on the imperfect UNDELETE command, try this:

 Create a TRASH directory in DOS. It's easy to do: just type **MD \TRASH.** Whenever you want to delete some file on the hard drive or on a floppy disk, first copy the file to the TRASH directory, then delete it from its original home. Later, when you want to

continues

Chapter 17: Computer Heimlich Maneuvers (Or, Help! My Computer Is Choking!)

354

continued

clean up your hard disk, you can always type **CD \TRASH,** and then **DEL *.*** *and delete everything in the TRASH directory.*

 Whenever you plan to rename or delete something from the DOS prompt, always hesitate before you press Enter. Stop and reread the line you just typed to make sure everything that should be in the command is there. The most common (and danger-ous) mistake is to type the delete command and forget **A:** or **B:** in the command.

If you don't want to do either of these things, use Windows' File Manager to delete files.

To save a file you've accidentally erased, you must undelete it as soon as possible. If you save any other work before trying to save your lost file, you reduce your chances of success. To use the UNDELETE command:

1. After accidentally deleting a file, type

   UNDELETE *C:\PATH\FILE*

C:\PATH\FILE is the drive, directory, and file name of the file you acciden-tally deleted. A list of deleted files are listed. In place of *FILE*, you can use wildcards, such as *.LET to display deleted files ending with the letters .LET.

2. For each file displayed, answer "Y" to those you want to undelete.
3. For each file, provide the first letter of its name.

If a file already exists with the same name, provide a different first letter.

Mirror, Mirror

Both the UNFORMAT and UNDELETE commands work much better if the DOS 5.0 MIRROR program is used. MIRROR.COM creates a file that records which files have been deleted.

To use MIRROR, add the following line to the last line in the AUTOEXEC.BAT startup file:

```
C:\DOS\MIRROR D: E: /TD /TE
```

C:\DOS is the drive and path to your directory of DOS files; *D:* and *E:* are the drives you want to protect. The */TD* and */TE* switches load the deletion-tracking portion of MIRROR for the drive letters you provide.

A small amount of your computer's memory is used when the /T switch is used (usually less than 7K). This memory used by the memory-resident portion of MIRROR is well worth it if you want to undelete almost any file.

You may want to disable MIRROR temporarily if you are about to delete or create many files you are certain you won't want to undelete. By disabling MIRROR, you can keep the PCTRACKR.DEL file from filling with this unwanted file information.

Catching Windows Errors

Microsoft Windows includes two ways to catch and diagnose Windows errors. First, Windows 3.1 includes a diagnostic utility called Dr. Watson.

Dr. Watson is installed by running DRWATSON.EXE. When an error occurs in Windows, Dr. Watson saves the commands leading up to the error in a simple text file called DRWATSON.LOG. From this text file, which you can browse in the Windows Notepad or other word processor, you can see what happened. If you can't figure out the problem, the text may help Microsoft technical support staff.

To install Dr. Watson, make the Startup group the active group. Select **N**ew from the **F**ile pull-down menu. Fill in **Dr. Watson** as the description and specify DRWATSON.EXE as the command line. When you restart Windows, Dr. Watson loads automatically. (Any icon in the Startup group is loaded automatically when you start Windows.)

NERDY
DETAILS

You can also use Dr. Watson with Windows 3.0. Simply download DRWATSON.EXE and TOOLBOX.DLL from the Microsoft Product Support Download Service at

continues

continued

206-673-9009. The file name is WW0440.EXE. To start Dr. Watson automatically, edit WIN.INI using SysEdit or Notepad. In the [windows] section, add DRWATSON.EXE to the **load=** line. If there is already a program being loaded, just add a space between it and DRWATSON.EXE. Your system's WIN.INI file should look like this:

```
load=DRWATSON.EXE
run=
Beep=yes
Spooler=yes
```

Dr. Watson helps only when using Windows. If you are having trouble simply getting into Windows 3.1, try loading Windows by typing

```
WIN /B
```

If Windows locks up again, a file called BOOTLOG.TXT is created in the Windows directory that looks like this:

```
[boot]
LoadStart = SYSTEM.DRV
LoadSuccess = SYSTEM.DRV
LoadStart = KEYBOARD.DRV
LoadSuccess = KEYBOARD.DRV
LoadStart = MOUSE.DRV
LoadSuccess = MOUSE.DRV
LoadStart = VGA.DRV
LoadSuccess = VGA.DRV
LoadStart = MMSOUND.DRV
LoadSuccess = MMSOUND.DRV
LoadStart = COMM.DRV
LoadFail = COMM.DRV Failure code is 02
```

The last line indicates which file failed to load properly. You can restore the corrupt file from the original Windows disks using the EXPAND utility.

By using these tips to restore your choking PC, you won't choke on a costly repair bill for something you could have fixed or prevented yourself. A little Heimlich goes a long way.

"JUST LET ME KNOW WHEN YOU'RE DONE."

I Can't Fix It Myself— What Next?

S ometimes you have to admit defeat just to avoid self-inflicted baldness or further embarrassment. After wrestling with a computer snafu for several hours, drenched in sweat, smart people pick up the phone to call in the cavalry. Chapter 17 described techniques to isolate and fix common problems. When you're stuck with an uncommon problem, you should look for uncommon help. This chapter uncovers the uncommon problem solver and also shows you:

 Where to get free help

 What to do before you call for technical support

 How to make the most of your technical support call and get the best service from the staff there

 How to prepare your PC for (gulp!) repair

Free (or Almost Free) Help— The Best Kind!

When your PC is under the weather, several sources of free help are available. Neighbors or co-workers, for example, may be a bit more knowledgeable about computers than you. They can provide a helping hand. At the very least, they can provide a shoulder to cry on.

A local computer user group is a wonderful source of help. These groups typically meet once a month, and the meetings often consist of a demonstration by a computer hardware and/or software vendor. Often, these groups have an "open access" portion to their meeting to answer any questions members may have. For a $30 to $100 per year membership fee, these groups provide ample sources of information, including a newsletter that lists people to contact for certain questions.

You can enlarge your universe of helpful friends by using a local bulletin board system (BBS) or on-line service, such as PRODIGY or CompuServe. These services have electronic bulletin boards on which you can leave public messages asking for help. For example, I used to oversee the Computer Club bulletin board on the PRODIGY service. Over 10,000 messages are placed daily on this one board alone!

Often, people who leave messages do not provide enough up-front information. They simply write: "HELP! My printer won't print. Can you help me?"

If you're in a pickle and you want to leave a message on a BBS, make sure you provide the following info:

- Brand and type of PC you have, such as an AST Research 386/33

- Amount of memory your system has

- Peripherals attached to this PC, such as a laser printer or a modem, and their brand names

- Version of DOS you are using (to find out which version you have, type **VER** at the DOS prompt)

- Software you were using when the problem occurred

- Any recent changes that led to the problem, such as installing a new software program or an electrical storm that passed by last night

With this information, you now can start a dialogue with those who can help you. Check daily for replies to your message. Those who want to help you may need further information from you before they can do so.

Getting Technical Support

If you already own a system, you may have paid for help. The technical support staff at your computer store and telephone support that comes with the purchase of a software package are two avenues for help. Technical support by phone should be used only after you have exhausted other means. In other words, don't rush to call a company's technical support department when you haven't even cracked open the manuals!

Pre-Call Preparation

Before you call a technical support department, prepare yourself by having this stuff available:

- If your PC includes a diagnostic disk, use it before you call. Even if the diagnostic routine doesn't give you enough information to fix the problem yourself, you can at least tell the technician you did use it and can provide him or her with information the diagnostic program uncovered.

- Try to isolate the problem. For example, look for patterns. Does the problem happen only when you use a particular program or at certain times of the day? What exactly were you doing when the problem occurred?

- Try to determine if the problem is a hardware, operating system, or software application. Knowing the type of problem may save you from being bounced around among three or more technical support staff.

- Watch for error codes. Jot down any error codes that may flash on your screen. These codes can be invaluable to a trained technician.

- If the problem occurs when running a particular software program, re-install it from the original disks. The problem often is caused by a file that was copied incorrectly from the disks.

- Know the version of DOS running on your PC. Simply type VER to discover which version of DOS you are using. Your PC will respond with a message such as MS-DOS Version 5.0.

- Print copies of the AUTOEXEC.BAT and CONFIG.SYS startup files. These could be the source of your problem and may help the technician find a solution. To do so, type these scary-looking lines at the exciting C:\> (yawn...) line:

TYPE C:\AUTOEXEC.BAT >PRN (and press Enter)

TYPE C:\CONFIG.SYS >PRN (and press Enter)

Have the printouts handy when you call.

 Bored yet? If your problem is related to Microsoft Windows, print copies of the WIN.INI and SYSTEM.INI files (Chapter 6 talks about them). Use the same technique as before by typing both of these hairy-looking lines:

TYPE C:\WINDOWS\WIN.INI >PRN (and press Enter)

TYPE C:\WINDOWS\SYSTEM.INI >PRN (and press Enter)

 You can also use Windows' SysEdit utility to display these files. In fact, this utility also prints the CONFIG.SYS and AUTOEXEC.BAT files. To print each file, select **P**rint from the **F**ile pull down menu, or press Alt-F and then P (print).

 Run the DOS utility CHKDSK and write down the information that appears on-screen. This gives you and the technician a quick check on total and available drive space, and total and free memory. To use CHKDSK, type **CHKDSK** at the stimulating C:\> prompt. To send the results to the printer, type **CHKDSK >PRN**.

 Have your original sales slip or invoice number, or the serial number of the PC or software on hand. (The PC serial number can be found in back.) In just a couple of seconds, some PC makers can pull up detailed information on your PC from these numbers. Every detail concerning your computer can be displayed.

 Have some simple tools available. In some cases, the technician may have you open up your PC or make some adjustment. A basic flat-blade screwdriver or Phillips-head screwdriver may be required.

Making the Call

Okay, now you're ready to make THE CALL... Nothing is more frustrating than trying to explain computer ills over the phone. It's a laborious process and one that can be costly if you are paying for the call. On the other hand, you can't enjoy your computer if it's not working, so muster up some courage and dial that phone. Several types of phone support exist:

 Unlimited calls and **toll-free.** You call as often as you like on their quarter, not yours.

Tolls calls. You can call for technical support but you are paying for the call. Avoid being on too long. I once waited 35 minutes to speak to a technician. If you find the delay unbearable, you may be offered a chance to leave a voice mail message. Don't expect an immediate reply to your message. I once left a voice mail call for help and received a return call... three days later.

 1-900 numbers. A more-expensive variation of the toll call is the 1-900 number. Instead of speaking with a sultry Swede, you'll likely be interfacing (nerds like this phrase) with a talky techie. Although unpopular and pricy, such services often provide instant access to a knowledgeable technician. For example, I once had a hard disk that refused to be partitioned (separated) into several hard disks. No matter what I told the DOS FDISK utility to do, the hard disk refused to save the information. After spending $5 on a 1-900 call to the drive's manufacturer, I had my answer. The IDE hard disk controller card was poorly manufactured, causing electronic "static" that prevented the FDISK information from being saved. I never would have guessed this was the problem without that technician's advice.

 Premium support plans. Some companies provide technical support for a yearly fee. Usually, sophisticated software—such as accounting programs or database software—requires such plans. Sometimes these support plans can be purchased above and beyond the typical phone support. For example, I decided to purchase the $149 premium support plan for Q&A, my database/word processor software. Instead of using the run-of-the-mill phone support, I use an 800 number to speak with more qualified staff. I also can access other services, including database critiques and tip sheets. Many companies offer such support plans as an additional source of revenue. Those customers who really need prompt, intelligent help will get it... for a price.

With a premium support plan, you often must wait to speak with a technician. According to Computerworld, the average number of minutes you may be on hold is three. Fortunately, over 80 percent of all problems are solved on the first call. The average wait to receive a return call is over one hour.

Companies have an average of 63 tech support telephone lines. Some companies have hundreds. Follow these tips to make the most of these resources:

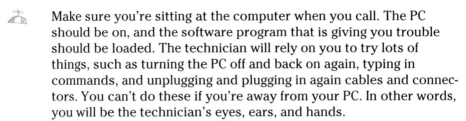 Make sure you're sitting at the computer when you call. The PC should be on, and the software program that is giving you trouble should be loaded. The technician will rely on you to try lots of things, such as turning the PC off and back on again, typing in commands, and unplugging and plugging in again cables and connectors. You can't do these if you're away from your PC. In other words, you will be the technician's eyes, ears, and hands.

Make sure you have enough time to solve the problem. Don't place the call right before lunch, an appointment, or at day's end. If a technician invests the time to answer your call for help, you should stay on the line until the problem is solved or all possible solutions have been exhausted.

Get the name of the technician as well as their phone extension, in case you have to call back. If you've spent 45 minutes describing and solving your problem, and the same problem occurs the next day, you'll save a lot of time and grief by asking for the same person you spoke with earlier.

Call between 9:30 and 11:30 a.m., or between 2:30 and 4 p.m., both Central time. These two times are when technicians have plenty of time to think carefully about your problem because the number of calls are fewest. Unless you have an emergency, wait to call during these times. The better service may be worth the delay.

If you have a non-critical problem, fax the details of your problem and your computer's setup information to the tech support department. Include a note asking them to call you on a certain day and time to work things out. With the information you provided up front, the technicians can research your problem, try to duplicate it on their test machines, and come up with good answers before they get on the phone with you. Provide a fax number, if possible; if the answer is simple, they can quickly send you a solution.

Rushing to the Repair Shop

If you must take your PC to the local repair shop or ship it back to Minnesota (or wherever it came from), you can take these steps to protect yourself:

Jot down everything you are sending—hard disks, memory, cords, monitor, and anything else. Next, record the serial number of each item. Sometimes the repair person may forget to put everything back into your PC. This way, you are assured you have at least a written record of what you sent. It's not a bad idea to include a copy of this list with your computer; that way the shop can make sure it's returning your whole kit and kaboodle. Some items, such as power cords and keyboards, do not need to be sent—unless these are a part of the problem. For example, if the keyboard works fine but the monitor is acting strange, you can assume the keyboard isn't part of the problem. Don't send it. If in doubt, ask the repair person.

If possible, make a backup of your hard disk or, at the very least, your work files before shipping your PC. Although rare, you'd hate to have a rookie technician destroy all your hard work.

You can find a good repair shop by asking around. Check with your local computer user group or club. You can also check under **Computers—Service & Repair** in your local Yellow Pages.

If your PC still is covered by a local store warranty, take it back. Typically, the labor is free, and sometimes the parts are as well. If your PC is no longer covered by a warranty, shop around for someone to fix it.

Every time you wreck your car (how recent was it?) you usually get a ton of estimates from automobile repair shops. You should do the same when your computer crashes.

Be aware of any minimum charges for simply examining your broken PC. Some shops charge up to $50 per hour to peruse your computer. When you get a reasonable estimate, proceed with the repairs. In most consumer-conscious states, you can be billed only for the repairs you've approved. The rest is free.

Pack your PC in its original boxes (if you still have them) before you bring it to the shop. Reinsert the plastic or cardboard floppy disk inserts that came with your PC. These keep the read/write heads from being damaged in transit.

Insist that the repair shop guarantee its work—parts and labor. (Twenty thousand disk spins or 20 power-ups, whichever comes first?) Don't simply accept the manufacturer's warranty for the parts they may use in repairing your PC. You want the shop to guarantee its installation of these parts, not the parts themselves.

Often, computer repairs take a few days. If you want immediate repairs, be prepared to pay a premium for that level of service. In some cases, you may be able to get a "loaner" PC. Hopefully with little effort, you can install your software onto this loaner and be up and running while your PC is recuperating.

When you get your PC up and running again, you can resume your work and put this pain-in-the-butt experience behind you. Statistically, you may not have another problem ever again.

PART 7

Upgrading Your Computer

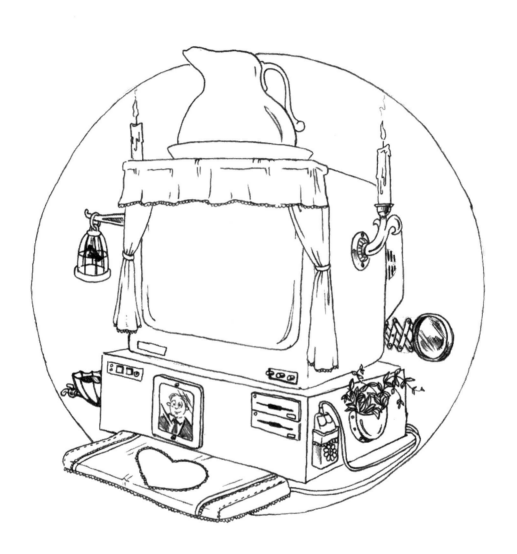

CHAPTER
19

Popular Things That Are Easy To Add to Your PC (You Don't Have To Take the Cover Off!)

F orget for a moment the few thousand dollars your PC cost. What about the fun, cheap, easy things you can add to it for $10 to $200? The addition of a few accessories can make your computer more powerful and easier to use.

You can add a cornucopia of computer contraptions (whew!) with little fuss or muss. In fact, you don't even have to look under your PC's hood! It's that simple. This chapter covers

- Buying your PC a pet and cleaning up after it
- An upright mouse versus a trackball (a mouse on its back)
- Making the right connections with a modem
- Game software + Joystick = cheap thrills
- Other accessories for the fashion-conscious PC

Most PC accessories simply plug into existing holes (called ports) on the back of your PC. At worst, you may have to load some software to bring the accessory to life. (See Chapter 13 for information on different kinds of ports.)

Adding a Mouse without a Peep

Most computer users have (or want) a plastic rodent called a mouse scampering all over their desk. (It sure beats the ones with actual hair.) The mouse looks like a bar of soap. Most mice have a "tail" that attaches to the back of the PC through either a mouse or serial port.

The mouse lets you use your software without contorting your fingers to type such key combinations as Ctrl-Shift-F or Ctrl-Z. With a mouse, you simply move the mouse body on your desk. A rolling ball in the mouse belly tells your PC to move the *mouse cursor* or *mouse pointer* (usually shaped like an arrow) on the screen. Move the mouse right, the screen arrow moves right; move left, it moves left.

A PC mouse, which has two or three buttons on its back, makes it easy to choose a menu and to initiate other actions. Imagine you have an important document to edit and you have to change a word. Without a mouse, you have to press the down arrow to move the cursor to your line. You then have to press the right arrow until you reach your word. With a mouse, you simply place the mouse cursor over the spot you want your cursor to be and press the left mouse button. Bingo! You're there!

Mouse buttons can also handle other functions, depending on your software. In most cases, you will use only the left mouse button.

Why aren't mice included with every computer? Because many software programs do not take advantage of the little creatures. You can't use a mouse from the DOS prompt, for instance. (You can click on the mouse all you want and the infinitely boring c:\> prompt will sit there.) All Windows software programs and a number of DOS programs now highly recommend using a mouse.

Mice come in two styles: serial and bus. Both work the same way but connect to your PC differently. A *serial mouse* simply plugs into one of your PC's serial, or COM, ports. (You usually have one or possibly two serial ports.) With one move, you can add a mouse. A *bus mouse*, on the other hand, plugs into a special card that comes with the mouse. This card is installed into your PC's expansion bus. Hence the name "bus mouse." You install this card into your PC by popping your computer's hood (this is covered in Chapter 20).

There are no advantages of one mouse over another. The serial mouse is less expensive because it doesn't require a bus card. Some people opt for the bus mouse to save their single serial port for another gizmo, such as an external modem (described later) or a serial printer. If you have a spare serial port, buy the serial mouse. You can plug it in and start working immediately.

NERDY
DETAILS

Some mice lack a tail. These *cordless mice* use the latest and greatest technology to send their signals to your PC. The mouse has its own transmitter to beam infrared or radio waves to a small receiving unit, which connects to your PC through a cable. Without a cord, your mouse won't be twisting its tail in the other cables behind your desk.

A cordless mouse requires batteries, so keep a spare set on hand. An infrared cordless mouse must be within a direct line of sight of the receiver. When the mouse misbehaves, the line of sight may be blocked.

Driving Miss Rodent

A mouse comes with its own software program. This program brings your mouse to life so that it can tell your PC where it's moving. The small software program is called a *mouse driver* because it "drives" your mouse. Common names for this driver are MOUSE.COM and MOUSE.SYS. Once installed, this software is started from your AUTOEXEC.BAT or CONFIG.SYS startup files.

TRICKS

If you only use Windows software, you don't need to load a mouse driver to use your mouse. Windows recognizes the mouse without it. The advantage of not using the mouse driver is that you can return the memory this driver would have used to your software programs. The extra memory can make your programs a little faster because they'll have more elbowroom in your PC's memory.

Danger: Mouse Area

Like real mice, a PC mouse needs a place to hang out. This area on your desk is called the *mouse area*. Sometimes your mouse, which has a rolling ball in its belly, may need some traction when it moves on a slippery surface. A *mouse pad,* a rectangular piece of plastic or rubber, solves this problem. Many computer stores sell "designer" mouse pads that have pictures of movie stars or artistic designs, but a plain white or blue pad works just as well. Some manufacturers give away these pads at computer trade shows or as a reward when you return their warranty cards. No matter which type of mouse pad you use, make sure it has a rough surface for the mice feet (little ball) to really dig in.

Always keep your mouse pad clean. Avoid spilling food or beverages on the pad, and occasionally wipe it clean. Don't use the mousepad as a placemat or coaster.

You may be all thumbs with the mouse at first, but it is easy to use. Gently place your hand on (not under) the mouse. Your fingers should hover over the buttons along the top. Don't let your fingers get lazy and press on the buttons. These buttons may be sensitive—you may accidentally do some-thing you didn't want to. You move the mouse by rolling it across your desk, or by pivoting your wrist.

NERDY
DETAILS

At a former job, a coworker purchased a mouse. She was stymied because she didn't know how to use it. She was sitting at her desk and holding the mouse at the far right edge of the desk. The mouse was about to jump off the pressed-wood precipice. "What do I do now?" she asked. "I'm at the edge here and my cursor still isn't where I want it." I had to explain, without laughing, that she could pick the mouse up, place it elsewhere on the desk and continue moving the mouse to the right.

If you're left-handed (as I am), your mouse software can accommodate your "specialty." In Windows, for example, you can use the Control Panel to swap the left and right mouse buttons. In my case, I learned to use a mouse with my right hand. If you are a lefty and new to mice, learn to use the mouse with your right hand. This will allow you to use other people's mice and com-puter desks without having to make any changes. Soon, using your right hand with the mouse will become a natural movement.

Your Mouse Has the Moves

Four basic mouse techniques include pointing, clicking, double-clicking, and dragging.

You can move the mouse to maneuver the cursor on-screen. Once the pointer is where you want it, click the mouse button to select the item. To click, simply press and quickly release the mouse button. *Double-clicking* means quickly pressing the button twice. If you wait too long between clicks, the double-click becomes two separate clicks.

Do not move your mouse in the process of double-clicking—you want to click on the same spot. Often, clicking is used to select an item and double-clicking is used to open it. Sometimes, you may need to move objects around your screen—this process is called *dragging*. To drag an object, place the cursor on an item, press and hold down the mouse button, and move the mouse while the button is pressed. In some programs, dragging may also enable you to select a portion of the screen.

Cleaning Your Mouse Ball (No Gloves Required)

The mouse ball can collect a lot of grime just by rolling around on your desk. One symptom of a dirty mouse is that the mouse slides more than it rolls or that the mouse pointer skips across your screen more than it glides.

To clean your mouse ball, you must remove the round cover from the bottom of the mouse. Typically these either turn or slide off. Once the cover is off, you can remove the ball and clean the lint and dirt sticking to the rollers the ball moves against. Use a pointed nonmetal object such as a toothpick to remove the dirt.

First pry off the larger chunks of dirt from each roller; then use a foam swab lightly dipped in isopropyl alcohol to clean off the remaining dirt. You can use a can of compressed air to clear loose dust and dirt from inside the mouse's body.

If your mouse gets dirty often, examine your work area. Do you leave food crumbs or spills on your desk? Is your mouse picking up paper dust from papers that get underfoot?

NERDY
DETAILS

From a service manual (honest!)...

"If a mouse fails to operate or should perform erratically, it may be in need of ball replacement... Before ordering, determine the type of mouse balls required by examining the underside of each mouse. Domestic balls will be larger and harder than foreign balls... Mouse balls are not usually static sensitive; however, excessive handling can result in sudden discharge... It is recommended that each servicer have a pair of balls for maintaining optimum customer satisfaction..."

Trackballs: Mouse on Its Back

An alternative to a mouse is a *trackball*. Trackballs work just like mice, but the ball is placed in the top center of the trackball and buttons are placed on the front. Instead of moving across your desk, the trackball stays in one place. You move the cursor by using your palm to roll the ball. To make a selection, press one of the buttons on the front. The trackball is ideal for those who have too much work on their desks to make room for a small rodent.

The trackball concept is also used in laptop computers. Instead of using the airplane window on which to roll your mouse (why ruin the view?), you clip the trackball to the edge of your laptop.

Messing with Modems

A modem can broaden your world. By letting your PC talk to other and often larger computers, a modem can increase your knowledge. I formerly worked for the PRODIGY on-line service and saw hundreds of people better their computer knowledge by sharing their questions with thousands of others. Today, I buy and sell stocks on PRODIGY and I can download software without leaving my home.

You can use either an external or internal modem. An external modem is shaped like an overgrown radar detector and even has similar lights. An internal modem is simply an expansion card you plug into one of your PC's vacant slots (such cards are discussed in Chapter 20). Like the internal-external mouse debate, little difference exists between the two. An internal modem is less expensive because you aren't paying for its fancy plastic case (or those cool digital lights).

An internal modem doesn't require a serial cable or power cord because it becomes a part of your PC. An external modem requires its own outlet and a bit of desk space, but does have some advantages. The row of lights on the front indicates when you are connected to another computer. External modems also have better speakers than internal ones. You can hear the modem dialing the phone number for you. If you get a busy signal, you'll hear it. Lastly, external modems can be carried to another computer or a friend's house.

A *modem* serves as a translator between two computers. It turns the digital lingo of your PC into analog sounds that can be sent over the phone line. On the receiving end, a modem converts the sounds back into digital. A modem cannot translate on its own. It receives instructions from communication software. Often, a modem comes with cheap software, letting you use it right away. Otherwise, you can buy top-notch communications software such as Procomm Plus or Crosstalk.

Most modems have two telephone jacks on their backsides (see fig. 19.1). You connect a standard phone cord from the phone jack in your wall to the modem jack marked "Line." You then plug your telephone into the modem's second phone jack. Whether your computer or modem is on, you can still use your phone. However, you can't use your phone while your PC is talking to another PC through the modem. In fact, picking up the phone may "garble" the conversation between the two. That's why it makes sense to have a separate phone line for your modem.

GEEK

The name "modem" is short for MOdulator/DEMdulator.

NERDY
DETAILS

For two computers to talk to each other, they must speak the same language. This is done by matching the following:

 Speed, or **baud rate.** Modems support one or more *speeds*. For two computers to communicate, the two modems must speak at the same speed. If not, the "conversation" may finish the same way a New Yorker talks to a Southerner—confusion. Popular speeds are 2400 and 9600 bits per second (bps), although no common standard for transmitting at 9600 bps is available. A modem's speed is also called its *baud rate*.

 Parity. Have you ever heard static during a phone conversation? This interference can be caused by sunspots, electrical generators, or simply bad karma. For a modem to speak clearly with another, a type of error-checking is used to eliminate such interference. This error-checking is called *parity* and it includes three types: odd, even, and none. When your modem is used, the communications software uses the parity to check that each character transmitted was understood.

NERDY
DETAILS

What is the difference between odd, even, and no parity? In a nutshell (this stuff is pretty technical), a transmitted character (which is a collection of bits) has an extra bit (parity bit) added to it so that the binary name for that character equals either an odd or even number (1 or 0). If you selected odd parity, for example, each character's binary name will end in a 1. If the received character ends in a 0, the receiving PC will know that the information got garbled in transmission and will ask for the character to be sent again. Sometimes, no parity is used, since the connection may be squeaky-clean or the communications software has built-in error-checking.

 Stop bits. Another way to ensure clear communication is to add a pause after each character is sent. This pause is called the *stop bit*. The number of stop bits inserted between each character of information may be 0, 1, or 2.

 Word length. Each character of information you send is made up of a bunch of codes called *bits* that say, "Hey, this is an A." To a PC, each character sent is considered a *word*, because the word is made up of several bits. The length of each word being sent by your modem is called the *word length*. The word length may be either seven or eight bits.

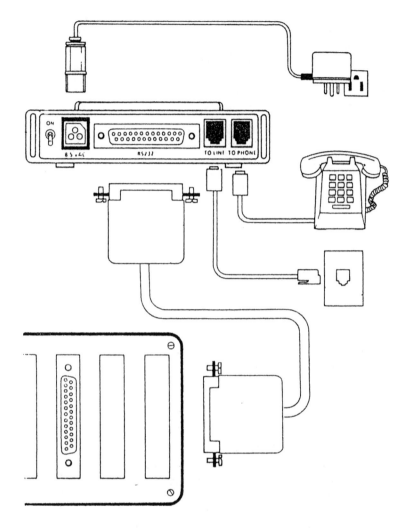

Figure 19.1

The back side of a modem. It's not that difficult to hook up.

When you set up your communications software to talk to another computer, you must match the preceding characteristics to those of the other computer. For example, when you want to transmit information to a friend, ask him or her how long the words are, what parity he or she is using (odd, even, or none), how many stop bits he or she wants, and what speed the modem is using.

Once you and your friend match, one computer can call the other and make the connection. To connect to an on-line service, such as CompuServe, you may need to set your computer to one stop bit, seven-bit words, and even parity. Sometimes this information is condensed into nerdy shorthand, such as 7,E,1 (seven-bit words, even parity, and one stop bit). Why isn't the speed mentioned in this formula? The typical baud rate is 2400.

Using Your Modem

Modems typically are used for two purposes:

 Calling on-line services

 Calling electronic bulletin board systems (BBSs)

An on-line service is simply a gigantic computer that can accept hundreds (if not thousands) of calls from other computers. For a monthly or hourly fee, you can access the resources of the gigantic computer, such as stock quotes, late-breaking news, soap opera updates, and more.

Once your modem dials an on-line service, you enter your user ID and secret password to begin using the service. PRODIGY, CompuServe, America Online, and GEnie are popular on-line services available nationwide and sometimes internationally. From the comfort of your chair you can be a world traveler. (For example, CompuServe is available in Japan and Europe.) Such on-line services offer hundreds of items of interest, including encyclo-pedias that never go out of date, accurate weather forecasts, and columns on a variety of subjects.

One unique part of on-line services is the *public forum* or *bulletin board*. In these areas, you can "post" a public message. Within hours, you can receive several public replies to your message. Some services even have live CB-like chatting so you don't even have to wait for a reply.

The dialog can become quite interesting and sometimes heated. When I worked for the PRODIGY service, I oversaw the Computer Club bulletin board. Each day, over 10,000 public messages about computers were posted. Often, insulting or profane messages had to be returned to the sender.

NERDY
DETAILS

Don't confuse public bulletins with private electronic mail messages. On a bulletin board or forum, every message is public and seen by everyone. Private electronic mail is seen only by you and the sender.

Some on-line services charge $12.95 per hour. You can get package deals, such as $7.95 per month, for up to five hours of use. Shop around and monitor your use of a service. Once you see how often you use it, you can pick the best price plan.

A *bulletin board system*—BBS for short—is a smaller imitation of an on-line service. Typically, a BBS is a single PC run by a computer nerd; the service is free or costs only a small fee. Many computer user groups have their own BBS for members to share information and their favorite software. (They do not share off-the-shelf software because this would be equivalent to stealing! Instead they share popular shareware, or try-before-you-buy software.)

Fax Away

Some modems double as fax machines. With a fax/modem in your PC, information is sent to the fax/modem in your PC rather than to a printer. Fax/modems also send whatever documents you have on your computer directly to other fax machines. Prior to sending, a pop-up box asks for you to enter various information, such as a phone number, recipient, subject, and a brief message.

Some fax/modems can only send faxes; these are called send-fax modems. Others can send and receive faxes. When you receive a fax, it is saved as a picture on your hard disk. Later, you can read it on-screen and decide whether to print it. You cannot pull the received document into your word processor unless you have special software called optical character recognition (OCR) software. OCR software converts the faxed message into text.

A fax/modem can be limiting in some ways. If you want to send a paper document, you can't do it unless you scan in the page (big pain). Other times, you may need to sign a document. With a fax modem, this is pretty difficult. There are ways around these problems, however.

For this book, for example, I received a non-disclosure contract I had to sign and return immediately. To do that, I converted the document to another picture format I could work with. Next, I scanned my signature with my handheld scanner (described in Chapter 20) and pasted it on the line I was to sign. Finally, I converted the finished picture back to a format I could fax. Whew!!!

Another drawback of fax/modems is that the software they require must always be present if you want to receive a fax on a moment's notice. Presently, such software requires a huge amount of memory. This memory could be put to better use. If you'll be receiving or sending several faxes, get a dedicated phone line and a real fax machine.

Pure Joy(stick)

Your computer is more than a tool. Color screens and fast, inexpensive computers make the PC ideal for gameplaying. Most computer games rely on a joystick instead of a keyboard. The best way to play flight simulation, combat, and car racing games is with a joystick.

Most joysticks have the same features. At least two firing buttons are included. One joystick provides buttons on both sides of its base for left-handed players. Selecting a joystick depends more on your individual hand size and shape. Some joysticks resemble a jet plane's flightstick. The Flight Yoke 2000 from Winner Products features dual grips so that you can use both hands to control your game vehicle.

Many joysticks include suction cups that attach to your desk. Unfortunately, you must have the desk space to use this feature. Don't have the room? Get a smaller joystick that fits in the palm of your hand.

NERDY
DETAILS

Joysticks usually provide vertical and horizontal controls with which to calibrate the stick. In your game, you often have a calibration choice.

Many computers come with a game port for a jostick. A game card is another option that provides the best control. A game card is an expansion card plugged into your computer. Why a dedicated game card? Some faster computers become confused by inexpensive game ports. During the heat of battle, for example, you may find your plane suddenly upside down or spiraling out of control. This is one sign that your game port is inadequate.

A dedicated game card also includes software that sets the correct speed and centers your joystick. Another benefit is most game cards have two game ports so that you can fly with a friend (a human, not computer, friend).

Other Goodies You Can Add

Your PC can also benefit from some simple protection and other fun additions:

 Surge protectors. Surge protectors protect your PC from sudden surges in electrical power. You insert a surge protector between your PC and the electrical outlet. These devices, which cost between 20 and 200 bucks, absorb the high-voltage spikes caused by nearby lightning strikes and power equipment. They only protect against power surges; they can't help when the power drops or dies completely.

Surge protectors are often built into multiple plug power strips. However, a multi-outlet power strip does not necessarily have surge protection. Look for three features in a surge protector:

 A status light that informs you when a large surge has occurred

 Support of the Underwriter Laboratories 1449 standard

 A circuit breaker that can be reset.

Any surge protector that meets these qualifications is a keeper. Surge protectors do not last forever; replace them yearly.

 Anti-glare screens. Want to protect your eyes? A filter of tinted glass or plastic can improve your monitor's contrast by darkening the screen uniformly. These are called *glare filters* or *anti-glare screens*. These filters are available for as little as $30.

Because of the filter, you may need to increase your screen brightness. You can get an inexpensive black mesh (nylon cloth) screen, but it may cause more trouble than it solves. These screens reduce glare by absorbing any light that isn't traveling perpendicular to the screen. Unfortunately, mesh screens absorb light that comes in at sharp angles from the side, producing glare. The coarser meshes also may interfere with the screen's images.

 Wrist pad. If you type a lot, you may want to get a wrist pad. These foam pads are placed in front of your keyboard. You can give your wrists a break by resting them on this pad. This way, you can reduce your chances of painful Carpal Tunnel Syndrome (CTS).

 Replacement keyboard. You may use your keyboard several hours each week. A keyboard is such a constant companion that you may want to invest in one that fits your needs.

You may want to purchase a replacement keyboard when you get a new PC. (The cheap ones that come with most PCs don't last long.) A favorite is the Northgate OmniKey/102—the function keys are placed on the left where you can easily reach them. You can also swap the Alt and Ctrl keys and move them where you like them. For under $100, you can select a keyboard that feels right for you.

 Keyboard cover and organizer. A keyboard cover to prevent dust and debris from lodging between your keys is available. The Keyboard Organizer from Curtis Manufacturing Co. is the Swiss Army knife of keyboard covers. A plastic unit with a built-in keyboard cover holds your keyboard. Ample slots and recesses hold the various items that always seem to float onto your desk. This organizer provides slots for 3 1\2-inch disks, pens, and paper clips. There's even a special holder for a mouse.

A keyboard drawer is also available. These allow you to place your keyboard under your PC's monitor when not in use. Not only does this keep your keyboard out of the way, but you can also place your monitor closer to eye level.

You can also get a keyboard "condom" that protects the keyboard while you are typing. A product such as SafeSkin from Merritt Computer Products places a skin-tight, see-through rubber cover over your keyboard. Even if you spill a cup of coffee on your keyboard, the board is perfectly protected.

 Dust covers. If you want extra protection or if you work in a dusty environment, you can buy plastic dust covers for your keyboard, monitor, and system unit. When finished for the day, cover your equipment until tomorrow's session.

 Mouse holder. When you want your mouse out of the way, a mouse holder can be useful. You mount a plastic rack for your mouse at the side of your desk. When you want to rid yourself of the mouse, you hang it up on the rack. Mice should not be seen or heard.

 Copy holder. A copy holder lets you place documents upright so that you can see the type more easily.

GEEK

NERDY
DETAILS

If your copy holder includes a magnet to hold the documents upright, throw the magnet away! The magnetic field could scramble the information on the disks.

Printer stand. If you own a dot-matrix printer, a printer stand can save you some space. The stand elevates and tips your printer; underneath, you place a stack of paper that feeds into the back of the printer.

 CPU stand. Many people have no room on their desks for their desktop PC. (Kind of an oxymoron, no?) A CPU stand lets you turn your desktop PC into a floor-standing PC. A CPU stand provides a stable base into which you can place your PC on its side. You can then place your PC to the left or right of your desk and use the newfound desk space for your work, a mouse, or a modem.

With these accessories, your PC will be a fashionable and reliable partner. (Just don't muss up the monitor when you kiss it.)

CHAPTER
20

Popular Things That Aren't Easy To Add to Your PC

D reaming about what to add to your PC is fun. Deciding whether to pay someone else $75 to install the item for you is not. Before you pay, ask yourself these questions: Can I use a screwdriver? Do I have a screwdriver? Can I avoid losing the screws in the carpet? If you answered yes to these questions, you can upgrade your own PC without bribing a computer nerd with a bag of corn chips.

In this chapter, you'll learn:

    How your PC works with expansion cards to improve itself

    How to install an expansion card without static cling

    The importance of jumpers and DIP switches (named after some nerd)

    How to improve your PC's memory without training

    Other available gizmos for your PC

Room for Improvement

One way to improve your PC is to add a new computer circuit board with enhanced capabilities. Such a board is placed into an *expansion slot* in your PC. This slot has connections to your PC's main circuit board, the motherboard.

The very first PC had five vacant slots, but yours may have between three and eight. The circuit boards that eventually fill those slots go by several names: *expansion cards, expansion boards,* or *add-on cards.*

Some of your PC's expansion slots may already be filled. Most PCs have a video card to run your monitor, a drive controller to command the hard disk, and an interface card to provide connections to your printer and mouse. The remaining slots enable you to add more cool features. You may want to add expansion cards that let you:

- Add a scanner so that you can scan pictures and text for use in your PC's word-processing system. (This is a scanner interface card.)

- Install a tape drive, which protects your work by duplicating the hard disk on a small tape that you store in a safe place. (This is called a tape drive interface card or tape controller card.)

- Add a CD-ROM drive so that you can access a wealth of information or simply play an audio CD. (This is called a SCSI controller card.)

- Play high-quality sound in games and other software programs. (This is called a sound card or sound board.)

- Receive and send faxes at your PC without wasting a single tree.

Danger! Static Kills

Whenever you open your PC and work on it, it basically is exposed. Your PC's worst fear is static electricity. When you are all "charged up" and touch your PC, the built-up electricity can cause your PC to restart itself, losing your current work.

When you touch the parts inside your PC or on an expansion card, you may either zap a part and kill it or cause it to fail prematurely. Before touching anything inside your PC, touch a metal object nearby, such as the inside of your PC's case, for a few seconds. This drains you of static electricity. When you handle an expansion card, don't touch any of the computer parts on it. Instead, grab the card by its edges or bracket.

Plug and Play

Adding an expansion card is like changing your oil filter—less messy, but just as important. (You won't have to lie on your back in the driveway.) You remove your computer's outer case, then remove a screw that holds a plate over an empty expansion slot. You then insert the expansion card into its slot and hold it in place with the screw you removed. Replace the case and you're finished.

Adding an expansion card typically requires less than 30 minutes. Below are the basic steps required to add an expansion card.

TRICKS

> If you're lazy like me, you may want to purchase a cordless rechargeable screwdriver. This makes opening and closing a computer really easy. Bzzzz. You're done!

Driving into the Garage

You first want to prepare your PC for its "oil change."

1. Turn off and unplug your computer from the electrical outlet.
2. Unplug all cables from your computer.

Many spaghetti-like cables are connected to your PC, such as those to the keyboard, modem, monitor, and more. Label each cable with some masking tape so that you know which port it should be reattached to. Grab each cable at its base and pull straight back (not at an angle) to avoid damaging it.

3. Gently move your computer to an area where you will have lots of room to work on it.

Pretend your PC is a loved one (to nerds, it is!). In other words, embrace it the same way a nerd would sleep with his or her computer. Don't hold the computer at arm's length; you could hurt your back. Bend at the knees to let your legs do as much of the lifting as possible.

Opening the Hood

Once you've moved your PC to a work area, you can now open it. Some computers, such as the IBM PS/1, have hoods that slide off after releasing a latch—no need to unscrew anything. Other computers require you to whip out the tools:

1. With a Phillips screwdriver, remove the screws that hold the case to your system unit.

The five or six screws at the rear of your computer should be the only obstacles to upgrading your PC. The screws are along the outside edges, at the corner and middle. Any other screws are usually meant to hold internal parts to the case. Four screws hold the power supply to the rear of your computer, for instance. Do not remove these! Set aside the screws you do remove so they won't be misplaced.

2. Firmly grasp the computer case from both sides and gently slide it backward, forward, or upward (depending on the type of case you have).

On desktop computers, the case usually slides forward. The case includes the bezel, the attractive front of your computer. On floor-standing computers, such as tower and mini-tower cases, the case is removed by sliding it backwards leaving the bezel behind. As you slowly remove the case, be wary of any resistance that might be caused by internal cables being snagged during its removal. Tuck in these cables as you slide off the case. Set the case aside where it won't be scratched or marred. It's best to lay it flat on the floor so it doesn't tip over. Get help if you need it. An extra pair of hands and eyes is always nice.

Taking Out the Old Filter

Sometimes you may have to remove an expansion card and install its replacement—like a brain transplant. You may be installing a color video card in lieu of your monochrome one, for instance. If so, you must remove the existing card and install its replacement. The current expansion card is held in place by one screw.

If you are adding a sound card, you can remove the screw of the empty slot. This screw simply holds a metal plate over the rear opening. Without the plate, the inside of your PC would be exposed to outside dust and debris.

1.   Remove the screw of the expansion slot into which you want to insert the new expansion card (see fig. 20.1).

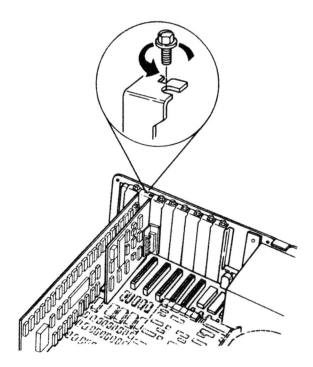

Figure 20.1

A single screw holds each expansion card in place.

Only one screw needs to be removed to free the metal bracket from the case. Set aside the screw where it won't be misplaced.

2.   Remove the existing expansion card, if needed.

These cards are not the easiest to remove. They are designed to keep a good electrical connection with the motherboard. To free the card, gently but firmly rock it back and forth along its length. In other words, don't twist the card from side to side but rather pull up alternately on each end.

STOP!

Grab the card by its edges or metal bracket. Do not touch any of the components on the card because any static electricity you may have can damage the card. After removing an expansion card, set it aside on a clean surface.

Putting On the New Filter

When you find a spot for the new expansion card, you can now insert it.

1. Select an empty expansion slot for your new card.

Your new expansion card may be either of two types:

8-bit (one-edge). This card has only one "tooth" that is inserted into the expansion slot connector.

16-bit (two-edge). A 16-bit card has two teeth that are inserted into the two expansion slot connectors.

NERDY DETAILS

A new design in some PCs is to bypass the typically slow expansion bus (into which the expansion card is inserted) and use what is called the *local bus*. In a PC that has a local bus, the expansion card talks to your PC at 32-bit speed, not 16 or 8.

This is like the "red phone" between Washington, D.C. and Moscow. Instead of placing a conventional call using secretaries and operators, the president can use the red phone to speak directly to his Moscow counterpart. Likewise, a local bus card directly "hot-wires" the expansion card to the processor. The local bus was first used for video cards but now includes cards that control the hard disk.

Expect huge gains in speed with local bus because the local bus video is not slowed to the typical 8MHz speed of a card, but to the top speed of your PC—25MHz, 33MHz, or faster. The new VESA (an industry video standards group) specification for local bus—VL-Bus Standard 1.0—allows for only three local bus slots in a PC.

Select a slot that matches the type of card you have. You don't want to put a 16-bit card (one with two connectors) into an 8-bit slot (one with a single connector), for example. A 16-bit card was designed to take advantage of the extra connection for faster performance. Let your 16-bit expansion card really sink its teeth into your PC by using both connectors. You can, however, place an 8-bit card into a 16-bit slot.

2.   Remove the new expansion card from its protective packaging.

Expansion cards are shipped in a special gray or silver anti-static bag. When you open this bag, carefully grab the card by its metal bracket and edges. Avoid touching any of the components on the card; any static electricity you may have can damage the card. Zap! Also, do not touch the gold (actually copper) edge connectors.

3.   Configure the expansion card.

You may have to set jumpers or DIP switches to customize, or configure, your card for your PC. However, each card is different. See the instructions that came with your card. (Later sections in the chapter discuss the purpose of jumpers and DIP switches.)

4.   Place the new expansion card into the expansion slot.

Keep going—you're almost there. Hold the card by its metal bracket and edges and place it in the expansion slot. Rock the expansion card back and forth along its length. There will be firm resistance as you press on the card—this is natural.

5.   Attach the screw that holds the expansion card in place.

Once the expansion card is installed, tighten the screw. (Don't overtighten it, though—you may need to remove it in the future.)

Pulling Out of the Garage

Once your new expansion card is in place, you can return your PC to normal operation. (Okay, go back to playing your game.)

1.   Replace your computer's case and tighten the outside screws or make sure the latch locks in place if you have a computer that uses a latch.

2.   Return your computer to working order.

Move your PC back to where it came from and reattach its cables and cords. This may be a good opportunity to untangle them.

3.   Install any software to run your new card.

Some expansion cards rely on small software programs called *drivers* to bring them to life. These drivers are usually loaded by your PC's CONFIG.SYS start-up file (see Chapter 6 for more information). Check the manual that came with the card for information on installing and using these drivers.

Ouch! The Burn-In

After installing an expansion card (you did it!), leave your computer on for 24 to 72 hours. This is called the *burn-in,* or *testing,* period. You don't have to do this but it's a good idea. Many PC makers burn in their computers for 48 hours. Believe it or not, this testing is good for the new expansion card. If the card fails during the burn-in period, you can return it or have it repaired or replaced before its warranty expires. If the expansion card passes the testing, it will probably last the life of your PC. When your boss asks you why you left your PC on overnight, you can reply with a techie-nerd line like, "Oh, I'm just burning in a new board." He'll probably walk away dumbfounded, and you can consequently add this new skill to your job description.

Telling an Expansion Card Where To Go

Most expansion cards are pre-set at the factory to work in most situations. Hopefully, yours won't be the exception. Sometimes, you must set *jumpers* or *DIP (dual-inline pin) switches* to get the most from your new card. My latest video card needed a change in the DIP switch so the card could work better with my NEC monitor.

A jumper is simply a short piece of wire, encased in plastic, that lets you make an electrical connection between two pins on your card. A DIP switch is simply a little box with a bank of switches you must set either up or down.

Jumpers and DIP switches also are the great peacekeepers. They can be used to give competing pieces of hardware their own "phone line." For example, after installing a new expansion card, you may find your mouse doesn't work. This problem is called a *hardware conflict*. The two pieces of hardware—the new expansion card and mouse—are trying to use the same phone line to talk to your PC. The result is nobody makes the phone call; they just argue. Four sources of such conflict are:

 Direct memory access (DMA) channel

Read-only memory (ROM) address

Input/output (I/O) address

Interrupt request (IRQ) line

Look up these phrases in your manual and see if you can use a jumper or DIP switch to change channels. A just-installed internal modem may be preset for COM1 (the first serial communications port), for example. This serial port occupies a specific I/O address. However, that same COM1 port may be used by your mouse. You will find that neither the mouse nor the modem works. The solution is to change a jumper or DIP switch on the modem to make it COM2. The conflict is then solved. Both mouse and modem are happy.

Mo' Memory

Adding memory to your PC may be the biggest improvement you can make. It can also be the least expensive. The cost of memory at the time of this writing was about $30 per megabyte—and falling. A small dose can be a big boost to your computer's performance. Windows, for example, loves lots of memory. The more you have, the more programs you can run simultaneously.

Giving your PC more memory is like giving yourself a bigger desk—you have more room to do your work and have the tools you need readily available. How do you add memory to your PC? You have two choices:

 Adding memory to vacancies on your motherboard.

 Replacing your current motherboard's memory with higher-capacity memory.

Your PC may still have room for more memory. Individual memory chips are placed into *memory banks*. This bank must be completely filled for it to work.

Most PCs have two memory banks (often called Bank 0 and Bank 1). In some cases, only one of these banks may be filled with memory chips; the other one is empty, begging for more memory to be installed. You simply fill this empty bank with matching memory chips. Some PCs, such as the new ZEOS models, have only one bank of SIMMs, but can still be configured with up to 64M of memory.

If both memory banks are full, you may still be able to add more memory. You can take out the memory chips in one bank and in their place install *higher-capacity* memory chips. The only drawback is that you end up having a handful of extra memory chips lying around unused. You may be able to sell them to someone who doesn't have two full banks.

Today's PCs use *SIMM (single in-line memory module)* memory chips. The SIMM is actually several memory chips on a small circuit board. In the old days (okay, five years ago), you had to install small memory chips one at a time. With a SIMM, you can install the equivalent of nine conventional memory chips in one step. No wonder the SIMM is so popular.

SIMMs come in four sizes: 256K (kilobit), 1M (megabit), 4M, and 16M. Typically, four SIMMs fill a memory bank. Table 20.1 shows the most popular combinations of SIMMs. When you fill any one memory bank with four of the same type of memory—you can't mix different sizes in the same bank—you get the multiplied number of bytes, not bits. For example, a memory bank containing four 256K SIMMs is equal to one megabyte of memory. Confused? It's really simple math: 4×256K = 1024K (kilobytes) = 1M (megabyte).

Table 20.1
Filled Memory Banks
Give You More Memory

Total Memory	Bank 0	Bank 1
1M	4×256K	empty
2M	4×256K	4×256K
4M	4×1M	empty
5M	4×1M	4×256K
8M	4×1M	4×1M

Total Memory	Bank 0	Bank 1
16M	4×4M	empty
17M	4×4M	4×256K
20M	4×4M	4×1M
32M	4×4M	4×4M

As you can see from Table 20.1, you can either add memory to an empty bank (if you have an empty one) or you can replace low-capacity memory with high-capacity memory. For example, I used to have 8M of memory in my PC. That is, I had two memory banks filled with 1M SIMMs. When I wanted more memory, I purchased four 4M SIMMs and placed them in the first memory bank. The total amount of memory I now have is 20M. (I recycled the four 1M SIMMs by placing them in my wife's computer.)

Taking It to the Bank

Like adding an expansion card, you must open your PC to add more memory. To install SIMM memory, follow these steps:

1. Turn off your computer, unplug it from the outlet, and remove its case. Use the previous procedure for installing an expansion card to open up your PC.

2. Locate your two banks of memory chips and the vacant memory bank.

Each memory bank holds four SIMMs.

3. Jot down the numbers on the SIMM memory chips present in the full memory bank and order additional memory for the empty bank.

The chips in the full memory bank are probably the type of memory chips you need to order. The current SIMM chips probably have these numbers within the chip's part number printed on its top:

SIMM Type	Size
1256	256Kx1 bit
14256	256Kx4 bits
11000	1024Kx1 bit
14400	1024Kx4 bits
41000	4096Kx1 bit
44000	4096Kx4 bits

If you have a vacant memory bank, you probably want to add chips that match the current ones. For accuracy, consult your owner's manual about the type of chips to add. If you don't have an owner's manual, consult the previous table of possible combinations for SIMM chips.

Besides the size of the memory chips you need, you must also consider speed. Memory chips are rated by their reaction time, which is measured in *nanoseconds*, or billionths of a second. How fast is a nanosecond? One nanosecond, abbreviated *ns*, is the time it takes light to travel 12 inches. Don't blink. The smaller this speed rating, the faster the chip. For example, a 60ns chip is faster than a 100ns chip. Generally, faster chips cost more.

The speed of a memory chip is printed on the surface of the chip. On the memory chips, you will see an identifying number. The last two digits after the dash (-) are especially important because they indicate the speed of the PC's memory. The last two digits indicate the speed in nanoseconds.

You should buy memory that matches the speed of the memory already installed in your PC. Faster memory won't help; your PC was set to run at a certain speed. Faster-than-required memory chips are unnecessary.

4.   Prepare the SIMM memory chips for installation.

Memory chips can be damaged by static electricity, so don't hold them and run across the carpet in your socks. Keep the memory chips in their anti-static packaging until they are needed. Before installing each SIMM, touch a piece of metal briefly, such as your computer's metal case, to drain yourself of built-up static.

5.   Install the SIMM memory into the empty sockets (see fig. 20.2).

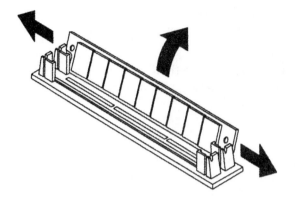

Figure 20.2

Insert each SIMM at a
45-degree angle and
snap it into place.

When installed, each SIMM must be pointing in a certain direction. Each chip has a polarity notch on one end of the circuit board. A SIMM has a notch cut into one side. These notches physically prevent the SIMM from being installed the wrong way. If the SIMM is reluctant to enter its socket, try turning it around.

Insert each SIMM at about a 45 degree angle, lining up the copper-colored connectors on the memory module with the socket on the motherboard. The chips on the SIMM should face away from the angle of the socket. Because four SIMMs must be installed into the bank, you must insert the modules in a certain order so that each subsequent SIMM has room to be inserted at this angle.

Firmly insert the SIMM into the socket. Next, pivot it backwards to an upright position until it touches the plastic latches on both sides of the socket. Carefully press the SIMM against these latches until they snap around the edges of the SIMM and clamp it firmly into place. Be careful not to break the SIMM slot! Those little plastic fingers can break off with too much enthusiasm.

6. Inspect your work.

Use a flashlight to inspect the installation. Make sure each module is not bowing out but is directly in line with its socket. You should see only the top rim of each contact finger at the top of the socket. If you see more, if one end of the SIMM is deeper in the socket than the other, or if the latches don't properly close around the SIMM, remove and reinstall the troublesome SIMM.

7.   Once all the chips are installed, attach your keyboard and monitor to the computer and plug your computer into the electrical outlet.

For now, leave your computer case off so that you can fix any chips that may have not been installed correctly. (Cross your fingers.)

8.   Turn on your computer.

Usually upon warming up, your computer will recognize that something has changed and then display an error message. From there, you can access your computer's built-in Setup program and make the changes. Sometimes, your computer will already guess how much memory your PC has but just have you approve the changes.

(GADS!) If your computer gives a message such as "Parity error" or does not recognize the new memory, you may either have a defective memory module or you may have installed it improperly. Inspect your work again.

Sometimes, adding new memory is not an end in itself. You often have to use software utilities, such as disk-caching software, to use the memory in speeding up your computer. Some software programs, such as Microsoft Windows, will recognize the new memory and use it automatically. Chapter 21 discusses software utilities that can use your PC's new memory to speed up your work.

Other Gizmos

Your PC can be improved with a plethora of paraphernalia. Some possibilities include:

 A larger, faster hard disk. You can add a second or larger and faster hard disk to your PC. You install the hard disk into your PC and attach it to your drive controller expansion card with a gray ribbon cable. Not for the faint of heart, replacing a hard disk is a one- to two-hour job. You must back up your current hard disk, open your PC, and (if you are replacing it) remove the original hard disk.

Once the new drive is installed, you may have to partition it using the DOS FDISK command and then format each partition. Finally, you can restore the backup of your hard disk to the new disk.

Whew! Installing a second hard disk is easier than replacing the original disk—assuming that you have the room inside your PC for it.

 CD-ROM drive. A *CD-ROM drive* lets you have access to mega-megabytes worth of information. One disk can hold the equivalent of 250,000 pages of information (660M). A CD-ROM drive is like a hard disk with two differences. First, you cannot save information to a CD-ROM. Second, a CD-ROM drive is much slower than a hard disk, up to 20 times slower. Unlike a hard disk, you can remove and insert various CD-ROM disks. You can even play your own audio CDs on these drives. A CD-ROM drive is required for *multimedia*, the combination of information, images, and sound.

NERDY
DETAILS

> The hottest CD-ROM technology going is CD-ROM XA. CD-ROM XA players are not the same as ordinary CD-ROM players. Ordinary CD-ROM players are "single session" players: they can only read CD-ROMs with a single recording on them. CD-ROM XA players are "multiple session" players: they can read joe-blow CD-ROMs (single session), audio CDs, and XA discs, which accept multiple additions to the original recording. Kodak's PhotoCD uses the CD XA technology.
>
> Although this information might seem useless, just remember a lot of computer salespeople are trying to push old merchandise, such as single session CD-ROM drives, out the door. If you're planning on adding a CD-ROM drive to your PC, check out *A Guide to Multimedia* (New Riders Publishing) before you let go of 500 bucks.

 Sound card. Your PC's built-in speaker is nothing compared to the sounds produced by a sound card. Adding a sound card to your PC provides stereo sound for computer games and Microsoft Windows. You simply insert the sound card into an expansion slot. Then, attach a pair of self-powered speakers to the stereo jacks on the back of the card. You can also use a microphone to record sounds, such as voice notes to your Windows documents. A $100 Thunderboard sound card from MediaVision gives you very good sound, for example—much better than your computer's anemic speaker.

Scanner card. If you want to scan pictures or text for use in your documents, you can add a scanner. A scanner expansion card is placed in your PC and then connected to the scanner. The scanner may be a small handheld model or a flatbed scanner that fits on a nearby table. Some scanners include optical character recognition (OCR) software. This software allows you to scan a page of text and turn it into actual words in your document. (Look Ma, no typing!)

 Game card. A game card gives you quick response to your joystick moves in many popular computer games. A game card (another type of expansion card) often enables two players to play a game at the same time. That way you can fly with a friend, or blast away at each other's tank.

 Tape drive. Tape drives are designed for backing up your hard disk. Instead of copying the contents of a 100M hard disk to almost 85 floppy disks, a tape drive can store the entire drive on one small tape cartridge. A tape backup system consists of a special tape drive mechanism, cartridge tapes to hold your data, and software to copy the files from your hard disk to the tapes.

 The least-expensive tape drives connect to your PC through the floppy disk cable. Otherwise, you can buy an optional tape drive controller card. This expansion card lets you back up data up to four times faster than the floppy controller. A tape drive can be located inside or outside your PC. An internal drive is installed like a floppy disk drive; the external drive has its own case and usually its own power supply. External tape drives are easiest to install. You simply put its controller card into an empty slot in your computer, close the case, and hook up the tape drive to the card's external connector.

Voilà! That's it for goodies you may have a tough time adding to your PC. Even though this hardware is a little more complicated to add, it actually is worth the trouble because it will make your PC more capable.

MORE RAM JUST WAS'NT ENOUGH FOR FRANKLIN

CHAPTER
21

Captain, I'm Giving Her All She's Got!

Your PC may not be giving you its all, even if you've had it for years and you think you know everything about it. If the PC you have is beginning to get a little gray around the expansion ports, you may want to get a new one. Although new models are always a possibility, you may decide to keep it by choice or because you're broke. No need to feel left out of the technological mainstream; save a few hundred bucks by upgrading the dinosaur (loan the money to a friend who went broke after he bought a new machine). If you have a computer and decide to upgrade, this chapter will pay for itself by helping you:

- Decide whether to upgrade your PC or replace it
- Set your buffers and files
- Use a RAM disk to speed up DOS and Windows
- Make the most of Windows' swap file
- Speed up loading your software with Fastopen and the path statement
- Use inexpensive disk caching, defragmentation, and print spooling to speed up your PC
- Add an OverDrive processor to your 486 PC (add a sixth gear to your computer's transmission)

Understand the importance of video accelerator cards, even if you don't care

 Understand how caching hard disk controllers work

 Replace Old Yeller's motherboard

When Upgrading Doesn't Cut It

How do you know when your PC can't cut the mustard? The signs are not always readily apparent; it won't sound a buzzer or a display a warning light, for instance. To determine just how viable your unit is, consider these questions:

 How many levels of technology have you passed up since you bought your current PC?

Today's hottest processor is the 80486. That model was preceded by the 80386, 80286, 8086, and 8088. If you have an 8088 processor (the one used in the first IBM PC in 1981), you probably know how limited this computer is.

 How often do your PC's capabilities limit your work?

Do you wait too long for your hard disk to load software? Does your screen make your eyes ache? Do your programs frequently indicate that your PC doesn't have enough memory? Does your hard disk groan and grind or occasionally lose your work? Do you want to play the latest PC games but can't because you need a VGA monitor?

Measure your PC's limits by the specific jobs you want to accomplish but cannot. You know that wish list of features you have for your dream computer (every aspiring nerd has one)? Put the list aside; those dreamboat features (ten zillion megabytes of RAM, a hard disk big enough for the Library of Congress) are the icing—this question is concerned with the cake.

 If you upgrade your PC, will it involve several hardware and software purchases?

The cost of upgrading your PC may be deceptive if you have to rework nearly your entire system. Not only do you have to install each part of the upgrade—and hope it works with the other components—but you also have to learn each component. Refurbishing your PC (or a mobile home) may make it an unstable friend.

 How often does your PC conflict with those of friends, family, or co-workers?

If you have a low-density, 5 1/4-inch disk drive, you may be unable to share information reliably with others who have 1.2M drives. Perhaps your monochrome (one-color) monitor doesn't display your friend's work properly.

 Take note of the most appealing features of each upgrade recommended in this book. How many of them are truly important to you?

Choose only those features you will actually use or need. Don't be distracted by bells and whistles, and don't be driven by the features of a co-worker or neighbor's PC. Instead of buying a larger hard disk, perhaps you could simply rid your drive of unneeded files. Be honest with yourself: how many features will really help you work smarter?

 How much work and time are you willing to devote to upgrading your PC?

Some of you have lots of free time—others have little. In a toss-up between money and time, you may prefer a little time and elbow grease to spending the money for a new PC or its repair. The replacement of your PC's motherboard—the main circuit board—is time-consuming, but beneficial if the old clunker needs a face lift.

 What are the real tradeoffs when upgrading or repairing your PC?

You may be sinking money that could be set aside for a new PC into old technology. Be selective about how far you want to go.

NERDY
DETAILS

Although inflation climbs at about 6 percent per year, computers are continually cheaper and more powerful. If you're having thoughts about upgrading whatever you can salvage from your senior citizen computer, stop, count to ten, and keep this in mind: new computers sometimes cost less than an upgrade to an existing computer. In other words, computers are almost disposable (not good for the environment).

What demands will your software or hardware upgrade make on your entire system?

Nothing is more irritating than upgrading your PC and then discovering that another component is needed. For example, the puny 135-watt power supply found in an older PC may need to be replaced to handle a new hard disk or other additions.

 Would a new PC, not merely an upgrade, better satisfy your heart's desires?

You may love your current PC but are having trouble recognizing when you've outgrown it. Suppose you decide to upgrade your older 80286 PC by purchasing a memory card and larger hard disk so that it can run Windows. All the cash you spent also could have been spent on a new 80386 PC that runs Windows in its optimum Enhanced mode. When the job at hand substantially outstrips your PC's capabilities, an upgrade probably won't help, however. It may be time to look elsewhere.

Improving your PC involves two things: software and hardware. You can purchase software programs (on floppy disks) that either solve problems or provide additional features. This method is the least expensive route to improving your PC.

You can also buy hardware to replace existing components in your PC, or to add more power. A couple types of hardware include a new hard disk or second floppy disk drive. Because PC hardware is a tangible, manufactured piece of equipment, you will pay more than you would for software.

The next few sections discuss many ways to speed up your PC. Each collection of tips has a different price range—from free to a few hundred bucks. Why torment yourself with an improvement beyond your means?

Free Stuff

Good news—you can speed up your PC without spending one dime. With a little effort, you can gain additional speed and preserve more memory for your main software. Often, PCs are misconfigured right off the showroom floor or as new software is added. In new software programs, your PC's two startup files, AUTOEXEC.BAT and CONFIG.SYS, are often changed. A few simple tricks can help you get more speed from your computer without investing in expensive hardware. Many of the following tips require you to create or change one of those two startup files.

How do you edit or create these files? DOS version 5.0 and higher includes a text editor called EDIT.COM. Even though it looks pretty boring, Edit lets you create simple text (also called ASCII) files. If you have DOS 5.0, you can type:

EDIT C:\PATH\FILENAME

C:\PATH\FILENAME is the drive, path, and file name of the file you want to edit or create. Press Alt-F-S to save your work when you are finished.

If you don't have DOS 5.0, use your own word processor. Open the file in the word processor and save the file as an ASCII, or text, file.

TRICKS

Whenever you change the AUTOEXEC.BAT or CONFIG.SYS files, you must restart your computer to make the changes effective. This is the same as cleaning the lint out of your clothes dryer after you've finished drying a load. You won't benefit from a clean filter until the next load.

To restart your computer, press Ctrl-Alt-Del or simply turn your computer off and then on again.

Type Softly and Carry a Boot Disk— The CONFIG.SYS File

How can you improve your PC using CONFIG.SYS? The following lines in the CONFIG.SYS file control different parts of your PC. You can change these lines so that the PC more closely matches the actual work you do. That way, no memory or extra processing time is wasted.

Before you attack these lines in CONFIG.SYS, make sure you have a boot disk on hand. Chapter 17 shows you what a boot disk is and how to create one in the section "Tools for a Troublefree PC—The Boot Disk." Make a boot disk first, then you can tinker with this file.

NERDY
DETAILS

If you don't have time or if you're too bored to create a boot disk, you can always use the original DOS floppy disks that came with your PC.

"Why do I need a boot disk?" If you misspell a word or leave out a character while you change these lines, your PC may not "boot" (work) when you try to start it again. The PC will not be broken; it just won't do anything. Be vewy vewy careful...

 BUFFERS=. This line is found in the CONFIG.SYS file, which is a file you probably shouldn't mess with unless you do exactly as I say. The BUFFERS= line controls the amount of memory DOS sets aside for programs. This memory stores information that the computer would normally have to access from the hard drive—a very slow process in the land of computing. The higher the number after the equal sign, the faster your hard disk.

If you feel adventurous, open the CONFIG.SYS file in a word processor or Edit, find this tiny line, and replace the number in the line from whatever it is (most likely 40) to something up to 99. If you are still reading and haven't fallen asleep yet, save the changes, press Ctrl-Alt-Del, then see if anything is faster. The changes should be little, but hey, it's free, right? If you are using a disk caching program (described later), reduce the number of buffers to two. The disk caching software does a better job of speeding up your hard disk.

TRICKS

If you have DOS 5.0 or greater and more than 2M of memory, select a buffer number of 44 or less. This allows the buffers to be placed above your PC's first 640K of memory. The saved lower memory can then be used for other programs.

 FILES=. If you're brave enough to open the CONFIG.SYS file, you probably have seen this line. When your PC starts, a certain amount of memory is set aside to track the number of computer files you are using. Your word processor, for example, may open five of its files. (These files are the program files the word processor needs, not any documents you created.) A value of 20 is adequate for most people.

Some programs, such as Microsoft Windows, require a higher number, such as 40.

You can save memory by selecting the bare minimum number of files. Reduce this number from 40 in increments of 10 to determine how many you need. If you lower the number too much, you will get an error message, such as "Out of files." Simply increase the number of files until your software is pleased.

If you try to start your PC after you change these buggers, and it looks as if the computer has crashed ("CRASHED!? IT DOESN'T #$%&@*^ WORK!"), save your hair and stick your emergency "boot" disk in the A drive to resuscitate it. If you don't have a boot disk on hand, call up a friend with a PC and ask to borrow his or hers (make sure your friend's PC has the same version of DOS).

Other Cost-Free Ways To Crank Up the Speed

Other built-in speed enhancements that only nerds know about are the FASTOPEN command and a nifty invisible gadget called a RAM disk. With the right hardware (plenty of RAM), a RAM disk will speed up your computer considerably. You might want to make this change:

 RAM disk. The no-cost *RAM (random-access memory) drive* is also known as a *virtual disk* or *RAM disk*. Your PC's DOS software comes with a utility called RAMDRIVE.SYS (or VDISK.SYS, depending on your DOS version and manufacturer). This utility temporarily creates a disk drive in your computer's speedy memory. To understand the advantages of a RAM disk, imagine your bathroom is underwater and you need to call a plumber. You can dial the number a lot faster if you remember the plumber's number rather than having to look through the yellow pages. Like your own memory, a RAM disk can provide information much faster than a hard disk.

A RAM drive is best used for storing temporary files required by Microsoft Windows, DOS, or other programs. The RAM disk utility is started from the spooky CONFIG.SYS file. The line that starts the RAM drive typically looks like this:

```
DEVICE=C:\DOS\RAMDRIVE.SYS 2048 /E
```

Pretty confusing, huh? (If you don't think so, you're a nerd!) The number following the RAM drive's file name is the size of the RAM drive in kilobytes (2048K). As a general rule, if your PC has 4M or more of memory, allocate about one-fourth of it for a RAM disk.

Once a RAM drive is created, it automatically is assigned the next available drive letter, such as drive D or E. Check your DOS or Windows manual or *Maximizing Windows 3.1* (New Riders Publishing) for information on making the most of the RAM disk.

 FASTOPEN. DOS can be quite a forgetful operating system. It searches for a file every time you request it—even if you just used that file. You can speed up DOS by using its Fastopen command, which has been available in all versions of DOS since version 3.0. Fastopen tells DOS to remember where it found files so it can find them again quickly, without doing a tedious search. Fastopen works best with database software.

To use the Fastopen command every time, you can add it to your AUTOEXEC.BAT startup file. Otherwise, you can simply type FASTOPEN at the DOS prompt whenever you want to use it. The command, given either from the DOS prompt or in your AUTOEXEC.BAT file, would be:

```
FASTOPEN C:=XX D:=XX
```

C: and *D:* are the drives you want to use Fastopen on and *XX* is the number of files to track. One rule of thumb is to give Fastopen one file for every megabyte on your hard disk. For example, if your drive C: is an 80M hard disk, you would want a setting of 80.

 Change the path. DOS organizes your hard disk into what is called tree-structured directories. The top directory, such as C:\, is called the *root directory*. Directories and subdirectories are then placed underneath the root directory. Tree-structured directories are a great way to organize your hard disk. For example, you probably have a directory called C:\DOS for just your DOS programs.

The PATH statement is used in your AUTOEXEC.BAT startup file to tell DOS where to search for your most popular program files. This way, you can type the program's startup command without having to go to the directory in which it is located. Your PC then looks to your PATH statement and finds the program file from among the directories listed. When you install new programs, these programs normally add their directory to your path. A typical path looks like this:

```
PATH C:\DOS;C:\WINDOWS;C:\BAT;C:\WP;C:\;
```

Although very useful, the PATH statement can get unruly. To locate your software program, DOS must search through layers of subdirectories. In other words, the longer the path, the longer it takes

DOS to find the program you want to run. You should limit your path to the bare essentials, such as C:\DOS and C:\WINDOWS. The fewer alternative paths, the less time it takes DOS to zero in on a program you want to run. Use the Edit program to change your PATH.

 Keyboard speedup. You can only type so fast, but sometimes you may like to move the cursor quickly to another line or position. Other times, you may want to have a certain key repeat more quickly. To take advantage of these possibilities, type the following command from your DOS prompt (C:\):

MODE CON: RATE=32 DELAY=1

You'll find the keyboard is easier to use. You can enter RATE values from 1 to 32; the default is around 20 (characters per second). The higher the number, the faster the keys will repeat. The value for the DELAY ranges from 1 to 4; the default is 2. The DELAY value denotes time in quarter-second increments.

NERDY
DETAILS

This MODE command stuff will not work on older 83-key, XT-type keyboards. You shouldn't be using these anyway, because they are so old, ugly, and loud (they click click you to tears).

If you like this faster keyboard, add the line you typed to your AUTOEXEC.BAT file so it is already loaded whenever you start your computer.

On the Cheap

Some improvements to your PC can be done for less than $100. Below are some highly recommended favorites. In some cases, you may have some of these utilities as part of your DOS or Windows software. (In other words, these improvements may be free.)

Warp Drive, Mr. Scott

A disk cache is the best way to improve your hard disk's speed. A *disk cache* is a program that places parts of your hard disk into your computer's memory. Once in memory, the contents can be read by your PC at warp speed. DOS versions 4.*x* and higher and Microsoft Windows include a disk-caching utility called SMARTdrive, although more advanced disk-caching utilities are available.

Unlike the buffers feature mentioned earlier, the disk cache has some intelligence. It anticipates what you want from your hard disk by retaining the information you most recently used. (The program assumes this information is what most likely will be needed next). A disk cache is generally more versatile than a RAM disk because it is dynamic; the contents of the cache change as you read other programs and work files.

All disk-caching programs copy frequently used parts of your hard disk into your computer's much-faster memory. The smarter caches *buffer*, or *delay*, writing to your hard disk. In other words, it saves information in its memory to your hard disk when your computer is not so busy doing your other work, usually waiting no more than one second. This is also called *delayed writing*. This waiting period adds significant speed but may cause information to be lost if your computer were suddenly turned off. Because of the small delay, often less than one second, this concern is minor.

A disk cache only helps with certain kinds of computer work. If your work generally loads entirely into memory and doesn't access the hard disk (as with spreadsheets and word processors, for example), disk caching won't improve performance.

Disk caching definitely helps software that uses your hard disk often. Almost any disk-caching utility makes a database software program run about three times faster.

Good disk-caching utilities let you adjust the size of the cache (bigger is usually better). Most disk caches are easy to install but provide extra options to fine-tune the cache for the best performance.

The size you set aside for the disk cache depends on how much memory you have (see table 21.3). As a general rule, if your PC has more than 1M RAM, set aside about one-fourth for a disk cache.

Table 21.1
Suggested Disk Cache Sizes

Total Memory	Cache Size When Not Using Windows	Cache Size When Using Windows
2M	1024K	512K
3M	2048K	1024K

Total Memory	Cache Size When Not Using Windows	Cache Size When Using Windows
4M	2048K	1024K
5M-6M	2048K	2048K
7M	2048K	2048K
8M	2048K	2048K
9M	2048K	2048K
10+ M	2048K	2048K

You may have free disk-caching software on your computer already. SMARTdrive is one such utility included with Microsoft Windows 3.0 and 3.1, and DOS 5.0. SMARTDrive typically appears as the file SMARTDRV.SYS. To load it, you must add the following line to your CONFIG.SYS startup file:

```
DEVICEHIGH=C:\DOS\SMARTDRV.SYS xxxx yyyy
```

The funky-looking *xxxx* and *yyyy* represent the size of the cache (in K) when running DOS programs and running Windows, respectively. Use the table above to select the best sizes based on your total memory. If your DOS directory is not called C:\DOS or you are using SMARTDRV.SYS from your Windows directory, you can replace it with the correct path.

A more recent version of SMARTDrive included with Windows 3.1 is faster and easier to use. In fact, its name has changed from SMARTDRV.SYS to SMARTDRV.EXE. By simply typing smartdrv from the DOS prompt, the program automatically guesses how best to work with your PC. If you have SMARTDRV.EXE (it should be in your Windows directory), you should add the following line to your AUTOEXEC.BAT file:

```
C:\WINDOWS\SMARTDRV.EXE 2048 1024
```

As mentioned earlier, the two numbers represent the size of the disk cache when running DOS programs and Windows, respectively. Change your two numbers based on the table above.

If you don't have SMARTDrive or prefer a superior disk cache, you can buy an off-the-shelf program for about $100. Commercial disk-caching programs include Multisoft Corp.'s Super PC-Kwik Disk Accelerator, PC-Cache, included with Central Point Software's PC Tools, and Norton Cache, included with Symantec's Norton Utilities. One popular shareware (try-before-you-buy) program is HyperDisk. Besides the cost of a disk-caching program, you may have to spend an extra $50 to $100 for more memory if your computer doesn't have at least 2M.

Scatterbrained

Every time you use your hard disk, it gets a little slower. Why? As your disk is used over time, its files are saved to various places on the disk. A perfectly normal process, this *fragmentation* occurs when a new file fills in the empty holes left after you delete old files. It also occurs when an existing file has outgrown the space it previously occupied because you added extra information to it. Although your files may be split into pieces and saved to various parts of your hard disk, your PC safely tracks which sectors each file occupies.

Unfortunately, finding and loading a fragmented file takes longer because the hard disk must search several places for the different pieces of the file. The more fragmented your disk, the slower it becomes. The remedy is to use a *disk defragmentation* software utility, also called a *disk optimizer, disk compactor,* or *hard disk compression* program.

A disk defragmenter gathers the scattered pieces that make up each file and saves them in one place as one chunk. (Nerds would call this *continuous, contiguous order.*) With the file in one piece, your hard disk can read it more easily.

The best defragmentation programs close up the spaces left by deleted files and let you place popularly used files (such as those ending with EXE or COM) and subdirectories (such as C:\DOS) at the front of the disk for faster access. A defragmentation program should also let you pick either a quick defragmentation or a full defragmentation. The benefit of optimizing your hard disk is great. Some benchmark tests have operated twice as fast after a disk is optimized.

Disk optimizers are typically included in hard disk utility packages such as Central Point Software's *PC Tools* and Symantec Corp.'s *Norton Utilities.* When my drive becomes 10 percent fragmented, I take the time for a full optimization using *Norton Utilities' SpeedDisk* (see fig. 21.1). If the fragmentation is less than 10 percent, I might do a quick compress in which *SpeedDisk* simply unfragments the individual files. Gaps where future files might be placed may still exist, however, causing future fragmentation.

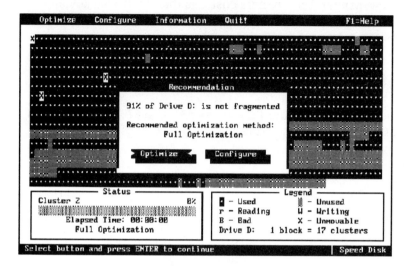

Figure 21.1

Norton Utilities' SpeedDisk visually shows how fragmented the hard disk is.

Print Now, Keep Working

When printing long or complicated documents, you may find yourself becoming mildly annoyed. That's because the printer must swallow the entire document before you can get back control of your PC and continue working.

One solution to this is a *print spooler*. A print spooler is a software utility that lets you print your entire document to your PC's memory. Then, you can get back to work while your printer is spoon-fed the document by the spooler.

A print spooler is often bundled with other software. PC-Kwik *Power Pak*, for instance, offers a collection of performance-enhancing utilities, including a print spooler, disk cache, RAM drive, command-line editor, and other goodies. PrintCache and PrintCache for Windows from LaserTools Corp. are well-known spoolers. Otherwise, your local computer club's bulletin board system (BBS) may offer a print spooler.

The speed improvements you get from a print spooler depend on your software and the work you do. The best results come with applications that print only in the foreground, locking up your computer from doing other work. A *Ventura Publisher* file that normally ties up a computer for 71 seconds, for example, can give the user control of the computer in 9 seconds thanks to a print spooler.

In lieu of print spooler software, you can purchase a print buffer. This small device connects between your printer and PC and swallows the document for feeding to your printer. Print buffers cost less than $100. One advantage of a print buffer is that you do not have to load the print spooler software, which requires part of your PC's precious memory.

High Brow, High Tech

Some gadgets for speeding up your PC may cost $100 to $700. If you want to hang on to that PC for a while and truly give it a boost, consider these ideas.

Double Time

You can give your 486 PC a brain transplant with Intel Corp.'s "Speed Doubling" technology. An OverDrive chip that uses this technology can double the speed of your PC's brain. You simply insert the OverDrive chip (which costs $300 to $700) into the internal socket of your PC. (This is also called the 80487SX math coprocessor or OverDrive socket.)

OverDrive sockets are available to 16- , 20- and 25MHz 80486SX computers. Once you plug in the new OverDrive processor, the original processor is shut off. (A true brain transplant.) For 80486DX PCs, the existing processor is replaced with the OverDrive processor. You cannot use an OverDrive with 386 computers.

NERDY
DETAILS

Your PC won't be twice as fast with an Overdrive chip. The OverDrive processor lets your PC's brain think twice as fast but still must talk to the rest of your computer at its originally designed speed. This is like drinking strong coffee in the morning; your thoughts are faster than your speech.

Fast-Flying Windows

Some video cards include a thinking chip that frees your computer from having to draw the screen. Such video cards are called *video accelerators* or *Windows accelerator cards* because they can speed up all Microsoft Windows software. A video accelerator card replaces the video card in your computer. In your DOS programs, they function as a normal VGA or SVGA card. When you work in Windows or another program that the video card supports, then you'll truly turn on the speed, possibly 10 to 40 percent.

A Real Disk Cache

Software-based disk caches are nice, but for hard-disk-demanding software such as databases, you should consider a disk-caching controller.

Most hard disk controllers include built-in memory to speed up your hard disk. These buffers tend to be between 8K and 64K. A *disk-caching controller* provides a hardware equivalent software disk-caching to the hard disk drive.

Unlike typical controllers, these disk-caching controllers provide more memory and their own on-board computer to manage the cache. This hardware approach to disk caching, however, is expensive—between $400 and $1500—and doesn't always offer a noticeable speed improvement over software disk caching. One advantage, though, is that a caching controller uses its own memory (your PC's memory is free for other things).

Old Case, New Computer

The motherboard is your computer's main circuit board. It contains your computer's processor, memory, and several other crucial components and forms the foundation for your entire system. In one fell swoop, you can give yourself a new computer in the same case. Don't worry about compatibility problems when you replace your motherboard; essentially, you are replacing your whole PC.

The decision to replace your motherboard has both pros and cons. The biggest drawbacks are the time and technical savvy required to replace it. Unlike other improvements, a motherboard replacement requires you to remove all expansion cards, disconnect all cables, extract all disk drives, and remove your power supply. Whew!

NERDY
DETAILS

Would you rather take up pit bull training than open that case? If so, you might know a nerd who would love to show off his or her talents at replacing a motherboard. As always, a good place for help is your local computer club. Computer nerds are very intimate with computers, and have no aversion to helping someone else. After all, what do nerds know better than anything else? Their own "mother"-boards!

If you are comfortable installing an internal hard disk in your computer, you can handle installing a new motherboard. If not, you may want to stick to adding extra memory. These improvements may be better for your PC (and your temper) than facing the unknown.

A new motherboard gives you new speed and extra features. If you want to run Microsoft Windows in its deluxe Enhanced mode, you need an 80386-based computer, for instance. Replacing your 80286-based motherboard with an 80386 model is about the only remaining option. Installing a new motherboard is very economical, costing as little as $75 (memory extra) and rarely more than $500.

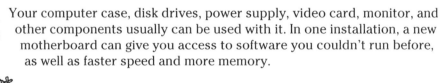

Your computer case, disk drives, power supply, video card, monitor, and other components usually can be used with it. In one installation, a new motherboard can give you access to software you couldn't run before, as well as faster speed and more memory.

Replacing your motherboard is also preferable to endless patching to an outdated computer. The computer may become a Frankenstein-like creation. (Get me a disk drive, Igor!) As you continue to upgrade your computer, you may run into hidden incompatibilities and problems.

Motherboard Problems

A new motherboard is great improvement but not a panacea. You'll still be using the same hard disk, monitor and power supply. For example, you may add the horsepower required to run Windows, but your current CGA monitor won't work with it. Likewise, the existing power supply rated at 135 or 150 watts may not be able to provide clean power to the new board.

To avoid these problems, replace your motherboard with one that is only a step ahead of yours. For example, replace your 80286 motherboard with one that uses the 80386; don't leapfrog from an 8088 to an 80846 motherboard. By doing this, you reduce your chance of facing such bottlenecks because the speed improvement is not that substantial. The case, power supply, and possibly even the hard disk, will work well with the 80386 or 80486 motherboard.

If you replace your entire motherboard, the most important concern is size. The new motherboard must match the layout and size of your computer's case. Basically, motherboards come in two sizes: XT (8.5 by 13.5 inches or smaller) and AT (12 by 13.5 inches or smaller). Because of their smaller size, XT motherboards are also called "baby AT" motherboards.

NERDY
DETAILS

If you own a genuine PC/XT or PC/AT, finding a motherboard is easy because these computers use standard sizes. Most other PCs also use the standard XT- and AT-sized motherboards. What matters is that the new motherboard isn't bigger than the space you have inside your case. Generally, these boards come drilled with enough holes that you can find a match for the posts and standoffs that hold your current motherboard.

XT motherboards typically are for 8088- and 8086-based computers. AT motherboards are for 80286-, 80386- and 80486-based computers. Although most XT-sized motherboards are designed to fit in place of an AT-sized board, the reverse is rarely possible because of constraints in case size. In other words, order an AT-sized motherboard only if your old PC has one. In other cases, you'll want an XT-sized board.

I Want a New Motherboard!— Step-by-Step Instructions

If you slaved through 900 pages of "The Computer Shopper" and finally found a replacement motherboard, follow these basic steps to stick it in your case. (If you want to be a true nerd, buy the Que book *Upgrading and Repairing PCs*, 2nd Edition by Scott Mueller. In 1400 pages, for an affordable price, you can learn all about motherboards.)

1. Back up your hard drive.

Before replacing your motherboard, you should have an up-to-date backup of your hard disk.

2. Before replacing your motherboard, record information about your computer.

You should first go into your computer's Setup program (also called CMOS), and print the screens or jot down the facts about your current computer, such as the amount of memory and, more importantly, the various parameters for your hard disk—cylinders, heads, sectors, etc. You will need to re-enter this information after the new motherboard is installed. To enter your setup program, you often have to press the Delete key or F1 as your computer warms up. Check your computer's manual.

3.   Open your PC and remove each expansion card.

As you remove each expansion card, place a piece of tape on each, noting its numbered position in the slots. For example, if you have an expansion card in the second slot, place a piece of tape with the number "2" on it.

Some expansion cards, such as your disk drive controller, may have gray ribbon cables that attach to your hard disk and floppy disk drives. Use tape to mark which cable is attached to which connector on the card. Mark these connections clearly because it helps when you put your computer back together.

4.   Remove your disk drives.

Each drive has two cables connected to it. One provides power to the drive; the other is for transmitting data read from the disk to the disk drive controller. Use a piece of tape to mark which connector is attached to which drive. Also note the order of the drives in your case. Is the 5.25-inch disk drive on top of the 3.5-inch drive? Is the tape drive in the third or fourth drive bay opening in your computer (if you have one)?

5.   Remove your power supply.

The power supply is probably the largest part of your computer. It probably has a sticker on it that says, "CAUTION: Hazardous Area." This chrome steel, box-like component must be removed for you to extract the motherboard. Before removing the power supply, you must remove any power cables connected to the motherboard itself.

You probably have removed the cables that attach to the disk drives. Next, remove the two sets of six colored wires that attach to the motherboard. These two power connectors are usually called P8 and P9, or P1 and P2. Note their position and how they are installed. Usually, the black leads on each connector face each other. Always grasp the connectors themselves; never pull the wires.

6.   Remove any other connectors.

There may be some electrical connectors attached to your motherboard. These may include wires for the speaker, keyboard lock, turbo speed, hard disk light, and reset button. Remove these.

7.   Remove the motherboard.

Once the expansion cards, drives, and power supply are removed, you can next remove the motherboard. It is held in place by two fasteners: retaining screws and standoffs—white plastic pop-in fasteners. First, use a screwdriver to remove the retaining screws and any insulating washers that are used with them. Next, use long-nosed pliers to squeeze the tips of the standoffs to free the motherboard. You may also have to slide the motherboard around to free it of the standoffs. Lift the motherboard up and out of the case and set it aside on a clean and antistatic surface.

8.   Position the new motherboard in your PC's case.

If your computer also uses plastic standoffs, put them into the case's slots first. When you install the motherboard, push the stems through the motherboard's mounting holes. If the new motherboard also uses screws, ensure you use insulating washers to separate the metal screw from the motherboard. Do not yet fully tighten the screws. You may have to shift the motherboard slightly for proper alignment.

9.   Reinstall everything you removed in reverse order.

10.   Test and set up your computer.

Attach your keyboard and monitor cables to the PC and turn it on. You should be given an error message and told to run the PC's Setup program. Go into the Setup program (usually by pressing the function key F1). This gives you the opportunity to tell your new motherboard about the type of disk drives, the amount of memory, and type of display you have.

11.   Return your PC to its normal working condition.

Although replacing the motherboard can be challenging, it is (hopefully) a one-time operation that greatly increases the speed and compatibility of your computer. In one move, you can extend the life of your computer by a few years, if not more.

INDEX

Symbols

* (asterisk) wild card character, 104-105
~ (tilde) character, 236
... (ellipsis), 127
¦ (pipe) character, 236
3.5" floppy disks, formatting, 110
5.25" floppy disks, formatting, 111
8-bit expansion cards, 390
16-bit expansion cards, 390

A

AC (alternating current), 206
accelerator keys, 125, 238
access speed, 40, 262
accounting software, 160
active-matrix screens, 310-311

adapters, null-modem, 325
add-on cards, *see* expansion cards
After Dark screen saver (Berkeley Systems), 226
aliases, ports, 269-270
alternating current (AC), 206
America On-Line, 31
analog monitors, 220
ANSI (American National Standards Institute), 231
antiglare lens, 213
antiglare screens, 225, 381
Apple Macintosh, *see* Macintosh computers
application windows, 120
applications, software, 158
arrow keys, 127, 233
asterisk (*) wild card character, 104-105

auto synchronous monitors, 220
auto tracking monitors, 220
AUTOEXEC.BAT file, 83, 170

B

backlit screens, 310
Backslash (\) key, 232
Backspace key, 234
backup software, 260
banks, memory, 198-199
Basic Input/Output System, *see* BIOS
BAT file extension, 99
battery drain, reducing, 309
baud rate, 375
BBSs (bulletin board systems), 167, 288, 379
beaming files, 329
BIOS (Basic Input/Output System), 184, 201-202

PCs WORDSEARCH

by Terry Hall

Find these PC words hidden in the puzzle below. Words may be hidden diagonally, horizontally, vertically, backward, or forward.

Hint: Some words share letters and may be found more than once. Can you find the 15 PCs?

T	A	G	V	R	E	P	U	S	E	I	R	O	T	C	E	R	I	D	S	H	P	P
R	A	M	E	L	B	I	T	A	P	M	O	C	M	B	I	A	T	A	T	R	C	T
O	A	U	T	O	E	X	E	C	B	A	T	R	U	S	T	N	O	F	A	E	T	D
P	I	R	R	H	C	N	I	R	E	P	S	T	O	D	D	D	W	A	N	M	I	E
L	H	O	O	E	M	U	L	T	I	S	Y	N	C	A	R	O	E	T	D	E	P	V
A	A	S	P	C	T	S	R	S	U	A	H	S	T	A	R	M	R	L	B	G	T	I
I	P	S	L	A	B	P	T	B	R	A	E	A	C	P	I	A	O	W	Y	A	O	C
R	P	E	E	F	F	A	A	E	R	L	T	O	A	C	L	C	P	S	P	B	D	E
E	L	C	L	E	M	S	D	D	I	R	E	G	R	P	A	C	G	X	O	Y	X	D
S	I	O	L	P	I	O	D	F	A	D	E	O	R	L	A	E	I	S	W	T	E	R
L	C	R	A	Y	H	I	P	N	I	S	S	O	A	S	X	S	K	S	E	E	O	I
A	A	P	R	T	S	U	S	V	P	O	C	R	C	P	Y	S	O	N	R	S	L	V
R	T	O	A	K	T	F	R	E	F	E	E	I	A	T	I	M	D	R	S	E	E	E
E	I	C	P	R	E	O	R	T	S	A	I	N	H	D	B	E	M	E	U	V	N	R
H	O	H	A	R	L	M	W	S	N	T	S	G	Y	P	D	M	C	V	P	I	N	S
P	N	T	R	O	I	I	I	E	E	I	I	P	S	M	A	O	Q	I	P	R	A	E
I	S	A	C	N	N	N	T	X	O	E	P	O	E	E	R	R	O	R	L	D	H	L
R	T	M	U	D	G	W	T	N	R	O	F	M	I	P	S	Y	G	D	Y	M	C	I
E	C	T	O	U	O	F	S	U	L	T	O	O	O	T	A	M	R	O	F	O	O	F
P	E	W	N	R	I	L	O	F	W	R	D	R	A	O	B	Y	E	K	E	R	R	V
E	S	I	K	L	O	F	R	A	Y	A	C	C	E	S	S	T	I	M	E	D	C	A
D	T	P	E	T	C	I	R	C	U	I	T	B	O	A	R	D	S	O	D	C	I	W
I	S	C	S	C	R	E	E	N	M	B	A	S	I	C	P	R	O	G	R	A	M	V

access time
applications
ASCII text file
autoexec.bat
BASIC program
cathode ray tube
CD-ROM drive
central processing unit
circuit boards
color video card
cps
Cray
CRC
CRT
data transfer rate
device driver
dir
directories
DOS
dot-pitch
dots-per-inch
driver
DTP
error
expansion slots
extended memory
fade
FAT
floppy disks
fonts
format
four-eighty-six
hard disk
IBM-compatible
IDE

ISA bus
keyboard
local area network
math coprocessor
megabytes
memory
MicroChannel
microprocessor
Microsoft Windows
MIPS
MTBF
multisync

OEM
pages-per-minute
parallel port
PC
peripherals
pins
power supply
print
RAM
random-access memory
RIP
ROM

screen
SCSI
serial port
software
standby power supply
start-up files
Super-VGA
tower
TSRs
typeface
video graphics adapter
wav files

PCs CROSSWORD

by Terry Hall

ACROSS

1 Parallel port
5 Backwards basics?
9 Memory access speeder
14 Restrain
15 Slanted type, for short
16 Academy Award
17 Capacitor memory
18 Computer clock reading: 2 wds.
20 Batch file comment
22 Disk tracks
23 Longfellow was one
25 Big Blue's design std.
26 Programmable electronic device
30 Slow mover
34 Bet. 640K and 1M
35 Popular user interface
37 Competitive operating system
39 Macintosh computer type
41 Place object
43 Ancient astrologers
44 Paste shortcut key
46 More certain
48 Big memory user: slang
49 Dealkalized clay soil
51 Chips' components
53 Test site
55 32-bit bus
56 Michelangelo and Dark Avenger, e.g.
60 Not raster
64 Multimedia player: 2 wds.
66 Shakespeare's famous question: 2 wds.
67 Scheduled program event
68 Arabian prince
69 College collection, in brief
70 T's predecessors
71 Power rating
72 Dramatic backgrounds

DOWN

1 Two below Navy captain: abbr.
2 Unadulterated
3 British streetcar
4 OS/2 utility, e.g.
5 Floppy
6 Municipality: var.
7 Storage media maker
8 Los ___, Calif.
9 Instruction
10 Amer. Soc. of Travel Agts.
11 Telecommunications standards setter
12 Amateur radio operators
13 Lest
19 Time periods
21 Soup thickener
24 Specialized words
26 Fashionable
27 Leaves out
28 Automated repeat steps
29 Pictured word
31 Mechanical extension
32 Potato state
33 Connect to a BBS
36 Spooky
38 Users' subgroups
40 Sick
42 Performs as promised
45 Disk labels
47 Extend vertically
50 Direct access storage device
52 Prickly plant
54 City near Cleveland
56 Monitors' moniker
57 Lens diaphragm
58 Caesar's city
59 Memory chip type
61 Color or sound quality
62 Death notice
63 Altered pgms.
64 Bee's follower
65 Industry shaker: infor.

This is to certify that

_____

is a graduate of the Non-Nerds School of PCs, and has successfully completed all training, testing, and behavior modification counseling necessary for this course.

But that doesn't mean much.

Awarded this _____ day of _____, Nineteen-hundred-ninety-_____

_____
Chief Executive Non-Nerd

NRP
NEW RIDERS
PUBLISHING

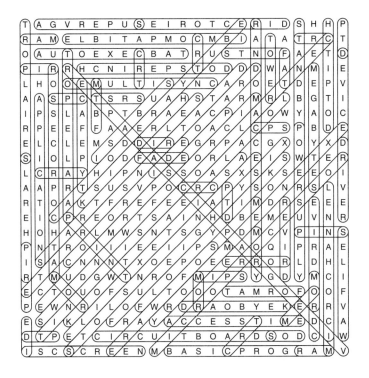

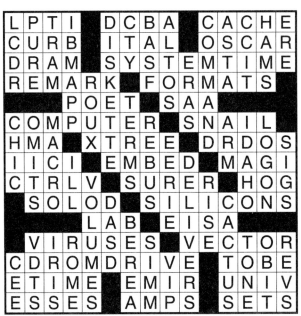

WANT MORE INFORMATION?

CHECK OUT THESE RELATED TITLES:

	QTY	PRICE	TOTAL
PCs for Non-Nerds. This lighthearted reference presents information in an easy-to-read, entertaining manner. Provides quick, easy-to-find, no-nonsense answers to questions everyone asks. A great book for the "non-nerd" who wants to learn about personal computers. ISBN: 1-56205-150-4.	____	$18.95	_____
DOS for Non-Nerds. This step-by-step, fun tutorial is easy to read and easy to understand. Perfect for beginning to intermediate DOS users who don't want a lot of technical jargon. Includes tear-out cards for quick reference to important information. ISBN: 1-56205-151-2.	____	$18.95	_____
OS/2 for Non-Nerds. Even nontechnical people can learn how to use OS/2 like a professional with this book. Clear and concise explanations are provided without long-winded, technical discussions. Information is easy to find with the convenient bulleted lists and tables. ISBN: 1-56205-153-9.	____	$18.95	_____
Windows for Non-Nerds. Windows for Non-Nerds is written with busy people in mind. With this book it is extremely easy to find solutions to common Windows problems. Contains only useful information that is of interest to readers and is free of techno-babble and lengthy, technical discussions. Important information is listed in tables or bulleted lists that make it easy to find what you are looking for. ISBN: 1-56205-152-0.	____	$18.95	_____

Name _____

Company _____

Address _____

City _____ State ____ Zip _____

Phone _____ Fax _____

☐ Check Enclosed ☐ VISA ☐ MasterCard

Card #_____Exp. Date _____

Signature _____

Prices are subject to change. Call for availability and pricing information on latest editions.

Subtotal _____

Shipping _____

$4.00 for the first book and $1.75 for each additional book.

Total _____

Indiana Residents add 5% Sales Tax.

New Riders Publishing 11711 North College Avenue • P.O. Box 90 • Carmel, Indiana 46032 USA

Orders/Customer Service: 1-800-541-6789
Fax: 1-800-448-3804

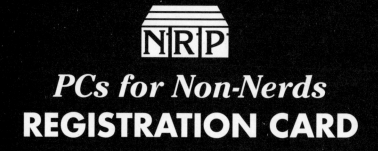

PCs for Non-Nerds
REGISTRATION CARD

Fill out this card to receive information about future Non-Nerds books and other New Riders titles!

Name _____ **Title** _____

Company _____

Address _____

City/State/Zip _____

I bought this book because _____

_____

I purchased this book from:

☐ A bookstore (Name _____)

☐ A software or electronics store (Name _____)

☐ A mail order (Name of Catalog _____)

☐ Some guy on the corner (Street Corner _____)

I purchase this many computer books each year:

☐ 1-5   ☐ 5 or more

I mostly use these software applications: _____

_____

_____

_____

I found these chapters to be the most informative: _____

_____

I found these chapters to be the least informative: _____

_____

Additional comments: _____

_____

☐ I would like to see my name in print! You may use my name and quote me in future New Riders products and promotions. My daytime phone number is:_____

Important PC Information

This card is your PC's "birth certificate." When you fill in everything, this page has everything other people need to know about your PC. When you need help or have questions, all the answers will be in one place. Go ahead and fill out this card, and keep it with your computer receipts.

What Do I Have Here?

In this section, you fill in your PC's specifications. You need this information if you ever call for technical support or for help with your hardware.

- Computer Model Name:
- Computer Model Number (usually on the box next to the serial number):
- Computer Serial Number:
- Monitor Model Number:
- Monitor Serial Number:

My computer has a 286, 386SX, 386, 486SX, 486, 486DX2 processor (circle one).

My computer has_____megabytes of RAM.

My computer has a(n)_____megabyte hard disk drive.

I bought the computer from:

_____

_____

_____

_____

Phone _____

This salesperson made all the promises:_____

I call here for help: _____

I have these peripheral items:

Item Name	Item Serial Number
_____	_____
_____	_____
_____	_____
_____	_____

I have these software packages:

Software	Serial Number	Support Number
_____	_____	_____
_____	_____	_____
_____	_____	_____
_____	_____	_____
_____	_____	_____